ONCE THERE WERE CASTLES

ONCE THERE WERE CASTLES

LOST MANSIONS and ESTATES of the TWIN CITIES

◆

Larry Millett

University of Minnesota Press
Minneapolis | London

Published by the University of Minnesota Press
111 Third Avenue South, Suite 290
Minneapolis, MN 55401-2520
http://www.upress.umn.edu

Library of Congress Cataloging-in-Publication Data
Millett, Larry
    Once there were castles : lost mansions and estates of the Twin
    Cities / Larry Millett.
        p.   cm.
    Includes bibliographical references and index.
    ISBN 978-0-8166-7430-5 (hc : alk. paper)
1. Lost architecture—Minnesota—Minneapolis metropolitan area.
2. Lost architecture—Minnesota—Saint Paul metropolitan area.
3. Mansions—Minnesota—Minneapolis metropolitan area. 4. Mansions—
Minnesota—Saint Paul metropolitan area. I. Title. II. Title: Lost mansions and estates of the Twin Cities.
    NA7511.4.M56M55 2011
    728.809776'579—dc23
                                                    2011023622

Design and production by Mighty Media, Inc.
Text design by Chris Long

Printed in the United States of America on acid-free paper

To Jodie

CONTENTS

ACKNOWLEDGMENTS

---◆---

This book would not have been possible without help from many people who share my interest in the history of the Twin Cities. Architectural historian Paul Clifford Larson, now of Stockholm, Wisconsin, was as always a tremendous source of information about matters large and small and also provided numerous photographs from his seemingly inexhaustible files. Another local historian of note, James Sazevich, passed along all manner of tantalizing information from his peerless research into the early days of St. Paul. Tony Krosschell at the Minnesota Historical Society helped greatly with the research by tracking down numerous photographs. Bob Glancy graciously made available portions of his extensive research into the history of the Charles G. Gates House in Minneapolis. Jay Pfaender provided similar help for another great estate, Oliver Crosby's Stonebridge in St. Paul.

Others I wish to thank include Mollie Spillman and the research center staff at the Ramsey County Historical Society; Susan Larson-Fleming at the Hennepin History Museum; Barb Bezat at the Northwest Architectural Archives at the University of Minnesota; Rollie Haywood at the Robbinsdale Historical Society; Larry Hutchings at the Carver County Historical Society; and the Westonka Historical Society.

At the University of Minnesota Press, Todd Orjala, Kristian Tvedten, and others did expert work in shepherding my manuscript through to publication.

Finally, a big thank you to my wife, Jodie Ahern, who not only read the manuscript but also provided much-needed encouragement on those many days when this project seemed like a mountain that could never be climbed. ◆

INTRODUCTION

Although urban renewal and the destruction of historic build-ings, homes, and neighborhoods is often thought of as a post–World War II phenomenon, the process is in fact much older than that. Consider these words, from an anonymous writer for the *Minneapolis Tribune*: "The casual pedestrian who walks about in a zone between Hennepin and Seventh avenue south, on the one hand, and Sixth street and Twelfth, on the other, cannot fail to note the many evidences that here was once a charming residence district of Old Minneapolis. Yet it requires a good deal of imagination to excavate that residence district now. Business offices, apartment houses, flats, hotels, and what not, have swept over it and buried it almost as completely as a flood of lava might. . . . A certain penalty is attached to progress in that the city must thereby sacrifice a good deal of its poetry—for its poetry, to a large extent, lies in its old residences."[1] The year of this lament was 1922.

The writer's comments could have applied just as readily to St. Paul, where an entire neighborhood of mansions had already been all but erased by the 1920s. Destruction of this kind has happened all across urban America, but that is of little consolation. The simple truth is that large sections of both Min-neapolis and St. Paul were once far more urbane and beautiful than they are today, or ever will be again.

The lost mansions of the Twin Cities constitute a graveyard of sumptuous dreams that extends into almost every corner of St. Paul and Minneapolis proper, and to Stillwater on the east and Lake Minnetonka on the west. It is hard to say how many great houses are gone, but at least five hundred can be accounted for in public records and photographic archives, while others exist only in the yellowing pages of obscure old atlases. Even the most magnificent mansions sometimes had shockingly brief lives. James J. Hill's first house in St. Paul stood for only fourteen years. The gigantic Charles G. Gates man-sion overlooking Lake of the Isles lasted for just two decades despite the millions poured into building it. Norman Kittson's sprawling home on the site of St. Paul Cathedral came down after just twenty-one years.

Whole neighborhoods are lost. In St. Paul, the Capitol

Hiram F. Stevens House, 15 Sherburne Avenue, and other mansions in the Capitol Heights neighborhood, St. Paul, about 1890. None of these homes still stands.

A. M. Reid House, Nicollet Avenue south from Ninth Street, Minneapolis, about 1908. Two years later the house was razed; a Target store now occupies the site.

Heights, College Avenue, and Lowertown mansion districts, once genteel gatherings of big houses and flowing lawns, have vanished virtually without a trace. In downtown Minneapolis, scores of mansions that once filled block upon block south of Seventh Street are gone. Farther south, Park Avenue is shadowed by the ghosts of mansions that for a time made it the Minneapolis version of St. Paul's Summit Avenue.

Mansion districts have long been a part of American cities, serving to display wealth through the medium of architecture and to confirm social status in a society where class distinctions are real but at times elusive. The peculiarly American idea of "arriving," whether through pluck and hard work or via the surer route of inheritance, is often marked by the building of a mansion. In the Twin Cities mansions began to appear as soon as settlers did, since some pioneers brought with them the financial wherewithal to live well even in a rough frontier environment.

There is no precise definition of what constitutes a "mansion." The largest and most luxurious houses built in the 1850s in the Twin Cities, for example, were much smaller than those that came later, and today they might hardly be viewed as mansions at all. Yet Jacob Bass's early house in the Lowertown neighborhood was certainly regarded as a mansion if only because it was for its time and place an unusually elaborate and costly home. "Estate" is also an elusive term, but it always suggests ample acreage in addition to an outsized house. Some of the grandest lost estates, spreading out over one hundred acres or more and bearing tony names like Highcroft and Katahdin, were along Lake Minnetonka's shores, where dreams of grandeur still flourish, if not quite on the scale of old. James J. Hill had the largest, if not the most lavish, estate of all, on five thousand acres north of St. Paul.

The first crop of Twin Cities mansions, those built before 1880, are almost all gone. In St. Paul only twenty or so mansions from this early period remain. Survivors include the David Stuart House (1858) and the Burbank-Livingston-Griggs House (1863),

both on Summit Avenue, and the Alexander Ramsey House (1872) near Irvine Park. In Minneapolis, even fewer pre-1880 mansions still stand. Most are located in the Fifth Street Southeast Historic District near the University of Minnesota's East Bank campus.

That so few early mansions survive is regrettable but hardly surprising. The bulk of these houses were constructed in or close to the downtown areas of St. Paul and Minneapolis, and that put them squarely in the path of future commercial development. As both cities grew, most rapidly in the period from 1880 through the early 1900s, downtown expansion claimed dozens of historic mansions, whose owners seldom succumbed to misty sentiment when the opportunity arose to sell their property for a handsome profit. Minneapolis banker Henry G. Sidle took an even more direct approach, replacing his brick mansion at Fifth Street and Nicollet Avenue with an office building that he named, naturally enough, the Sidle Block.[2]

Mansions were not always torn down to make way for progress. In 1883, Daniel Robertson moved his mansion off a lot facing West Seventh Street in St. Paul so that he could put up a commercial building. Both Robertson and his mansion were then relocated just around the corner on a quieter street. Even heavy brick houses were occasionally moved, although most of the travelers were of the lighter, wood-frame variety.

All told, at least seventy-five early-era mansions in downtown St. Paul and one hundred or more in downtown Minneapolis have vanished. Today, no mansions survive in downtown St. Paul. In downtown Minneapolis, the Hinkle-Murphy House (1887) still stands on South Tenth Street, although it is no longer used as a residence, and a handful of historic houses also remain in the traditionally mixed-use Loring Park and Elliot Park neighborhoods.

"Teardowns," as they are known today, also sent a number of first-generation mansions to premature graves, especially along Summit Avenue, where ten or more early residences were replaced by larger houses in the late nineteenth century. Other houses succumbed to sheer extravagance, their upkeep

Henry G. Sidle House, Fifth Street and Nicollet Avenue, Minneapolis, 1876. No sentimentalist, Sidle replaced the house two years later with a more profitable commercial building.

costs simply too much to bear once their original owners died. Railroad expansion (most notably in the Lowertown area), road and freeway construction, urban renewal, and the occasional fire were among other forces that added steadily to the toll of lost mansions. These forces were not unique to St. Paul and Minneapolis. Absent special intervention (such as the law enacted in 1936 to preserve New Orleans's fabled French Quarter), "progress" in one form or another led to the destruction of historic residential districts in virtually every American city.

The visual history of mansion districts in the Twin Cities begins, curiously enough, with an image of two far-from-wealthy drivers of a dogsled. Known only as Tarbell and Campbell, the men

arrived in St. Paul in the winter of 1858–59 as part of a "dogtrain" carrying furs and other goods down from the Red River valley. Pioneer St. Paul photographer Joel Whitney caught up with the pair near present-day Seven Corners and posed them for a picture with their dogs, their sled, and, for added charm, a small boy well bundled against the cold. The photograph's real revelation, however, is what stands behind the dogsledders, atop the steep bluffs where Summit Avenue begins its long run through

Dogsledders near Seven Corners, St. Paul, about 1859. Six early mansions of Summit Avenue are visible above, looking west. The Reverend Edward Neill House at far right was located where the James J. Hill Mansion now stands at 240 Summit Avenue.

St. Paul. Six large houses are visible along the crest of the bluff, forming one of the earliest mansion districts in the Twin Cities.[3]

Mostly built just before the devastating financial panic of 1857, the houses belonged with one exception to the kind of men—entrepreneurs, lawyers, political figures—who formed the vanguard of early mansion builders in the Twin Cities. The exception was the Reverend Edward D. Neill, pastor of House of Hope Presbyterian Church and later the founder of Macalester College. In about 1855 Neill built the Italianate-style house visible at the far right of the photograph. Neill's house, the oldest in the photograph, was also one of the first to vanish, coming down in the late 1880s to make way for James J. Hill's daunting brownstone mansion, still the greatest of all the avenue's residences.

Oddly enough, the smallest house in the photograph (third from the left) was home to the most prominent man among these Summit Avenue pioneers—Henry Mower Rice. A fur trader, real estate speculator, and later U.S. senator (as well as the namesake of downtown St. Paul's best-known park), Rice built the first house on Summit in 1851, according to research by St. Paul historian James Sazevich. Too far south to be seen in the dogsled photograph, it was located at what is today about 400 Summit, next to Lookout Park. The home was eventually incorporated into the Carpenter House Hotel, built on the site of the park in 1879. A year later, the hotel burned down, taking the old house with it. By then, Rice had already been in his second house—the one visible in the photograph at 288 Summit—for twenty-three years. In 1882 he would go on to build a third, larger mansion directly across the street at 285 Summit. All of Rice's houses were gone by 1900, making him perhaps the only Twin Citian whose legacy includes three lost mansions within eyeshot of one another.

The other four houses planted atop the bare bluff belonged to a flour miller (a not uncommon occupation in early St. Paul before Minneapolis took over the trade), a lawyer, a lumberman, and one owner of unknown means. The lumberman was David Stuart, and his house at 312 Summit, which dates to 1858, is the only one of the original six that remains. None of the others survived past 1903, by which time the blufftop stretch of Summit had filled in with houses far larger than those built by the pioneers.

The Summit six, as they might be called, were indeed quite modest compared to the huge, sumptuously appointed houses that would eventually replace them. Few of the first-generation of mansions built in the Twin Cities between the 1850s and early 1870s appear to have exceeded five thousand square feet in size, whereas Hill's 1891 mansion encompassed about thirty-six thousand square feet. The early mansions also lacked, in most cases, the sophisticated design of those built in the 1880s and later. Like other Twin Cities mansions of the time, the Summit six were the work of master builders, as opposed to formally trained architects. These builders often adapted their designs from plan books featuring homes in the then-popular Italianate and French Second Empire styles.

The early mansions scattered around the Twin Cities were built from a fairly limited palette of materials. Until the 1870s, gray or yellow Platteville limestone, quarried at many sites around the Twin Cities, was used for the most substantial mansions. Others were constructed of locally made brick or were sided in wood from nearby sawmills. At least one—George Farrington's extraordinary octagon house of 1857 on College Avenue in St. Paul—was constructed of concrete, then a novel material.

Deluxe interior furnishings and finishes were available, however. Jacob Bass—whose house, started in the late 1850s, was among the largest in the long-vanished Lowertown mansion district—featured custom millwork made in Cincinnati and shipped to St. Paul via riverboat. Although numerous riverboats reached St. Paul (twenty-four were docked on one day alone in May of 1857, the peak year for traffic), the big paddle wheelers were slow and cumbersome, and could not operate in winter. It was not until the arrival of railroads, which by 1870 linked the Twin Cities to Chicago and points east, that a wide range of materials and furnishings became readily available to local mansion builders.

Plumbing, heating, and mechanical systems were surprisingly advanced in many of these early mansions. Water was often brought in from wells, springs, or cisterns and then pumped up to zinc-lined attic storage tanks. Central furnaces were also in use by the 1860s. Bass's house, which had both central heat and running water, set the standard. A mansion built next door in 1860 by banker Horace Thompson also featured indoor plumbing and was reputed to have the city's first bathtub. Even so, reliable plumbing in most cases had to await the arrival of municipal sewer and water systems.

The Summit six demonstrate one other characteristic of the early mansion era, which is that even the most solid-looking houses were often built on treacherous financial ground. The pioneer age in the Twin Cities, as elsewhere in urban America, was a giant real estate casino in which almost everyone who had a few dollars to spare participated. The winners won big, and the losers fell hard, all at a time when large property owners tended to be leveraged to the hilt. One account of the wild scene in St. Paul in 1856 sounds much like what happened 150 years later: "The buying of real estate, often at the most insane prices, and without regard to its real value, infected all classes. . . . Honest labor was thrown aside for more rapid means of wealth. Farmers, mechanics, laborers, even, forsook their occupations to become operators in real estate, and grow suddenly rich, as they supposed."[4]

Once the inevitable crash occurred, as it did in 1857, foreclosures were distressingly common. The Summit six were not immune to this reality, and half of the homes pictured in the dogsled photo fell into foreclosure within two years of their completion, forcing out their original owners.

The lower portion of Summit Avenue remains the most intact nineteenth-century mansion district in the Twin Cities despite the loss of so many early houses. Lowry Hill in Minneapolis has also retained its cachet as prime mansion territory, although many of its finest homes date to the early twentieth century. Summit and Lowry Hill are, however, exceptional survivors because most of the dozen or more historic mansion districts once sprinkled around the Twin Cities are either gone or radically altered by redevelopment.

In 1952, the Charles Colter House, built in the 1870s, was marooned amid parking lots at 472 Sibley Street in downtown St. Paul. Colter owned a butcher shop on nearby Jackson Street. The demolition of the house likely occurred soon after this photograph was taken.

St. Paul, by virtue of its distinctive topography and date of settlement, had more early mansion districts than Minneapolis. The city's compact downtown, extending back from the Mississippi River, is ringed by bluffs on the east and west and less precipitous hills to the north. Wealth craves altitude, and the high spots overlooking downtown quickly sprouted clusters of mansions. "Our notice has been attracted to the number of new residences in progress of erection and already completed on the bluffs surrounding our city," one publication noted in 1857.[5] "These handsome and sightly locations will in a few years all be occupied by elegant private mansions, the abode of wealth and luxury, ornaments to our city and evidence of its prosperity."

Not everyone headed for the hills, however. In the early days, when roads were muddy paths and transportation options were limited, many of St. Paul's wealthiest men built their homes in Lowertown, in an area that today consists of a maze of railroad tracks, freeways, and industrial buildings. Before rail lines transformed the area, it offered beautiful natural scenery in the form of Trout Brook valley as well as distant views of the Mississippi. Pioneer lawyer and later St. Paul mayor Edmund

Stone house built in 1854 at 62 East Twelfth Street in downtown St. Paul, 1936. It came down in 1954, seven years before its next-door neighbor at left, Central Park Methodist Church, was razed to make way for Interstates 35E and 94.

Rice (Henry's brother) had a forty-eight-acre estate in the valley with an eight-bedroom house at the center of it. Lowertown's finest homes were along all-but-vanished Woodward Avenue, which once ran a block north of Grove Street east of present-day Lafayette Road. Mansions continued to go up in the Lowertown–Trout Brook area until about 1880, after which railroad and industrial development drove the wealthy residents away to Summit Avenue and other more attractive environs.

The terraced hills east of downtown St. Paul (today's Dayton's Bluff neighborhood) were home to another collection of early mansions, some of which occupied grounds the size of a city block or more. Lyman Dayton, a real estate speculator whose personal attributes included a surpassingly strange hairdo, gave his name to the neighborhood after building a house near present-day Mounds Boulevard around 1850. The most splendid of the neighborhood's lost mansions was the James Thompson (later Patrick Kelly) House, a double-towered stone residence built in the 1860s. Only three pre-1870 mansions—the Smith-Davidson-Scheffer House (1850s and later), the Reverend Cyrus Brooks House (1860), and the Munch-Heidemann House (1869 and later)—remain in Dayton's Bluff, albeit in much modified form.

North of downtown, around the present state capitol, mansions began appearing in the 1850s, mainly designed in the then-popular Federal and Greek Revival styles. Among these early mansions was a curious New Orleans–style balconied house, built by a certain Mrs. Cochran, who hailed from that city. Its grounds were said to include one of the finest gardens in the city.[6] The most magnificent mansions, including the John Merriam House (home to the Science Museum of Minnesota for many years), were built in the 1880s, along and just south of Sherburne Avenue in an area known as Capitol Heights. Other substantial houses overlooked Central Park, a vanished swath of greenery now the site of a parking ramp behind the Centennial Office Building. Not a single historic mansion survives in the capitol area.

A small mansion district also developed along portions of nearby College and Summit Avenues. One of the first notable mansions built on College, originally much longer than it is now, was Farrington's octagon house. Others followed in the 1860s and 1870s, among them the Charles H. Bigelow House, a French Second Empire pile that stood for nearly a century before being demolished. A four-block stretch of Summit that once extended from near the St. Paul Cathedral east to Wabasha Street was also home to mansions. Much of this part of Summit was lost to freeway construction in the 1960s and later, while only a fragment of College survives near Kellogg Boulevard.

Some of the very earliest mansions in St. Paul were not built on the hillsides but instead occupied the level ground below the Summit Avenue bluffs along West Seventh Street and around Irvine Park. Two columned Greek Revival–style mansions—the Daniel Robertson and Alpheus Fuller houses, both from the early 1850s—once adorned the Seven Corners neighborhood. Another small area of mansions could be found along Pleasant Avenue. Among them was the Charles Flandrau House (1871), home to a celebrated jurist and later two well-known authors. The Alexander Ramsey House, an outstanding example of the French Second Empire style near Irvine Park, is the best-preserved of this area's surviving mansions, which include the Wright-Prendergast House (1851 and later) and the Joseph Forepaugh House (1870 and later), now a restaurant. East of Seven Corners, around Rice Park, there were also some large houses, but most were more on the order of townhomes than full-fledged mansions.

Elsewhere in St. Paul, mansions blossomed here and there atop the West Side bluffs, near Como Lake, in St. Anthony Park, and along and near the Mississippi River gorge at the western edge of the city, where engineer and inventor Oliver Crosby built his incomparable Stonebridge Estate in the early 1900s.

With the exception of Lowry Hill, Minneapolis lacked the commanding heights that appealed to so many of St. Paul's mansion

Deaconess Home (originally Charles H. Bigelow House), 181 College Avenue West, St. Paul, 1916. The eighteen-room mansion was razed in the 1960s after also serving as a girls' club.

Alpheus Fuller (later Lafayette Emmett) House, 279–81 West Seventh Street, St. Paul, 1936, six years before it was razed. Legend holds that Emmett's brother, Daniel, perhaps dreaming of southern warmth, wrote the song "Dixie" here.

builders. Because it was not founded until the 1850s and did not surpass St. Paul in population until 1880, Minneapolis never had as many pre-1870 mansions as its older rival.

The village of St. Anthony, which grew up on the east side of the Mississippi in the 1840s and finally merged with Minneapolis in 1872, was home to some of the earliest mansions, mainly near St. Anthony Falls and in the university neighborhood. The Ebenezer West House (1859), at 200 Second Street Southeast, was among the most prominent of these mansions. It is long gone, as are a pair of late 1860s mansions—the William Eastman House and the Charles Loring (later William King) House—that once occupied large lots on Nicollet Island. In 1879, millionaire miller and university patron John S. Pillsbury built the largest

William Judd House, Fifth Street and Chicago Avenue, Minneapolis, about 1885. Built in 1873 for a prominent miller, it became a boardinghouse before it was razed to make way for the Minneapolis Armory.

mansion in this part of the city at 1005 Fifth Street Southeast. It came down in the 1960s. Today, the houses in the Fifth Street Southeast Historic District constitute the best remaining collection of mansions on the east side of the river.

Across the Mississippi, in Minneapolis proper, mansions were strewn about rather haphazardly in the 1850s and 1860s. There was no zoning in those days (like St. Paul, Minneapolis did not approve a comprehensive zoning code until the 1920s), and in the free-for-all of the real estate market big houses could crop up almost anywhere. Still, most of the city's early mansion builders looked for sites away from the bustle, noise, and horse-manure enriched streets of the downtown core, then concentrated in the Gateway area around Hennepin, Nicollet, and Washington Avenues.

Vast personal fortunes accumulated with particular speed in Minneapolis because the city—perfectly poised to exploit the region's natural resources—grew so quickly. Flour milling, lumbering, manufacturing, and later railroading were among the most reliable routes to riches for Minneapolitans, but in many ways real estate was the most lucrative business of all. The buying and selling and financing and subdividing and developing of fresh new urban dirt was the great money sport of the time, propelled ever upward on heavily leveraged wings until the inevitable crash occurred. "The truth is that not even the wealth of a Rockefeller poured out upon this territory could have made the great Minneapolis of which these promoters dreamed," wrote one historian. During the height of the real estate frenzy in the 1880s, it was said that the young city could boast of thirty-eight millionaires, at least on paper.[7] Some of Minneapolis's finest nineteenth-century mansions were built by real estate developers like Samuel Gale, whose towered stone Italianate villa (1864) on Fourth Street was an early downtown landmark.

By 1875, a mansion district of sorts had begun to coalesce along downtown's southern and eastern flanks, in an area roughly bounded by Nicollet and Park Avenues, and Fifth and

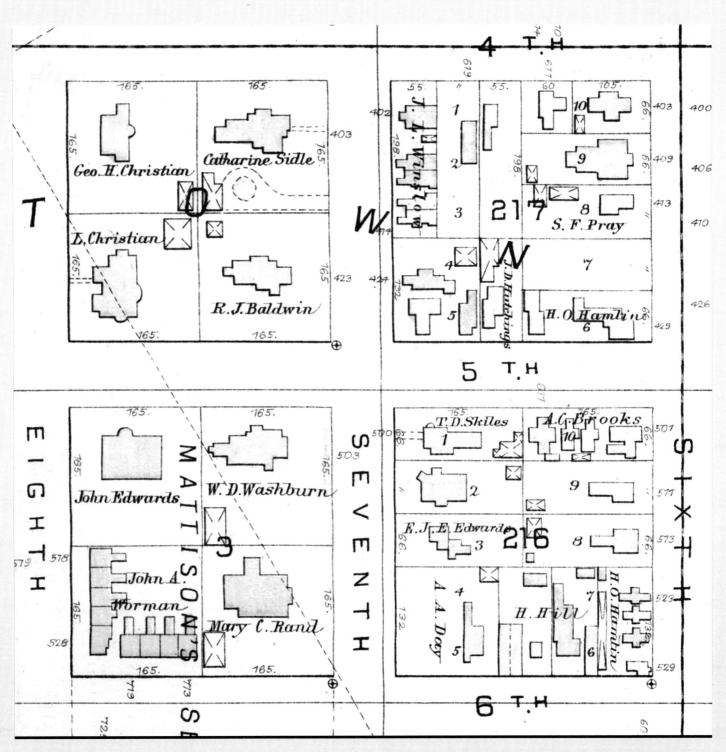

Real estate atlas showing mansions in downtown Minneapolis, centering on the area of Fifth Avenue South and Seventh Street, 1885. Many of the homes occupied lots that were a quarter block or more in size.

Eleventh Streets. Millers, merchants, real estate dealers, and professional men built houses here. The blocks around Third Avenue South and Tenth Street, where two members of the Pillsbury family constructed large houses in the late 1870s, were particularly choice, as was another node of mansions near Tenth and Nicollet. The last sizable house in what might be called the south downtown mansion district went up just before 1900, by which time other, more distant neighborhoods such as Lowry Hill, Loring Park, and Park Avenue had already gained favor among the city's financial elite.

The closely related Italianate and French Second Empire styles dominated the architectural conversation in the south downtown mansion district until a variety of other Victorian styles took over around 1880. The mansions here typically occupied lots a quarter block or larger in size, and some, like the William Judd House at Fifth Street and Chicago Avenue, had entire blocks to themselves. As the downtown commercial core expanded southward in the 1890s and into the early 1900s, the mansions and their big yards gradually gave way to office blocks, stores, hotels, and other commercial buildings. The homes that remained were often sold by their owners to be converted into rooming houses or some institutional use. Few mansions here survived past the 1920s, when a building boom reshaped large portions of downtown.

As the south downtown mansion district faded, the Loring Park and Lowry Hill neighborhoods began to fill in with large houses. Although Loring Park was not formally established until 1883, mansions had begun to populate the area by the 1860s. The park and its lovely pond made the neighborhood even more desirable, and a number of leading businessmen built houses nearby in the 1880s and 1890s. Among them was Samuel Gale, who vacated his mansion at Fourth and Marquette to build an astounding stone fortress on Harmon Place. By this time, mansions were also going up on Lowry Hill, a steep ridge named after streetcar mogul Thomas Lowry. A home built by Lowry in 1874 was the hill's first prominent mansion.

To the north, mansions appeared on Hennepin Avenue near Tenth and Eleventh Streets, and around Hawthorne Park, a vanished square now buried beneath ramps leading to and from Interstate 394. Lawyer-politician Eugene Wilson's estate, built in the 1870s a decade before the park's creation, was one of the area's showpieces. Another lawyer, William W. McNair, also had a large home here. Near Sixth Avenue North (now Olson Highway) and Lyndale Avenue, Samuel Gale in 1880 platted an enclave of winding streets known as Oak Lake. It was intended to be an upscale residential district, but most of the houses were not quite big or luxurious enough to qualify as full-fledged mansions.

South of downtown, however, two significant clusters of mansions, a few of extraordinary size and quality, developed around what is now Washburn–Fair Oaks Park and along Park Avenue. The two square blocks that form the park were once the estate of William Washburn. His vast stone house, which arose from the estate's beautifully landscaped grounds in 1884, was probably the largest mansion up to its time in either Minneapolis or St. Paul.

Washburn was not the first wealthy resident of the neighborhood, which even in the 1880s was still considered to be fairly remote from downtown. Dorilus Morrison—a flour miller, entrepreneur, and the first mayor of Minneapolis—built an estate known as Villa Rosa in the 1850s on a large parcel at Third Avenue South and Twenty-Fourth Street. Morrison's property eventually became the site of the Minneapolis Institute of Arts.

But it was Washburn's home and the equally impressive John W. Johnson (later Charles E. Pillsbury) House on Stevens Avenue that firmly established the neighborhood as a choice mansion district. Before long, other men of wealth—including members of storied flour-milling families like the Pillsburys, Crosbys, and Christians—joined the crowd. George H. Christian built the area's last mansion (now the Hennepin History Museum), at 2303 Third Avenue South, in 1919. Although a goodly number of the old mansions near the park remain, most have been converted to institutional use.

By contrast, many of Park Avenue's mansions, originally concentrated between about Eighteenth and Twenty-Eighth Streets, have not survived. At least twenty of the avenue's big houses are gone, including a pair of delightfully over-the-top Queen Anne–style homes: the Edwin R. Barber House at 2313 Park and the John E. Bell House at 2401 Park, both built in the mid-1880s. Many of the demolitions here occurred in the 1950s and 1960s, a period when historic buildings were often viewed merely as impediments to progress.

The streets west of Washburn–Fair Oaks Park, extending to Nicollet Avenue, also filled in with big houses, many dating from the 1880s and 1890s. The largest estate here was owned by

Chester Simmons House, 2741 Park Avenue, Minneapolis, about 1898. Built in 1891, the stone-walled, Chateauesque-style mansion was one of the avenue's major residential monuments until its demolition in 1959.

Richard Mendenhall, a banker turned florist, who in the 1870s built a mansion in what was then described as a "rural" area near First Avenue South and Eighteenth Street. The property, which included large greenhouses, was sold and subdivided after Mendenhall's death in 1906.

The most spectacular of all lost mansions in Minneapolis was in the Lake District, much of which was not developed until the early twentieth century. The mansion, on the east shore of Lake of the Isles, belonged to Charles G. Gates, heir to a vast fortune. Nearly forty thousand square feet in size and luxuriously outfitted, the house was finished in 1914, only to be demolished less than twenty years later.

A number of communities that now form part of the greater Twin Cities metropolitan area have also seen mansions come and go. In Stillwater, lumber barons, among others, built big houses as early as the 1850s. Many of these historic homes remain, but others have disappeared, most notably the hilltop mansion built in the late 1860s by lumberman Isaac Staples.

To the west, White Bear Lake became the summer resort of choice for wealthy St. Paulites in the 1880s, although very few of the big houses occupied Lake Minnetonka–sized estates. Even so, leading local architects like Cass Gilbert, Clarence Johnston, and Allen Stem designed fine homes. Dellwood and Manitou Island were the favored locales. Just to the west of White Bear Lake was James J. Hill's North Oaks Farm, established in 1883. It was by far the largest country estate in the history of the Twin Cities.

In suburban Minneapolis, Lake Minnetonka attracted the bulk of mansion builders. One of the first was Charles Gibson, a transplant from St. Louis, who acquired 108 acres of lakeshore in what is today Deephaven and built a mansion known as Northome in 1877. Estates of baronial proportions continued to spring up around the lake in the 1880s and 1890s, culminating in Highcroft, built by Minneapolis grain merchant Frank Peavey on Wayzata Bay in 1895.

Two of the most architecturally significant of all lost Twin Cities mansions were also at Lake Minnetonka. The Edward Decker House (1913) in Wayzata was designed by Minneapolis architects William Purcell and George Elmslie, leading practitioners of the so-called Prairie School style created by Frank Lloyd Wright. Wright himself designed the Francis Little House (1914) in Deephaven. It was Wright's last great Prairie School house, and its dismantling deprived the Twin Cities of an architectural masterpiece.

At least two other remarkable suburban estates appeared in the early twentieth century, both on the Minnesota River bluffs in Bloomington. The first belonged to Marion Savage, owner of the legendary pacer Dan Patch as well as a stock food company that made him millions. Savage's Classical Revival mansion looked directly across the river to the stock farm where he maintained an elaborate barn and racetrack. Not as well known was another blufftop estate, to the east, built by Minneapolis coal dealer Charles Wales. It included a mansion, an observation tower, a clubhouse, a barn, and other outbuildings.

Few of the Twin Cities' lost mansions could fairly be described as singular works of architecture. Instead, most were designed, with varying degrees of skill, in the popular styles of their times and were not greatly different from mansions built elsewhere in the Midwest. The pre-1880s mansions were generally smaller and less sophisticated than those that came later, although even in the early days there were houses exceptional either for the quality of their design or their use of novel structural techniques.

The late Victorian decades, from 1880 to 1900, produced some spectacular mansions, especially after the powerful Romanesque Revival style pioneered by Boston architect Henry Hobson Richardson became popular in the mid-1880s. By this time, truly gifted architects were practicing in the Twin Cities—Cass Gilbert and Clarence Johnston in St. Paul, Harry Jones and Franklin Long in Minneapolis, among others—and at

Alfred F. Pillsbury's sprawling summerhouse on Lake Minnetonka, off Ferndale Road in Wayzata, about 1904. The house was built in 1888 for Alfred's father, John S. Pillsbury, and was razed in 1954.

their best they produced houses on a par with the finest work elsewhere in the country.

Still, the golden age of mansion building in the Twin Cities did not come until a bit later, between about 1900 and 1920. Ranging in style from Art and Crafts to Classical Revival to all manner of exotic hybrids, the houses of this period remain unexcelled in terms of their overall quality of design, their often exquisite detailing, and their use of long-lasting and beautiful materials. Their likes will never be seen again.

The Modernist era, which in the Twin Cities began in the late 1930s but did not reach fruition until after World War II,

Charles G. Gates's palatial home at 2501 Lake of the Isles Parkway East, Minneapolis, about 1920. It cost $60,000 a year to maintain the house, which was completed in 1914 and succumbed to its own excess only nineteen years later.

also produced many handsome and well-planned houses. Grandiose new mansions were quite rare, especially in the 1950s and 1960s, when a rather Spartan aesthetic prevailed, and the rich seemed genuinely to believe that less was more. It was not until the 1980s, when more became everything, that the biggest new mansions began to rival some of the great estates of old in size, if rarely in quality. Fortunately, almost all of the best mansions of the Modernist era in the Twin Cities remain. The greatest loss is undoubtedly the Philip and Eleanor Pillsbury House in Wayzata, designed in 1963 by Minnesota's own master of Modernism, Ralph Rapson.

All houses are precious vessels filled with history, and in the case of mansions the stories of their owners tend to be especially fascinating, if only because they are founded on the twin American obsessions of money and status. Mansions are validations to the world of their owners' success, and in the beginning dreams pour into them like summer sunlight. Sometimes the dream holds and sometimes it fades, and when mansions come down, memories always float like airy fugitives amid the dust and debris. So it is with the lost mansions of the Twin Cities. Their stories range from the fantastic saga of Marion Savage to the continent-spanning conquests of James J. Hill to the lethal despair of early Como Lake developer Henry McKenty to the all but forgotten tragedy of Olaf Searle, a poor immigrant turned millionaire who found and lost a dream in the middle of Lake Minnetonka.

A newspaper writer long ago captured the special sense of loss that comes with the destruction of a house, regardless of its size: "Year in and year out . . . wherever cities grow strong and lusty and sprawling . . . the wrecking crews tear down old houses. All kinds of old houses these are: humble, weather-worn cottages, through whose windows, now broken and begrimed, untroubled eyes of children once peered, watching for 'Dad' and his tools and dinner-pail; larger, more pretentious dwellings which, with the march of progress . . . degenerated into rooming houses; old time mansions standing aloof and almost deserted, which have grown gradually shabbier and more lonely, like tired old men. And so the wrecking crews tear them down, one by one, these fine old houses. . . ."[8] ◆

ST. PAUL

CHAPTER 1

LOWERTOWN and DAYTON'S BLUFF

◆

In 1923, a writer for the *St. Paul Pioneer Press* took readers on a nostalgic tour of a vanishing world. "In the shadows of large commercial buildings in the once fashionable Lower Town district of St. Paul is desolation as grievous to certain of the city's pioneer residents as war-devastated places in France. . . . Homes that once were the abode of the well-to-do and hopeful . . . have disappeared before the encroachment of railway trackage and other things of commerce." Among the last holdouts was an Italianate-style stone house on East Eighth Street. Built in the late 1860s for George Peabody, it had been home for thirty-seven years to jeweler Edwin Brown, who had "remained in the old home until the time of his passing" in 1922 so that he could "live with familiar walls and furnishings."[1]

Brown's house, finally demolished in 1930, was among fifty or more mansions that once occupied portions of Lowertown, which in the pre-freeway era extended well to the east of its present boundaries. The finest homes were located northeast of Interstates 94 and 35E in an area now given over entirely to commercial, industrial, and institutional uses, leaving few visual clues that might explain why so many of St. Paul's elite—including James J. Hill, Amherst Wilder, and Henry Sibley—chose to live there long ago.

Part of the neighborhood's appeal was the scenic Trout Brook valley. Although rail lines first penetrated the valley in 1862, the brook and its surroundings retained much of their pastoral beauty until the 1880s. Now largely channeled underground, the brook was then a riffling stream. Its broad green valley attracted lawyer and railroader Edmund Rice, who built a country estate along the brook in the early 1860s.

By that time, St. Paul's population exceeded ten thousand, and its first generation of merchants, manufacturers, and bankers had already begun to amass fortunes. A brief building boom in mansions ensued. The heights of Summit Avenue and Dayton's Bluff were still considered a bit distant, whereas Lowertown was easy to reach and offered enough land for large lots. After 1872, it was also one of the first neighborhoods connected by horsecar to downtown.

Woodward Avenue, which once ran a block north of today's

George P. Peabody's Italianate-style mansion at 286 East Eighth Street, shortly after its completion in 1869. Jeweler Edwin Brown was later a long-time occupant of the house, which was razed in 1930.

Lafayette Park, southeast corner of Lafayette Road and Grove Street in the heart of the old Lowertown mansion district, about 1888. A parking lot now occupies the site.

Grove Street, was Lowertown's premier address. Hotel owner Jacob Bass's house was the first to appear, in 1857. His neighbors soon included banker Horace Thompson and entrepreneurs John Merriam and Amherst Wilder. Merriam, whose house sat on a triangle of land at Grove and Willius Streets, owned an adjacent block, which he and neighbors used as a playground. The city acquired the block in 1886 and turned it into Lafayette Park (gone), a pleasant little square with a central fountain.[2]

Eighth, Ninth, and Tenth Streets were also popular venues for mansions. One of the first, built on Eighth in 1856 and greatly enlarged in 1867, belonged to John S. Prince, a businessman of many interests and a five-time mayor of St. Paul. James J. Hill's mansion, at Ninth and Canada Streets (an intersection now buried beneath Interstate 94), was among the last to be built in the neighborhood. Railroads such as Hill's own Great Northern were the prime cause of Lowertown's undoing as a mansion district. By the mid-1880s, tracks had already filled Trout Brook valley and were chewing away at the bluff along Woodward. With the tracks came smoke, soot, and clamor from an army of coal-burning locomotives. Wealthy residents began leaving for more pleasant locales. Wrote one historian, "The lower town region, once so attractive, became too contracted . . . and too noisy for comfort, and a rapid hegira for the hills was well underway."[3] Merriam decamped to the Capitol Heights area in 1887, while both Wilder and Hill relocated to Summit Avenue.

In 1903 the *Pioneer Press* reported that "not much was left to Lower Town but the memories of departed grandeur." Some mansions were already gone by then. Others were lost to a tornado that tore through Lowertown in August 1904 after first knocking down part of the Smith Avenue High Bridge. Then, in 1917, the Great Northern began clearing away six square blocks for a new freight terminal (now a warehouse) at Eighth and Pine Streets.[4] More than 250 houses, along with schools and churches, were demolished in the process. By the time two interstates and Highway 52 consumed even larger chunks of Lowertown in the 1960s, no mansions remained.

To the east of Lowertown, the terraced hills of Dayton's Bluff offered splendid views but were hard to reach from downtown in the early days, and so attracted only a modest number of mansion builders. The neighborhood was platted by Lyman Dayton, who in 1849 bought five thousand acres along the blufftops. A few years later he built a large house near Conway Street and Mounds Boulevard. Other prominent men followed, including bankers James Thompson (Horace's brother) and Gustav Willius (one of many Germans who settled in the area), and "Commodore" William Davidson. Most of the mansions were along or near Mounds Boulevard, originally known as Hoffman Avenue. The Thompson House (1863), later owned by Patrick Kelly, was the most prominent of these early Dayton's Bluff estates, its twin towers visible for miles.[5]

Access problems prevented the neighborhood from rivaling Lowertown as an early mansion district. Separated from downtown by the boggy lower reaches of the Trout Brook–Phalen Creek valley and its accumulation of railroad tracks, Dayton 's Bluff did not fully develop until East Seventh Street was regraded from downtown via a series of bridges, cuts, and embankments in the early 1880s. The new grade allowed cable cars and later streetcar lines to operate. By this time, wealth in St. Paul was already concentrating along Summit Avenue and in the adjacent Hill District. Most homes built in Dayton's Bluff in the 1880s and 1890s were for the middle class, and the neighborhood's old mansions were subdivided into apartments, converted to institutional uses, or torn down. Construction of Interstate 94 in the late 1960s further reshaped the blufftops, claiming Lyman Dayton's old house, among many others.[6]

Edmund Rice Estate ("Trout Brook"), northeast of Phalen Boulevard and Mississippi Street, 1862 to 1883 (razed)

Edmund Rice was a Vermonter who put down roots in St. Paul in 1849 and founded one of the city's first law firms. His older brother, Henry Mower Rice, was by then already well established in the city and owned much of the land around the down-

Children at Edmund Rice's Trout Brook estate in the late 1870s, a few years before Rice sold the property to the railroads that still run through the valley. The brook has been diverted underground along much of its former course.

RES. OF EDMUND RICE ESQ.
New Canada Minn.

Phot by Illingworth.

Edmund Rice House, east of Mississippi Street between Granite and Acker Streets, 1867. Amenities included running water that was pumped from a basement cistern and stored in a tank in the attic.

town park that bears his name. Railroading turned out to be Edmund Rice's real passion, and by 1862 he was president of the St. Paul and Pacific, which laid the first track in Minnesota, through the Trout Brook valley from St. Paul to Minneapolis, in 1862.

Edmund Rice House and grounds, late 1870s. The estate took in nearly fifty acres and was one of the largest in early St. Paul.

Conveniently for Rice, he already owned a good chunk of the valley. Within a year or so of his arrival in St. Paul, he had borrowed $400 to buy 160 acres of land along the brook a half mile or so north of Lowertown. The seller was Edward Phalen, an ex-soldier of disreputable character who needed to unload the land in a hurry because he had committed a murder and was understandably eager to leave town. The property turned out to be a wise investment on Rice's part. When he sold off the last of it to the Northern Pacific Railroad in 1883, his total proceeds approached $400,000.[7]

A few years after buying the property, which remained outside the city limits until 1872, Rice fenced in about forty-eight acres to create what was probably the largest estate of its day in the vicinity of St. Paul. At the center of it, atop a windy hill, was a house built in 1862 and designed, according to one account, by an architect from the East. Clad in board-and-batten siding and Italianate in style, the house, where Rice and his wife, Anna, raised eleven children, was the family home for twenty-one years. The surrounding estate, landscaped with gravel walkways and rustic bridges, included a plum orchard, a horse barn, an icehouse, and a boathouse on a small lake created by damming the brook. The estate's animal life included cows, horses, chickens, and two beloved black labs named Moody and Sanky, who in winter were harnessed to pull a sleigh for the children.

In 1953, the Rices' last surviving child, Maria Rice Dawson, then eighty-eight years old, wrote a wonderful letter to her grandchildren describing life at the estate. The house itself, she recalled, was "spacious and comfortable."[8] The downstairs consisted of a drawing room where visitors were entertained, living and dining rooms, a library, a sitting room, a kitchen, and servants' quarters. Fireplaces with marble mantels adorned several rooms, but wood-fired stoves provided most of the heat.

Upstairs were eight bedrooms and three bathrooms with running water—a rare amenity in the pioneer era. The water descended from a tank in the attic after being pumped there from a basement cistern. Dawson remembered that the water pipes often froze in winter, making the bathrooms unusable. Her father addressed this problem by building a heated, three-stall outhouse equipped with a device for releasing "chemically treated red earth" after every use. It was, Dawson reported, "a very satisfactory arrangement," not to mention an early example of eco-toilets in action. Three house servants, plus several men to tend to the animals and grounds, were required to keep the estate going. "The laundry was a tremendous task," Dawson wrote, "and usually took three days each week. On sunny days it was a pretty sight to see the whole side of the hill covered with lines of white and colored clothes."

Described by one chronicler of St. Paul as "a large, commanding figure" with a "courtly bearing" and calm disposition, Rice encountered his share of reverses in the notoriously treacherous railroad business.[9] It was not until he finally sold the estate that he achieved financial security. Before then, he had offered to donate part of his property as a park, but the city turned him down. Well-liked in the community, he served twice as mayor of St. Paul and one term as a U.S. congressman before his death in 1889.

The site of Rice's estate is today a busy rail corridor, and the brook where his children once played was channeled underground long ago. Still, all may not be lost. When Rice's mansion was torn down in 1883, wood and other material salvaged by the wreckers was used to build six small houses, according to Dawson, and so it is possible that somewhere in one of St. Paul's old neighborhoods remnants of the beautiful Trout Brook estate survive to this day.

Woodward Avenue Mansions

Jacob W. Bass (later Henry H. Sibley) House, 417 Woodward Avenue, T. R. McConnell (Cincinnati), (started 1857) 1860 to 1896 (razed)

Horace Thompson House, 383 Woodward Avenue, John D. Pollock, 1860 to 1904 (razed)

Amherst Wilder House, 427 Woodward Avenue, John DeGraw, 1863; remodeled, ca. 1879 to ca. 1901–3 (razed)

These three houses, built within a few years of one another, once formed the finest row of mansions in St. Paul, each occupying well-wooded grounds of an acre or more on the north side of Woodward Avenue above Trout Brook. Only one photograph of the avenue at its height is known to exist. Taken in the 1880s, it shows the homes behind their low walls and high iron fences, while a carriage waits in the street as if to underscore the neighborhood's genteel elegance.

Jacob W. Bass began building the first mansion here in 1857. His timing was inauspicious—a financial panic soon engulfed the city—and he was not able to finish the house until 1860. Bass had arrived in St. Paul in 1847, five years after marrying Martha Brunson (brother of pioneer surveyor Benjamin Brunson, who laid out St. Paul's original downtown streets and whose 1855 house still stands in St. Paul's Railroad Island neighborhood). She was just fourteen when they wed (he was twenty-seven), but her young age does not seem to have provoked much comment at the time. The couple moved from Ohio to Chippewa Falls, Wisconsin, where Bass started a lumber business only to have it wiped out by a flash flood. Martha wrote that her husband was "perfectly prostrated at first" by the loss of his business, but that "he soon rallied and began to look around for some new enterprise."[10]

He found what he was looking for in St. Paul, where he bought a log building at Third and Jackson Streets, near the steamboat landing, and turned it into the city's first hotel,

Woodward Avenue, east from Lafayette Road, about 1887, with the Horace Thompson House at left. Woodward's days as a tony residential street ended when railroads came to dominate this part of Lowertown.

the St. Paul House. Sporting "a right smart tavern," the hotel became a popular spot, and in 1849 it was the scene of a meeting to organize the Minnesota Territory.[11] Bass sold the hotel in 1852 and branched out into other business ventures. One biographer described Bass as "a man of exalted purity," which certainly would have made him a rarity among tavernkeepers.[12]

Like almost everyone else with a beating heart in those days, Bass speculated in real estate, and in the 1850s he bought eighty acres on Woodward Avenue near Trout Brook. In 1857 he set aside two acres to build a sixteen-room stone mansion, at a reputed cost of $40,000, which was probably the largest home yet built in St. Paul. Although one newspaper cited the house's "magnificent proportions and exquisite workmanship," it soon became known as "Bass's Folly" because of the high cost of maintaining it.[13]

Mixing the Greek Revival style with the popular new Italianate look, the house had twelve-to-fifteen-foot-high ceilings,

Henry Sibley House and its well-shaded yard, 417 Woodward Avenue, about 1888. The house was considered the finest in the city when it was built for Jacob W. Bass in the late 1850s.

enormous front bay windows said to have cost $1,000 each, and expensive fittings such as silver-plated doorknobs. The house culminated in an octagonal cupola with a swirling domed roof right out of the *Arabian Nights*. A newspaper story claimed that this observatory, as it was usually called, was "large enough to hold a company of twenty or thirty persons inside, and on the outside many more. The view from this is unsurpassed."[14]

A master builder from Cincinnati named T. R. McConnell designed the house and supervised construction, living for a time in the kitchen with his wife. Many of the home's furnishings came from the East via riverboat, as did the Pennsylvania pine used throughout the interior. The home's amenities included a basement furnace that heated all but two of the rooms, and running water piped in from nearby springs.

Directly west of Bass's house, thirty-three-year-old banker Horace Thompson completed in late 1860 an even more interesting limestone mansion, designed by local master builder

Horace Thompson House, 383 Woodward Avenue, about 1880. The Bass-Sibley mansion next door may have been larger, but Thompson's house, in the Italian Villa style, was a more graceful design.

John D. Pollock at a cost of $10,000, a very substantial sum at the time. Unlike Bass's squarish house, Thompson's home was a dynamic exercise in the full-blown Italian Villa style, complete with an arcaded porch, heavy window hoods, prominent quoining at the corners, and a lovely three-story tower. Andrew Jackson Downing's *Cottage Residences* of 1842 may well have inspired Pollock's design. Little is known about the house's interior arrangements, other than that Thompson and his family enjoyed central heating, gas lighting, and indoor plumbing.[15]

Like Bass, Thompson hailed from Vermont. He was a newcomer to St. Paul at the time he built his house, although an older brother, James, had arrived in the city a year earlier. In 1863 the Thompson brothers organized the First National Bank of St. Paul, and Horace later served as its president.[16]

The third member of Woodward Avenue's mansion row was the Amherst Wilder House, located just east of the Bass-Sibley property. Wilder migrated from New York State to St. Paul in 1859 and gradually amassed a fortune from lumbering, railroading, banking, and other enterprises. His name still retains great currency in St. Paul through the foundation established in his name in 1906.[17]

He and his wife, Fanny, built their brick mansion, a rather conventional example of the French Second Empire style, in 1863, replacing or possibly enlarging an earlier house on the site. The designer was John DeGraw, yet another of St. Paul's early master builders. Described by one newspaper as "modest, yet commodious," the twelve-room house, which the Wilders expanded and remodeled in 1879, featured a rather gawky tower and a wraparound veranda.[18] It also had central heat and six upstairs closets, which must have pleased Fanny. The Wilders and their daughter stayed in the home until 1887, when they moved into a far grander mansion on Summit Avenue.

Although Bass, Thompson, and Wilder were all well known, Woodward Avenue's most famous resident was undoubtedly Henry H. Sibley. In 1864 Sibley bought Bass's house for $25,000, leaving the home (still standing) he had built twenty-six years earlier in Mendota. Dubbed by an admirer as "the first gentle-man of Minnesota," Sibley had come to Mendota as a fur trader in 1834, beginning a long career that ultimately involved him in business, politics, and war. As a treaty negotiator and later as a military commander in the Dakota War of 1862, he presided over the removal of the Dakota people from much of Minnesota, yet also sired a daughter by a Dakota woman. He served as the state's first representative in Congress and first governor, had a hand in many businesses, and even enjoyed some renown as a writer of outdoor sketches.[19]

A visitor to Sibley's house described it as being lavish: "The interior of the mansion with its high ceilings, large doors, broad staircase, heavy rails, elaborate chandeliers, frescoes and fine tapestries, reminds one of baronial times. There are oil paintings on the walls of his living room, one of 'Mendota in 1836,' and of his favorite hunting dog, 'Lion.'"[20] Yet the house also held awful memories, particularly of a night in 1867 when a young servant, Maggie Murphy, turned into a human torch after a kerosene lamp exploded. Sibley, his wife, Sarah, and his sixteen-year-old daughter Augusta were all burned—Augusta seriously—trying to put out the fire. Murphy died a few hours later, "in agony" as the newspapers put it, and Sibley never forgot the horrific scene.[21]

One day in 1888 a minister stopped by the house to see Sibley, who was then in his late seventies, in poor health, and thinking, as old men do, about his legacy. Sibley startled the minister by announcing that he was "very sad" and that he considered his life "a failure." He said, "I am nearing the end of my course, and as I look back, the only thing that gives me real satisfaction is the little good I have done. And I have neglected so many opportunities."[22] Despite his own misgivings, Sibley was greatly respected, and when he died in 1891 the *St. Paul Pioneer Press* described him as "the foremost man in Minnesota," although later historians have found less to admire, especially in his dealings with the Dakota people.

The mansion itself, a newspaper writer remarked in the 1880s, "suggests taste, comfort, elegance and permanency," but in fact was not destined to last much longer than Sibley himself.

*Amherst H. Wilder's first St. Paul house, 427 Woodward Avenue, about 1880.
Seven years later he built a far grander mansion on Summit Avenue, confirm-
ing his status as one of the city's nabobs.*

By the time of his death, Woodward Avenue's great residential days were over, and railroads ruled Trout Brook. Even so, Sibley's mansion managed to make some interesting history during its final years. In 1893, a couple obtained permission to move into the vacant home as caretakers. They and their children stayed until the mansion was demolished in 1896. Before leaving, the couple salvaged wood, window casings, and fixtures from the mansion, then used the material to build a small house nearby. They also salvaged an iron chest that contained many of Sibley's personal papers, which were later turned over to the Minnesota Historical Society.[23]

Monroe Sheire House, Ninth and Olive Streets, about 1870. Sheire was a contractor who designed and built some of St. Paul's best-known early mansions, including the Alexander Ramsey House near Irvine Park.

Today, all of Woodward except for a short stub off Payne Avenue has vanished, but the blufftop site where the three mansions stood survives as a little patch of urban wilderness, thick with cottonwoods, and it is still possible to imagine the old world there, where stone houses towered above shady lawns and Trout Brook flowed fast and clear below.

Monroe Sheire House, 357 East Ninth Street, Monroe Sheire, 1866 to ca. 1916 (razed)

Before academically trained architects from the East Coast and abroad began working in the Twin Cities in the 1880s, so-called master builders—essentially contractors who doubled as designers—were responsible for many of the early mansions in Lowertown and elsewhere in the cities. In St. Paul, among the most successful of these master builders was Monroe Sheire, whose own home on Ninth Street served to showcase his work.

Born in 1834 in New York State, Sheire was the son of a contractor. He appears to have been largely self-educated, learning firsthand from his father and also working for a time in Detroit, where he may have apprenticed in various architects' offices. In 1860 he found his way to St. Paul and within two years became a partner in a design-build firm. His younger brother, Romaine, came aboard four years later.[24]

Sheire's first big project in St. Paul was a Gothic-style stone chapel (gone) for the First Baptist Church, completed in 1862. Thirteen years later he built, but did not design, the congregation's present church, at Ninth and Wacouta Streets in Lowertown, a half block away from the earlier chapel. The Alexander Ramsey House near Irvine Park, completed in 1872, and the West Side home (1875) of brewer Anthony Yeorg Sr. are Sheire's other surviving works in St. Paul.[25]

The house Sheire designed and built for himself in 1866, combining French Second Empire with Italian Villa elements, suggests that while he was faring quite well, he was not as rich as many of his clients. Stone and brick were then the preferred materials for mansions in Lowertown, but Sheire built his fifteen-room house of wood, which was less expensive, at a final cost of about $9,000.[26]

Like much of Sheire's work, the house was not especially svelte, but its inset corner tower, which included two charming balconies, must have cut quite a figure at the corner of Ninth and Olive Streets. The house also had a wraparound front porch and the usual mansard roof with ornate dormers. Not much is known about the interior, but Sheire would have been able to furnish the house with all of the usual Victorian goodies. A wood picket fence, rather than the iron variety gracing many Lowertown estates, surrounded the property.

Sheire remained in the home until about 1880, when he moved into a row house he had built nearby. By the mid-1880s, many well-trained architects were working in St. Paul, and it is likely that Sheire's business at that point had turned exclusively to contracting. Sheire died of tuberculosis in 1887 while summering at White Bear Lake.[27] It is not known exactly how long his house stood, but it could not have lasted past 1917, when a new Great Northern Railway freight terminal filled the site.

Dayton's Bluff Estates

Truman M. Smith (later William F. Davidson, Albert Scheffer) House, 908 Mound Street (also 52 Bates Avenue), 1856 to 1858; enlarged and remodeled, ca. 1860s; remodeled, Millard and Ulrici, 1885; extant but greatly altered

James E. Thompson (later Patrick H. Kelly) House ("Fairview"), 230 Mounds Boulevard, John D. Pollock, 1863 to ca. 1908–14 (razed)

The older of these two Dayton's Bluff houses qualifies as a lost mansion even though it still stands. Used for many years as a nursing home, it bears little resemblance now to the mansion it once was. In its nineteenth-century prime, it was one of St.

Paul's landmarks, poised atop a high hill and encrusted with a two-story porch decorated in a gaudy version of the Eastlake style, which one writer in the 1950s dubbed "Steamboat Gothic." The house's long history, threaded with episodes of financial ruin, offers fascinations of its own, including one sale accomplished by means of a raffle.

Although the fifteen-room house was built for John Burns (namesake of nearby Burns Avenue), the first occupant was Truman M. Smith. When he arrived in St. Paul from Wisconsin in 1851, Smith was twenty-six years old and, by his own account, had "the enormous sum of six dollars seventy cents" to his name. Within a few years, however, he had opened a debt collection agency and was building a real estate portfolio, undoubtedly on borrowed money. In February 1857, he started a bank, and the next month he and his wife bought the nearly completed house on Mound Street for $9,500. Built of local limestone, the house was a Greek Revival–Italianate mix with no great ornamental flourishes, but was well appointed inside, with marble fireplaces and floors, frescoed ceilings, and a bathroom complete with tub and shower.

By October 1857 a publication hailed Smith as "one of the richest men in the Northwest." In fact, he was about to become very poor, very quickly. A speculative bubble burst that same month, plunging St. Paul and the nation into a monumental credit crunch. Smith's bank failed. Flat broke, he managed to stave off foreclosure of his mansion until 1864, even though marshals once forced their way in and confiscated his house keys. Smith was eventually able to forge a new career as a market gardener.[28]

The next occupant was William F. Davidson, who purchased the property in 1865. Davidson, who operated a packet boat company, was variously known as Commodore or Captain. Among other improvements to the mansion, he added a rooftop observatory resembling the pilothouse of one of his riverboats. The home's "Steamboat Gothic" decoration, however, was the work of a later owner. In 1871, Davidson sold the house for $24,000 to the *St. Paul Pioneer Press*, which in turn raffled

it off as part of a promotional campaign promising "$65,000 in premiums for 65,000 subscribers." The winner, who got the house for five dollars, was a certain Dr. J. H. Murphy, who quickly leased the property to a military academy.[29]

In 1885, the house came under the ownership of Albert Scheffer. Born in Prussia, he served in a Wisconsin regiment in the Civil War before beginning a long career as a banker in St. Paul. It was during Scheffer's tenure that the mansion achieved its ornamental apogee, the porches sprouting an extravaganza of sawn and turned woodwork designed by St. Paul architects Denslow Millard and Emil Ulrici. Views from the enormous wraparound porch, which was 151 feet long, must have been spectacular. Scheffer also landscaped the grounds, adding a small fountain and pond. Then, in 1893, yet another financial panic came along, and a bank started by Scheffer failed. In 1897 he was tried in St. Paul for embezzlement but ultimately acquitted. By 1899 Scheffer and his family had moved elsewhere, possibly because of a foreclosure.[30]

In about 1955, when the property became a nursing home, the porches were stripped of their Victorian finery and filled in with windows, and the old stone walls were covered with stucco.[31] Commodore Davidson's "pilothouse" is long gone as well. The lot has also changed dramatically, with houses now occupying the lower portion of the old estate along Bates Avenue.

A few blocks to the northwest, yet another banker, Vermont native James E. Thompson, built an even more impressive mansion in 1863, a few years after moving to St. Paul from Georgia, where he had done well as a merchant.[32] He and his brother, Horace, both commissioned mansions after arriving in St. Paul. James preferred the blufftops, while Horace settled in Lowertown. Known by the not very original name of Fairview, James's limestone mansion, near where Mounds Boulevard now crosses Interstate 94, was in the same towered Italian Villa style as his brother's. The houses also shared the same designer-builder, John D. Pollock.

According to one account, Thompson's wife, Susan, "took a

Albert Scheffer House and its elaborate porch, 908 Mound Street, about 1885. Truman M. Smith and William F. Davidson were earlier owners of the house, which once sold for five dollars in a raffle.

great interest" in the home's construction, "and, in fact, looked after many of the little details, so that everything was of the best." The house contained about fourteen rooms, was heated by steam, and had hot and cold running water. There are no known interior photographs, but the house must have been elaborately finished. All the doors, for example, were said to be made of solid oak three inches thick, an indication that few luxuries were spared. One newspaper said the house cost $30,000, which would have made it among the most expensive of its time in the city.[33]

James Thompson died of a heart attack while fishing near the St. Croix River in 1870, and around that time wholesale grocer Patrick H. Kelly acquired the house. Kelly, a native of Ireland, began in the grocery business in St. Anthony in 1857 before moving to St. Paul in 1863. He later went into partnership with Bruno Beaupre, and their warehouse at Third and Sibley Streets was one of the largest in Lowertown until it burned down in 1880. Kelly also became active in politics, wielding "great power in the (Democratic) party's affairs in the Northwest," according to the *New York Times*.[34]

After acquiring the house, Kelly bought more property around it so that the lot, defined by a handsome stone wall, eventually took up an entire square block bounded by Euclid Street, Mounds Boulevard, Hudson Road, and Maria Avenue. An 1891 map shows several outbuildings on the grounds, a fenced chicken yard, and a fountain set in the middle of a curving driveway.

Situated as it was, the house afforded Kelly and his family one of the best vantage points in the city. "P. H. Kelly may sit upon the spacious veranda of his stone mansion on Dayton's Bluff and look almost directly down upon every business house in St. Paul," *Northwest Magazine* reported. "From the cupola of the dwelling one may enjoy a bird's-eye view of the entire city, while Fort Snelling is in full view up the Mississippi . . . and the lower valley of the river is followed by the eye for a distance of more than twenty miles." The magazine added: "Mr. Kelly's house is, architecturally, much like the famous grocer—square and solid to look upon."[35]

Kelly and his family vacated the house in about 1892, eight years before the grocer's death. The house was later used as a sanitarium, a church home, and, in 1907–8, headquarters of an organization known as the Tuxedo Club. By that time, a group of houses, three of which still stand, had been built along Maria Avenue on the eastern side of the mansion's old grounds. The mansion itself was razed sometime before 1914, when the bulk of the property became a city playground. Interstate 94 now runs through the site.

Above Swede Hollow

Theodore Hamm House, 671 Greenbrier Street, Augustus Gauger, 1887 to 1954 (burned)

Samuel Mayall House, 735 East Seventh Street, 1881 to 1916 (razed)

Just east of Trout Brook, another stream, known as McLeod and later Phalen Creek, tumbled down to the Mississippi through a narrow valley called Swede Hollow, where breweries, mills, and a variety of makeshift houses occupied mostly by poor

James E. Thompson House, 230 Mounds Boulevard, about the time of Thompson's death, 1870. The second owner, Patrick H. Kelly, was a prominent wholesale grocer and Democratic Party stalwart.

immigrants jostled for space. Far above, however, on the high eastern rim of the hollow, there was a radically different world of mansions, gardens, and manicured lawns.

The house that lorded over the hollow above all others was the Theodore Hamm mansion, a busy Queen Anne pile culminating in a high-hatted tower, which was a St. Paul landmark for more than half a century. Hamm's son, William, began building the house in 1886 as a present for his father and mother, who presumably were surprised to see it when they returned from a long tour of Europe. The house posed in improbable splen-

dor above Hamm's ever-expanding brewery, which by the 1880s filled much of the hollow along Minnehaha Avenue.[36]

Born in Germany, Hamm had fallen into the beer business in 1864 after foreclosing on a mortgage he held for what was then known as the Excelsior Brewery. Hamm turned out to be a brilliant businessman, and by the 1880s he had made a fortune

Theodore Hamm House, 671 Greenbrier Street, towering above the brewery and Swede Hollow, about 1900. Hamm's son, William, built the house in 1886–87 as a present for his parents.

with the help of a talented brewmaster named Jacob Schmidt, who would one day go on to establish another of the city's great breweries. Hamm appears to have been a liberal and well-liked employer, once even urging his workers to form a union and vote for a president to represent them, only to learn afterward that he had won the election.

Hamm's fourteen-room mansion was designed by another German, Augustus Gauger, a St. Paul architect whose work seldom sank into the tepid depths of understatement. Built of red brick with terra-cotta and white stone accents, the house was like a shrunken version of one of the castles Hamm would have seen along the Rhine River during his tour abroad. When they moved into the house, Hamm and his wife, Louisa, by all accounts a formidable woman, had six surviving children—five daughters and a son. The home's interior, as shown in numerous historic photographs, was a classic example of Victorian decor, with dark heavy drapes, oriental carpets, floral patterns

Hamm House and terraced grounds, about 1890. There was a large flower garden on the east side of the house off Greenbrier Street.

Dining room of the Hamm House, about 1890. The fancy carved and turned woodwork was typical of deluxe Victorian interiors.

adorning walls and ceilings, carved woodwork, stained glass, and eight tiled fireplaces.[37]

As befitting its status, the mansion occupied large, terraced grounds. A meticulously maintained flower garden drew visitors, who could reach the house from Greenbrier (originally Cable) Street or via a winding drive and staircases that led up from the brewery. The Hamms staged an annual picnic at the house for the brewery's employees, whose benefits included free beer while on the job.[38]

Hamm died in 1903, by which time William had been running the brewery's day-to-day operations for many years. William moved into the house after his father's death. Other

family members were already living nearby in big houses built mostly in the 1880s and 1890s, forming a family compound along Greenbrier. William Hamm remained in the house until his death in 1931. His widow died there in 1933, the same year that William Hamm Jr., who had assumed control of the brewery, was kidnapped near the house by members of the Barker–Karpis gang. He was released unharmed four days later after the family paid a $100,000 ransom.[39]

By 1954, Hamm's was the fifth largest brewery in the nation, but the company's success did not extend to the old mansion. After a stint as a nursing home, the house became vacant, and in April of that year a fourteen-year-old boy got inside and started a fire. The old brick walls survived the flames, but the roof and interior were burned away, and the mansion had to be demolished. The brewery itself, which the Hamm family sold in 1965, continued in operation under several different owners until 1997. Today, most of the old brewery buildings stand vacant, while the site of Theodore Hamm's mansion, marked by a plaque, is now known as Upper Swede Hollow Park.

Before the Hamm mansion rose over the hollow, the neighborhood's residential showpiece belonged to Samuel Mayall. In 1881 he built a towering house on East Seventh Street just a block south of the Hamm property. Yet Mayall's house, which reputedly cost $35,000, never acquired the notoriety of the brewer's mansion. Perhaps it was because Mayall, though well known in St. Paul's business community as a lawyer and real estate investor, lacked what today would be called a high public profile. Instead, he seems to have been something of a stealth figure, quietly acquiring houses and commercial buildings until he became one of the city's biggest property owners.[40]

A native of Maine, Mayall served as a congressman from that state and played a role in founding the Republican Party before migrating to St. Paul in 1857. He left in 1862 to fight in the Civil War, serving two years as a captain. After returning to Minnesota he dabbled in politics, running twice as the Prohibition Party's candidate for governor in the 1870s. Real estate was his

Theodore Hamm and his grandchildren at the house, about 1903, shortly before his death.

Ruins of the Hamm House after fire, 1954. The home was vacant when a four-
teen-year-old boy found his way inside and ignited the blaze.

Samuel Mayall House, 735 East Seventh Street, when it was the Nugent Institute, a drug treatment center, about 1903. Mayall was once among St. Paul's largest property owners.

chief interest, however, although it does not seem to have been an especially happy career choice. A sympathetic newspaper article in 1888 noted that Mayall's "struggle to keep his realty has been an exceedingly unpleasant one and for years he has been fighting his way through lawsuits, struggling with mortgages, paying interest, taxes, and assessments, being defeated and swindled by cheating, dishonest tenants, and generally fleeced whenever any knave could get a hook in on him."[41] The story's spectacularly aggrieved tone suggests that Mayall himself may have had a hand in composing it.

Despite all of the scoundrels apparently intent upon sabotaging his efforts to make an honest dollar, Mayall must have done well for himself judging by the size of his house, a brick mansion of the French Second Empire persuasion dominated by a tall central tower and a broad front porch. Cruciform in shape with an unusually long rear wing, the house had sixteen rooms, although not much is known about how they were arranged and decorated. The grounds occupied about half a square block facing East Seventh Street.

Mayall died in 1892, but his family—he left behind a wife and three children—apparently stayed in the home for several years before a succession of institutions moved in. Among them was the Nugent Institute, which offered programs intended to cure alcohol and drug addiction. The institute proudly advertises itself in one of the few surviving photographs of the mansion, taken around 1905. Another tenant, beginning in 1907, was the city's Detention Home and Parental School, which the newspapers, with unblinking honesty, referred to as the "home for bad boys."[42] A variety of other private and public agencies occupied the house until about 1916, when one of Mayall's daughters donated the property to the Home for the Friendless (later known as the Protestant Home), which completed a new building in 1917. That building now forms part of a large nursing home on the site.[43] ◆

CHAPTER 2

CAPITOL HEIGHTS, CENTRAL PARK, and COLLEGE AVENUE

In May 1948 the *St. Paul Dispatch* reported, with a palpable sense of melancholy, the destruction-in-progress of yet another grand old Victorian-era mansion: the George Benz House, located behind the State Capitol. An official of the upcoming Minnesota Territorial centennial celebration was quoted as saying it was "a disgrace and a shame that St. Paulites are not interested enough in the city's early history to preserve such a fine building for posterity," but he might as well have been conversing with the wind.[1]

The fate of the Benz House was, or soon would be, the fate of all the other mansions, easily fifty or more, that had once been scattered around the Capitol area in an arc extending from now vanished Central Park on the east to the hills north of University Avenue to College and Summit Avenues on the west. Not only are all the mansions once there gone, but so, too, are many historic streets. Four block-long sections of both College and Summit Avenues east of today's Kellogg Boulevard were lopped off in the 1960s to make way for Interstates 35E and 94. Construction of the Capitol Mall in the 1950s obliterated several other streets.

The first mansions in today's State Capitol area appeared in the early 1850s, although most of the bigger houses were not built until the 1870s and later. Among the pioneer residents was William L. Ames, member of a famous Massachusetts family that owned the largest shovel factory in the world and also helped build the Union Pacific Railroad. In 1852, Ames, who later operated a three-hundred-acre stock farm a few miles east of downtown, built a Greek Revival–style house near Cedar Street and Bluff Street (today's Rev. Dr. Martin Luther King Jr. Boulevard), where the State Judicial Building now stands.[2] The house was greatly expanded in the 1880s and given a Queen Anne makeover by its second owner, lawyer Uri Lamprey, before being demolished in 1915. By the 1870s, mansions were also scattered along St. Peter, Wabasha, and Cedar Streets near the present-day interstate, and along the now vanished portions of College and Summit Avenues.

Mansions on Capitol Heights, north from Wabasha Street, about 1896, as work was beginning at the site of the new State Capitol. The John Merriam House, near University Avenue and Cedar Street, is at right.

Uri Lamprey House, Cedar Street and the present Rev. Dr. Martin Luther King Jr. Boulevard, about 1900. Built in 1852 for William L. Ames and greatly enlarged in the 1880s, the house was razed in 1915 to make way for what is now the Minnesota Judicial Center.

Peter Berkey (later Morris Lamprey) House, 137 College Avenue West, 1937. The massive stone house, a fine example of the Italianate style, was razed in 1944.

College, so named because it was once the location of an Episcopal mission school, followed a low ridge overlooking downtown, and those views made it attractive to early mansion builders who did not want to venture too far from the city's commercial core.[3] George Farrington's octagon house, built in the 1850s, was one of the first big homes to appear on College.

By the mid-1870s, the avenue's north side had become an outpost of the French Second Empire, with a row of mansarded stone and brick mansions set in large, hilly yards. Other mansions, including a foursquare limestone house built for Peter Berkey in 1864 at 137 College and later sold to Morris Lamprey (Uri's brother and also a lawyer), settled for less grandiose Italianate styling.

Two other mansion clusters in the Capitol precinct did not fully develop until later. Central Park (now a parking ramp

Central Park, south toward downtown, 1898. A parking ramp behind the Centennial Office Building at 658 Cedar Street now occupies the site of the park.

behind the Centennial Office Building near Cedar and Twelfth Streets) was created in the 1880s from land donated by several prominent businessmen, including banker William Dawson and wholesaler William Lindeke, who occupied mansions on nearby Bluff Street and wished to buffer themselves from what one newspaper described as a "repulsive" and "forbidding" neighborhood of run-down houses just to the south. The narrow, block-long park opened in 1886, just in time to become the site of St. Paul's first Winter Carnival ice palace. By 1890 a

half dozen or so new mansions, among them the superb Stone-Blood-Hardenbergh Double House, surrounded the park.[4]

Farther north, along University and Sherburne Avenues at the crest of the hills above downtown, the 1880s saw construction of some of the finest mansions ever seen in St. Paul. In 1882 William Merriam, who would become governor of Minnesota

John Merriam House (left) and William Merriam House, north on Cedar Street from University Avenue, 1888 (the year William was elected governor of Minnesota). William's house burned down in 1896, but the elder Merriam's home remained here for many years.

by the end of the decade, built a Queen Anne–style mansion near the northeast corner of University Avenue and Cedar Street. A few years later, William's father, John Merriam, built the neighborhood's undisputed masterpiece, a magnificent sandstone fantasy just to the west across Cedar. Other large Victorian homes lined up along Sherburne Avenue to the north. Around 1890 a handsome overlook was built at the east end of Sherburne, where Benz's house and its round tower struck a romantic pose.

A variety of forces, beginning with the decision in 1894 to build a new State Capitol a block from Central Park, doomed the neighborhood's lavish homes. Completed in 1905, the Capitol was a white marble missile shot into the heart of the mansion district, ultimately causing vast urban rearrangements. New buildings for Mechanic Arts High School (1911) and the Minnesota Historical Society (1917) soon appeared at the northern edge of Central Park, inaugurating a pattern of state and institutional expansion that continues to this day. New apartment buildings also sprang up around the park even as some of the old mansions took on second lives as rooming houses. The same trend occurred along College Avenue, where Farrington's mansion and several others were gone by 1920.

Two massive modern-era interventions—the State Capitol Mall, completed in 1954, and the construction of Interstates 35E and 94 a few years later—wiped even more historic homes, buildings, and streets off the map. By the early 1960s, when the John Merriam House was destroyed to make way for a new state office building, the neighborhood's transformation was complete. Today, a few old stone walls and staircases in the area around Cass Gilbert Park at Cedar Street and Sherburne Avenue are all that remain of what was for a brief time one of St. Paul's most elegant residential environments.

William F. Mason House, 542 North Wabasha Street, 1869 to 1954 (razed)

Most of the Italianate mansions built in the Twin Cities were either simple decorated boxes or towered affairs in the romantic manner of country villas. This rugged, L-shaped limestone house was neither. Despite such typical Italianate trappings as bulky stone window hoods and paired brackets along the eaves, the house's broad massing, low-slung hipped roof, and scaled-down third-story windows gave it the feel of a small Florentine palace from the Renaissance, somehow transplanted to faraway St. Paul.

Its builder and long-time occupant, William Findley Mason, was a native Philadelphian who arrived in St. Paul in 1858 at age twenty-one. He had already had some experience in the clothing business and within a year established what one publication described as the "first hat, cap and fur store in Minnesota," at Third and Wabasha Streets. By the early 1860s he had also married and purchased a large parcel of land at the northeast corner of Tenth and Wabasha, across from the First State Capitol.[5]

A portion of Mason's lot, right at the corner, was already home to a Greek Revival–style cottage built around 1850 by James Day, a pioneer building contractor. The usual protocol among mansion builders of the time would have been to tear down the cottage, but Mason kept it as a revenue-producing rental property. It stood until 1907, when Mason made plans to replace it with a two-story commercial building.[6]

Mason waited a few years before beginning work on his mansion, which was not completed until 1869. The house was large for its time, with eleven rooms on the first floor, ten on the second, and six on the third. Unfortunately, no interior images or plans of the house have been found, and the layout of the rooms is not known. An impressive stone wall surmounted by a low iron fence ran along the front of the property on Wabasha and around the corner on Tenth. Unlike some other mansions

of the period, the house initially had no central heat, but Mason remedied this deficiency in the 1880s by piping in steam from boilers in an apartment building he had constructed nearby.[7]

Mason and his wife, Isabella, raised three children in the house, which by the 1880s would have been near many other mansions along Wabasha and St. Peter Streets north of Tenth. The house must have been comfortable because Mason never moved. In 1908, while putting up screen windows, he fell off a ladder and died of his injuries.[8] Afterward, his widow and grown children moved to Summit Avenue, and the old mansion was sold. It became a rooming house in 1911 and may also have been a brothel at some point.

William Mason House, 542 North Wabasha Street, with the old James Day cottage from the 1850s still standing at the corner of Tenth Street, 1890. The horsecar passing by on Wabasha would soon be replaced by electric streetcars.

By the late 1940s, the neighborhood around the house had become ripe for urban renewal as part of the new State Capitol Mall and its approaches. In 1953 the city of St. Paul acquired the mansion, then home to about twenty roomers, and tore it down the next year.[9] Three years later, the city built a Public Health Center, which, with its parking lot, takes up the entire block where the mansion once stood.

Mason House, divided into apartments, 1941. Built in 1869, the twenty-seven-room limestone mansion may have been a brothel at some point during its long history.

Drawing and plans of an octagon house by Orson Squire Fowler, from his book published in 1854. Fowler believed eight-sided houses were models of efficiency, but the floor plans tended to be highly impractical.

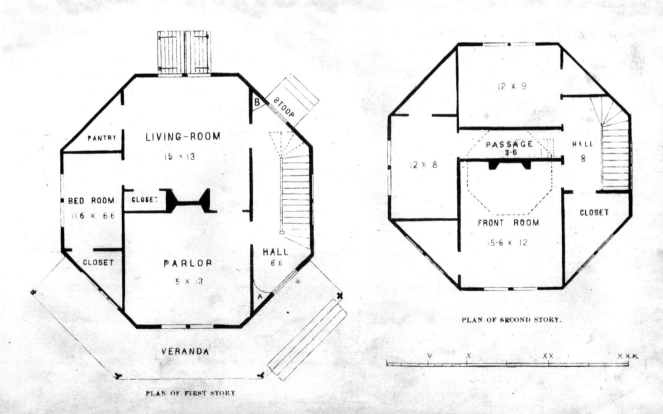

PANTRY

LIVING-ROOM
15 × 13

BED ROOM
11 6 × 6 6

CLOSET

CLOSET

PARLOR
5 × 13

HALL
6 6

B

STOOP

A

VERANDA

PLAN OF FIRST STORY

12 × 9

12 × 8

PASSAGE
3-6

HALL
8

FRONT ROOM
15-6 × 12

CLOSET

PLAN OF SECOND STORY.

COLLEGE AVENUE

George W. Farrington House, 125 College Avenue West, 1857 to 1917 (razed)

Erasmus M. Deane (later Reuben Warner) House, 173 College Avenue West, 1868 to 1943 (razed)

Implausible as it may sound, houses in the shape of octagons enjoyed considerable popularity in the latter half of the nineteenth century, thanks to a dreamer from New York State with the wonderful name of Orson Squire Fowler. In 1848 he wrote a book called *A Home for All, or the Gravel Wall and Octagon Mode of Building*, in which he extolled the many virtues of living in an eight-sided environment.[10] The book, which was also a detailed construction manual, inspired at least a thousand adventuresome souls, mainly in the East and Midwest, to build their own octagons. Today, 1850s-vintage octagon houses can still be found in Hastings and Red Wing, just south of the Twin Cities, and in nearby Hudson, Wisconsin, but none remain in St. Paul or Minneapolis proper.

Among those caught up in octamania was George W. Farrington, who with his brother, John, arrived in St. Paul in about 1850. He plunged into a variety of business ventures, served on the city council and in the state legislature, and in 1857 built St. Paul's first and only octagon house for himself and his family.[11] He used a concrete-wall system, as Fowler recommended, since the octagonal shape made standard wood framing difficult and costly. The concrete was poured into forms that could be raised as the wall grew higher, with a coat of plaster providing the final finish.

Although concrete had been employed extensively by the Romans, it was considered a novel material in the mid-nineteenth century, and Farrington's use of it stirred considerable comment in St. Paul. "George W. Farrington is building an octagonal two-story house . . . of concrete, the walls of which are completed," a newspaper reported. "This home of Mr. Far-

rington's is an experiment of his own, to see if a good house cannot be built of concrete. His experiment is successful in the opinion of Mr. F. and is worthy of the attention of those who intend to build, being much cheaper than either stone or brick, while it makes a solid and not unhandsome wall."[12]

No formal photographs of the house exist, but a distant view taken in about 1916 shows that it had a large wraparound wooden porch and a foursquare rear wing, which may have been an addition. Little is known about the home's interior, but it probably followed one of the plans in Fowler's book. Despite Fowler's claims to the contrary, the octagonal form made for clumsy interiors, with numerous small leftover spaces, often triangular in shape, that would have been all but impossible to furnish.

Farrington stayed in the house for less than a decade, moving on to Wisconsin and eventually to California. The house itself survived until 1917, when it was razed to make way for Miller Hospital. Today, the Minnesota History Center occupies the site.

The Erasmus Deane House, located along the only portion of College Avenue that still exists (between old and new Kellogg Boulevards), was far more conventional than Farrington's octagon. Part of an imposing row of stone and brick mansions, Deane's house was textbook French Second Empire, sporting a front tower decorated with iron cresting, a high mansard roof, and a broad front porch. Deane built the house in 1868, six years after arriving in St. Paul. He was best known in St. Paul as president of the St. Paul Harvester Company, a manufacturer of farm machinery that once employed more than five hundred workers on the city's East Side.[13]

The house's second owner, Reuben Warner, was another successful entrepreneur. He established an auction business with his brother, John, in the 1850s and later became a partner in Lindeke, Warner & Schurmeier, a dry goods wholesaling firm.[14] Warner died in 1905, but family members remained in the house until the 1920s, when it finally became apartments.

George Farrington House, 125 College Avenue West, southeast from Summit Avenue, about 1916. Its concrete walls were a novelty when the house, St. Paul's only residential octagon, was built in 1857.

Erasmus Deane (later Reuben Warner) House, 173 College Avenue West, at center, with Charles Bigelow House (left) and Ursiss Borer House at corner of Sixth Street, 1937. The Cathedral of St. Paul loomed over the houses, now long gone.

Known as Warner Flats, it was razed in 1943, as was an adjoining mansion to the east. Today, the house's site is a parking lot used by the nearby Catholic Education Center.

CAPITOL HEIGHTS MANSIONS

William R. Merriam House, 25 University Avenue East, Clarence Johnston, Queen Anne, 1882 to 1896 (burned)

John L. Merriam House, University Avenue at Cedar Street, Mould and McNicol, 1887 to 1964 (razed)

George Benz House, 5 Sherburne Avenue, Emil Ulrici, 1888 to 1948 (razed)

Around 1880 a developer leveled off the crest of what was then known as Sherburne Hill, a ridge just north of where the State Capitol now stands, and began to offer choice lots for wealthy homebuilders. A few big houses had been built in this area as early as the 1850s, but the mansions that blossomed in the 1880s were far larger and more luxurious. Among the first to colonize this new mansion district was William R. Merriam, whose house, built in 1882 at a cost of $30,000, occupied a superb site above University Avenue. Merriam was just thirty-three years old at the time, but he was already head cashier and soon would become president of the Merchants National Bank of St. Paul.[15] His happy circumstances were not entirely the result of dazzling talent, since the man he succeeded as bank president was his father, John, one of St. Paul's richest men.

Merriam chose architect Clarence Johnston to design his house. Today, Johnston is well known as St. Paul's premier designer of mansions, with more homes to his credit on Summit Avenue than any other architect. In 1882, however, Johnston was just starting his career, and Merriam's house was his first meaty commission. Johnston responded with an intriguing Queen Anne–style design based on English models. Built of red brick with white sandstone trim, the house was predictably picturesque, sporting an outsized bay window, porches adorned with delicate spindle work, a porte cochere, and much architectural theater along the roofline.[16] The interior offered a small forest's worth of oak, maple, butternut, and cherry woodwork, along with one especially eye-catching feature in the form of broad plaster wall friezes studded with sea shells. The effect of this oceanic ornament so far from sea salt must have been quite startling.[17]

A year after moving into the house with his wife, Laura, and their children, Merriam was elected to the Minnesota Legislature. In 1889, at age forty, he became the state's youngest-ever governor, serving two terms during which, according to one unimpressed historian, he "grappled with few large issues as measured against the problems of the times."[18] Merriam, whose rather odd nickname was "Spooky," loved to hunt, fish, and party, and his home was the scene of many lavish gatherings.

The good life at his mansion did not last for long. In April 1896 the house burned down while his family was away in Georgia.[19] A few years later Merriam headed off to Washington, D.C., to direct the 1900 census. He later moved to Florida, where he died in 1931. Today, Cass Gilbert Park occupies the site of his mansion, although some of the estate's old limestone walls still stand along Cedar Street.

While William Merriam's House was striking, his father's mansion, built just to the west across Cedar in 1887, was extraordinary. Constructed of rough-faced blocks in two shades of reddish Lake Superior sandstone, it was designed in the powerful style pioneered by Boston architect Henry Hobson Richardson (1838–86), who drew his inspiration from the medieval Romanesque architecture of France and Spain. The style—marked by the use of monumental stone walls, round arches, and leafy Byzantine-derived ornament—was especially popular in the Twin Cities from about 1885 to 1895. Minneapolis City Hall remains the greatest surviving local example of the style.

William Merriam House and overlook off Sherburne Avenue, west from Robert Street, about 1888. Portions of the stairway and retaining walls can still be seen today in Cass Gilbert Memorial Park.

Parlor with shell-studded wall frieze in the William Merriam House, about 1890. Merriam and his wife, Laura, hosted many parties in the house, especially during his two terms as governor.

John Merriam House, northeast across University Avenue toward Cedar Street, about 1890. The William Merriam House (far right) and other large houses nearby once made Capitol Heights a prestigious mansion district.

Intricately crafted sandstone walls of the John Merriam House in 1964, during its last year as home to what is now the Science Museum of Minnesota. The Romanesque Revival–style house was among the finest of all St. Paul mansions.

John L. Merriam, son of a New York iron manufacturer, reached St. Paul in 1860, two years after he had enhanced his business prospects by marrying Amherst Wilder's only sister, Helen. Before long, Merriam and Wilder were running a stagecoach line, the first of many partnerships. The men worked together so often, said a newspaper, "that it is almost impossible . . . to refer to the one without speaking of the other."[20] Merriam gradually added railroading, banking, and real estate (St. Paul's Merriam Park neighborhood is named after him) to

his résumé. He also served in the state legislature. By 1885 he was worth millions and decided it was time to leave his Lowertown house, an ungainly pile that hardly qualified as one of the city's ornaments. Merriam hired architects Charles Mould and Robert McNicol, who practiced in St. Paul for only a few years before moving on, to design his new mansion at cost of at least $75,000.[21]

Main staircase of the John Merriam House, 1937. Dark—some might say oppressive—woodwork was a standard feature in Victorian mansions.

Set on an entire square block, the mansion—with its chunky round tower, yawning arches, mysterious carvings, and checkerboard stonework—was massive, dark and dramatic, a castle built by commerce. The house evoked money and power, and as if to underscore the point, a grotesque winged dog perched atop one corner, guarding the riches. At the center of it all was a deep-set arched entrance, black as the mouth of a cave, and promising wonders within.

And wonders there were. "The house is a palace," reported the *St. Paul Pioneer Press* upon its completion in August 1887. Each of the main rooms was finished in a different wood, with mahogany, baywood, antique oak, cherry, and butternut among the anointed species. The main staircase, winding up through a balconied entry hall, had few peers in the Twin Cities. Italian marble fireplaces, stained-glass windows, and other luxurious appointments filled the house, which Merriam had only eight years to enjoy before he died.[22]

Above the Merriam mansions, at the crest of the hill on Sherburne Avenue, George Benz built a grand house in 1888. Like his fellow German immigrant Theodore Hamm (one of whose daughters married one of Benz's sons), Benz was in the liquor business, only he specialized in wine and distilled spirits. Benz landed in St. Paul in 1856, opened a billiard hall and restaurant, then went into the wholesale liquor business. He married in 1861, and he and his wife, Rosa, eventually had eight children. With its large Irish and German populations, St. Paul was a thirsty city, and Benz prospered. By 1868 his company was headquartered in a building on Third Street that included a 175-foot-long wine cellar dug out of sandstone thirty-five feet underground. Benz's sons later joined him in the business, which included ownership of a Kentucky distillery that produced whisky under such labels as "Old Blue Ribbon" and "Jack Silver."[23]

The lot Benz chose for his mansion offered some of the city's best views but was already occupied by a large brick house built a few years earlier. Benz solved this problem by buying the house and moving it to the rear of the lot. His new thirty-room mansion, among the most prominent on Capitol Heights, rose above a stone-walled cul-de-sac (called Merriam's Lookout) that included a small fountain and a staircase leading down to Robert Street (portions of these stairs are still visible). Designed by architect Emil Ulrici, an obscure figure who worked in St. Paul for only six years, the red brick house was pure Victorian romance.[24] Its octagonal corner tower, crowned by a steep conical roof, harbored a viewing platform that allowed the Benzes to take in the full sweep of the city below. There was also a wraparound front porch.

Within, the main floor offered a sequence of ornate rooms with fifteen-foot-high ceilings, a grand walnut staircase described by one newspaper writer as "a sight never to be forgotten," a ten-by-twelve-foot mural depicting two frolicking cherubs, fireplaces inlaid with patterned tiles, and the usual complement of fancy woodwork. Upstairs there were eight bedrooms and several bathrooms of extraordinary size (the largest was twelve by twenty feet). The third floor included a billiard room said to be "the finest private sports room of its kind in the Northwest." Practical amenities included a kitchen "larger than that of many a restaurant," a dumbwaiter, and an elevator.[25]

Benz died in 1908, but his descendants continued to occupy the house right up to the end. Its destruction came in 1948, by which time many of the mansions on the hill had already been relocated to landfills.[26] On Sherburne the last mansion to go was another towered Victorian from 1888, the Charles H. Petsch House. It came down in 1952 and was replaced by what is now the Education Minnesota Building.

Perhaps fittingly, the greatest of the Capitol Hill's houses, John Merriam's, was the last to fall. After Merriam's death in 1895 at age seventy, his widow, Helen, stayed on. Around 1905 she offered the home to the state as a governor's mansion. The state, unfortunately, said no—a marvelous opportunity missed. In 1927 the mansion became home to the St. Paul Institute,

George Benz House, 5 Sherburne Avenue, north from Merriam's Lookout, about 1915. The house, built for a prominent distiller, struck an exceptionally romantic pose.

forerunner of today's Science Museum of Minnesota. Despite adding a rear wing in the 1930s, the museum ultimately outgrew the house and moved into a new downtown facility in 1964.

Early that year, the *St. Paul Dispatch* reported matter-of-factly that "a St. Paul landmark, the brownstone building, north of the Capitol, which houses the Science Museum, will be a victim of progress."[27] So it was. The state of Minnesota, which had acquired the house in 1959, wasted no time tearing it down. Wrecking crews began their work in October 1964, and the house soon disappeared into rubble, although many of its deluxe interior features were salvaged. The State Administration Building, built in 1965, now occupies the site.

George C. Stone (Thomas L. Blood–W. Adams Hardenbergh) Double House, 665–67 Central Park Place West, Willcox and Johnston, 1887 to 1956 (razed)

This brick double house, one of the finest of its time in St. Paul, was the first residence built on the west side of Central Park. As was the case with many Victorian-era double houses, its original occupants were all related by blood or marriage.

The man behind the house was George C. Stone, a colorful character who sailed through life on a sea of bright expecta-

John Merriam House, north from roof of State Capitol, 1961. A bland state office building replaced the mansion after its destruction in 1964.

tions, undaunted by an occasional bankruptcy. He bounced around the Midwest as a young man, trying his hand without great success at banking and other endeavors before landing in Duluth in 1869 as an assistant to the local agent for Jay Cooke, the celebrated New York financier. Cooke's empire, an incomprehensible arabesque of leverage and creative bookkeeping, collapsed in 1873, and Stone found himself, at age fifty-three, broke once again. But he soon found a new dream, iron ore, and he spent the next decade rounding up money, supporters, and land. By 1883 he was general manager of the Minnesota Iron Company, which tapped into the rich ore of the Vermilion Range, the first of Minnesota's great iron mining areas.[28]

Although still based in Duluth, Stone spent $40,000 to build the double house in St. Paul as a gift to his two daughters and their husbands. The northern side went to his daughter Clara, whose husband, Thomas Blood, ran a paint business in St. Paul but was also secretary of Stone's iron company. The other side was given to daughter Ella and her husband, W. Adams Hardenbergh, a leather goods wholesaler. The gift came with a catch: Stone and his wife, Kate, reserved a second-floor apartment in the house for their own use. Whether this arrangement proved satisfactory to all involved is unknown.[29]

The house, like four others facing Central Park, was designed by Clarence Johnston and his then-partner William Willcox in the Richardsonian Romanesque style. In keeping with the Victorian love of the picturesque, the architects made sure

George C. Stone (Thomas L. Blood–W. Adams Hardenbergh) double house, 665–67 Central Park Place West, about 1888. Stone built the house for his two daughters and their husbands but also set aside an apartment for his own use.

to vary the exterior treatment of the two connected houses. The Hardenberghs' side included a corbelled tower and an inset arched entry reached from a small terrace. There was no front tower on the Bloods' portion of the house, but it did have an elaborate stone porte cochere as well as a charming oriel window on the second floor. Both sides, however, featured identical semicircular terraces overlooking the park. Little is known about the interior appointments, but it is unlikely they were spartan.[30]

Stone died in 1900, in Duluth. The Hardenberghs and Bloods apparently stayed in the double house until about 1905, by which time the new State Capitol had been completed and apartment buildings were beginning to dominate the area around the park. Over the next fifty years, the neighborhood slowly declined as mansions turned into rooming houses and the park grew scraggly. The creation of the Capitol Mall was the final blow. In 1956 Stone's splendid family gift was demolished by the state, and two years later the Centennial Office Building rose in its place.[31] ◆

CHAPTER 3

SUMMIT AVENUE
and THE HILL DISTRICT

◆

No street in the Twin Cities is more associated with mansions than Summit Avenue. Henry Mower Rice built the first house on Summit in 1851, and within two decades another twenty-five or so homes, most of them big enough to be called mansions, filled in along the avenue. All but a few were located on the prime blufftop portion of Summit between Selby Avenue and Ramsey Street. Topography and location made Summit especially appealing to mansion builders. The avenue offered a commanding height, was less than a mile from the heart of downtown, yet was well removed from Lowertown's sooty rail and industrial corridor.

Despite these natural advantages, it took a while for Summit to solidify its place as St. Paul's most desirable mansion district. Getting there was the problem. The steep bluffs that made Summit so alluring also made it, and the nearby Hill District, hard to reach. "It was difficult to get into the hill district from downtown; there was then no Oakland [now Grand] avenue, and no Ramsey street," an early resident recalled. "We reached

our homes either by going up Third street hill, or by going first to Rice Street and then up Summit Avenue. In winter it was especially hard."[1]

Horsecar service from downtown finally reached Summit and its environs in 1880, when a line was built up the hill on Third Street and then along Marshall Avenue. The service proved far from ideal, however. An extra mule was required to pull a car up the hill, but even then passengers sometimes had to get out and help push.[2] Still, the arrival of public transportation, along with street improvements, combined to make Summit more accessible than it had ever been before. At the same time, St. Paul was poised to begin a decade of unprecedented growth; the result was a building boom on Summit.

During the 1880s, about sixty mansions—half of them along the blufftop portion of the avenue—were built on Summit. Rapidly rising land prices were one indication of the avenue's growing prestige and popularity as a residential address. Noting how expensive lots had become, the *St. Paul and Minneapolis*

J. H. Allen House, 335 Summit Avenue, about 1900. By this time Summit Avenue had secured its position as St. Paul's great repository of mansions.

Pioneer Press said in 1883 that "the only plausible excuse for this advance is that there is only one Summit Avenue in St. Paul."[3] By 1890, most of St. Paul's ultrawealthy families—including the Hills, Wilders, and Kittsons—owned or were building mansions on Summit. By this time, too, a cable car line was operating on Selby Avenue. Electric trolleys soon replaced the cable cars, but the challenge posed by the precipitous grade up to Summit was not completely overcome until the Selby Avenue streetcar tunnel opened in 1907.[4]

Because so many houses remain, Summit is not usually thought of as a lost mansion district, but it is. All told, at least sixty houses that once stood on the avenue have been lost to either demolition or fire. Many of the avenue's early houses were demolished to make way for new, much larger mansions.

Edward Neill House, 242 Summit Avenue, a few years before its demolition in 1887. The house became one of many early "teardowns" on Summit Avenue when it was razed for James J. Hill's mansion.

There were eight such teardowns in the 1880s. James J. Hill's mansion at 240 Summit, completed in 1891, replaced two older homes on the property: Edward Neill's 1855 house (visible in the dogsled photo) and a later house built by George W. Armstrong. Hill's neighbor, Amherst Wilder, followed the same pattern, buying and demolishing the 1860s-vintage George L. Otis home before putting up his mansion. The decade from 1910 to 1920 saw the most demolitions on Summit, with eleven houses coming down.[5]

Among the lost mansions of Summit, two in particular stand out. Norman Kittson's vast house, which brought a gaudy conclusion to the French Second Empire era in the Twin Cities,

Houses on Cathedral Place designed by Cass Gilbert (left) and Clarence Johnston, 1890. These homes and Cathedral Place were swept away in the 1960s to make way for what is now St. Paul College.

Copyright 1904
by C. F. Gibson
St. Paul

Amherst Wilder House (left), looking southeast from tower of Norman Kittson House, 1903. The two great mansions once formed a remarkable urban set piece at the head of Summit Avenue.

was demolished in the early 1900s to make way for the St. Paul Cathedral. Half a century later, the St. Paul–Minneapolis Archdiocese razed Amherst Wilder's mansion, one of the largest houses ever built on Summit, and replaced it with a new chancery and residence.

In the 1960s a four-block-long section of the avenue, extending from today's Kellogg Boulevard to Wabasha Street, was lost to construction of Interstates 35E and 94. This part of Summit was never prime mansion territory, but it did provide a direct connection to downtown. A nub of what might be called old Summit remains just east of Kellogg, and it was on this block that the Arnold Kalman House, a remodeled Queen Anne extravaganza, once stood.

To the west and south of Summit lies the so-called Hill District, which also saw a wave of home building in the 1880s. Most of the houses were built for an upper-middle-class clientele and are not quite large enough to merit mansion status. Even so, a number of houses rivaling those on Summit did appear here, especially atop the bluffs east of Dale Street in what is commonly called Crocus Hill. At least two exceptional mansions have been lost in this neighborhood: the Russell Dorr and Theodore Schurmeier houses, which once stood side by side at 5 and 6 Crocus Hill, respectively.

At the northern end of the Hill District, a good many houses were lost to highway and urban renewal projects in the 1950s and 1960s. In one case, an entire street vanished. Summit (later Cathedral) Place once ran just north of the St. Paul Cathedral and was the site of houses designed by Cass Gilbert, Clarence Johnston, and other prominent St. Paul architects. The street and its houses were cleared away in about 1960 to make way for St. Paul College. On nearby Marshall Avenue, urban renewal in the 1950s claimed the Charles E. Dickerman House, a fabulous hunk of Victoriana that overlooked Summit Park.

Giants of Summit Avenue

Norman W. Kittson House, 201 Summit Avenue, Abraham Radcliffe, 1884 to 1906 (razed)

Amherst H. Wilder House, 226 Summit Avenue, Willcox and Johnston, 1887 to 1959 (razed)

For a span of just eighteen years, these two mansions—one a rather brutish but undeniably imposing pile, the other a grand exercise in Victorian eclecticism—stood across from each other at the head of Summit Avenue. The life of Kittson's house was short and unhappy, and its late French Second Empire styling gave it a rather antique air even when it was new. Wilder's house, by contrast, was easily among the most accomplished designs on Summit. Yet it, too, failed to survive the eroding forces of time.

The two men were as different as their houses. Norman Kittson, born in Canada in 1814, was a rough-and-tumble character who began his career in the fur trade, arriving at Fort Snelling in 1834 and later establishing a post at Pembina, North Dakota. In 1854 he moved to St. Paul, where he linked up with James J. Hill in various business ventures, including a company that operated steamboats on the Red River of the North. Thereafter, he became known as "Commodore" Kittson. He was also involved with Hill in railroading, owned large tracts of land in St. Paul, and by 1880 found himself in possession of an enormous fortune.[6]

Kittson spent a lot of his money on horse flesh. In 1881 he built the Kittsondale stables and racetrack in St. Paul's Midway area, and he also owned a large horse farm in Pennsylvania. When not tending to his money, Kittson was busy in the bedroom, reputedly siring twenty-six children by at least three wives. Clearly, he was a man in need of a large house, but his old homestead on Jackson Street just north of downtown was a modest affair, and so in the early 1880s Kittson, then approaching seventy years of age, built the biggest mansion yet seen in St. Paul, on the crest of what was then known as St. Anthony Hill.

Norman Kittson House, 201 Summit Avenue, in 1886, two years after its completion. The large yard included at least one statue.

Pioneer St. Paul architect Abraham Radcliffe was called on to design the mansion, and he produced a retro French Second Empire design that, sniffed one critic, "was erected, unfortunately for its beauty, at a time when poor attempts at classicism were the rage."[7] It did not lack for bombast, however. Kittson spent at least $125,000 on the three-story house, which enclosed twenty thousand or more square feet under its mansard roof. Built of limestone quarried near Mankato, the mansion included a four-story corner tower (with a chimney bursting through its roof) that may have been the most massive ever built for a private residence in St. Paul.

Within, the house was a wood-heavy fairy tale, each of its main rooms decorated in a period style. French and German Renaissance, "Henry VIII," and "Roman" were among those identified by the *St. Paul Daily Globe*, which devoted an article to enumerating the home's wonders.[8] Costly details abounded, including six stained-glass library windows depicting famous authors, a staircase made of hand-carved English oak, tapestries and damask curtains, wall and ceiling paintings executed in oil, overwrought chandeliers that were hideous even by Victorian standards, and all manner of custom millwork in cherry, sycamore, maple, oak, and mahogany. It is not clear how many rooms Kittson packed into his palace, but there must have been thirty or more. Two of the largest, a ballroom and a billiard room, were on the third floor. The kitchen and other work quarters were in the basement, and heat was piped in from a boiler located in an eight-stall carriage house on the property.

Pretty much everything about the mansion shouted overkill, and it is perhaps not surprising that Kittson seems to have

Dining room of the Kittson House, about 1888. Like most Victorian interiors, the room did not lack for decoration.

Amherst Wilder House, 226 Summit Avenue, about 1908. The red brick and brownstone mansion occupied a three-acre lot offering some of the finest views in St. Paul.

spent very little time there, preferring life on the road. In 1888, just four years after completing the house, he was aboard a train speeding through Wisconsin when he dropped dead at age seventy-four.

Kittson's will mentioned only eleven of his children, an oversight that occasioned considerable dispute among the heirs, and the untangling of his estate brought much employment to the legal profession. The mansion proved too much for Kitt-

Wilder House, second-floor corridor, about 1958. Deluxe woodwork was featured in many of the mansion's twenty-five rooms.

son's official widow, Mary, or his children to cope with, and by the mid-1890s it had become the fanciest boardinghouse in St. Paul. Its choice location soon attracted a buyer with big plans. Archbishop John Ireland, looking for place to build a new St. Paul Cathedral, kept his eye on the property and bought it in 1904 for $52,500, less than half of what the mansion had cost to build. Two years later the house came down, although many interior items were salvaged and can still be found here and there in St. Paul.[9]

Amherst Wilder was much less flamboyant than his neighbor across Summit, but he was nearly as rich. Described as a rather cold man who lived for his work, he, like Kittson, had started early in the transportation business, thanks in part to family connections (his cousin James Burbank founded a stagecoach line and operated steamboats on the Red River before Kittson and Hill took over the enterprise). Banking, wholesaling, and lumbering added to Wilder's wealth, and as the money flowed in, he decided to move up to Summit Avenue from Lowertown.[10]

In the mid-1880s Wilder purchased a three-acre site on the bluff side of Summit near Selby Avenue that included a house built in 1863 by lawyer George Otis. Wilder had the old house razed before he set about building his $130,000 mansion. Whereas Kittson had settled on one of the city's old-time architects to design his house, Wilder hired the recently minted firm of Willcox and Johnston. William Willcox was an experienced East Coast architect who had migrated to Minnesota, while Clarence Johnston was just beginning what would be a long and prolific career in St. Paul. The firm turned out to be a powerhouse, producing many outstanding buildings, including nearby Laurel Terrace (1887), the finest of all Twin Cities' row houses.[11]

The Wilder project began with construction of a superb, double-towered carriage house. Once it was done, work started on the mansion, which the *St. Paul Pioneer Press* described as a "baronial castle . . . grand in its proportions, picturesque and

Wilder House, partial view of two-story central hall, 1898. Plaster friezes, polychromed ceilings, and stained-glass windows were among the home's ornamental flourishes.

Wilder House demolition, 1959. A chancery and residence complex built for the St. Paul–Minneapolis Archdiocese in 1963 now occupies the site.

stately in its architecture and commanding in position."[12] Built of red brick and sandstone in an eclectic mix of styles derived from French and English sources, the mansion was indeed a rich man's castle. Among its extraordinary features was a three-level rear porch set at an angle beneath a conical tower. For many years the tower and porches posed in striking fashion above the steep Selby Avenue hill where streetcars climbed out of downtown. The house's main entry was sheltered beneath a Gothic-arched porte cochere reached via a winding driveway from Summit.[13]

Inside, the twenty-five-room mansion was organized around a galleried two-story-high hall modeled on those in English country estates. A gigantic fireplace presided over the hall, from which an elaborate screened staircase led up to the second floor. A panoply of Victorian decorative arts—polychromed ceilings, carved woodwork, stained glass, and plaster friezes—animated the mansion's deluxe series of rooms. Interior photographs suggest that the house was more open and certainly less suffocating than Kittson's overstuffed mansion.

Wilder lived in his mansion on the hill for just seven years, dying in 1894. His wife, Fanny, and sole child, Cornelia, remained in the house until 1903, when they died within three months of each other (Cornelia was just thirty-four). Their deaths touched off a legal challenge to their wills, which called for establishing the charitable trust that became the Wilder Foundation. Cornelia's husband—an elegant but dubious character whose name, Dr. T. E. W. Villiers Appleby, was perhaps more impressive than his medical credentials—fought the longest. The doctor's goal was to overturn a prenuptial agreement that limited him to a yearly income of $10,000 from the Wilder family fortune so long as he did not remarry. He lost and was finally booted out of the mansion in 1907 after four years of litigation.[14]

The St. Paul–Minneapolis Archdiocese acquired the house in 1918 for use as the archbishop's residence. Maintenance costs proved to be a burden, however, and the house slowly sank into decrepitude.[15] By 1958, it was vacant, and in June of that year the *St. Paul Dispatch* reported that the mansion would soon be torn down, noting that "demolition crews will find that vandals have already done much of their task for them, with most of the windows broken, building stones torn loose, everything not fastened down strewn about the building."[16] It was a sad ending to a magnificent house that very probably would have been preserved and restored had it lasted into the 1970s.

Around Summit Park

Osgood McFarland (later Arnold Kalman) House, 192 Summit Avenue, 1870; enlarged and remodeled, 1885 to ca. 1920 (razed)

Charles E. Dickerman House, 183 Marshall Avenue, Augustus Gauger, 1887 to 1955 (razed)

Although Summit Park still exists along John Ireland Boulevard, it bears little resemblance to its predecessor, established on part of the same site in the 1880s. Today's park, empty except for the Soldiers and Sailors Monument installed in 1903, has the feel of a leftover space, and its immediate surroundings— St. Paul College, a few old houses and apartments, and wide streets carrying heavy traffic—are not very attractive. The old park, which took in the southern half or so of the current one, was one of the city's beauty spots, occupying a triangle bound by Summit and Marshall Avenues and a now vanished street called Summit (later Cathedral) Place. Mansions ringed the park, which offered a central fountain, walkways, gardens, and numerous shade trees.

The two most notable mansions directly overlooking the park belonged to Arnold Kalman, a German-born banker and investor who arrived in St. Paul in the early 1880s, and Charles E. Dickerman, a prominent real estate broker and developer. Both houses were eclectic excursions into the picturesque, sporting the usual Victorian array of towers, turrets, gables, bays, balconies, and porches.

Summit Park, looking northeast from steps of the Norman Kittson House, about 1890. Across the park, the towered Charles Dickerman mansion rises above the trees.

Kalman's rambling brick house, at the southeast corner of Summit and what is today called Old Kellogg Boulevard, was actually an instance of remodeling on a grand scale. Beneath its Victorian finery was a simple brick Italianate house built in 1870 by Osgood McFarland, who managed the nearby Park Place Hotel (gone) and later became a wholesale grocer. In 1882 McFarland resettled in western Minnesota and sold the house to Kalman, who was then living in New York but planned to move to St. Paul. Kalman hired an unknown architect to enlarge the house and update its styling to reflect the latest Queen Anne trends, at a cost of $8,000.[17] Among the new features was a tall round tower placed rather incongruously in the middle of the home's busy front facade. A more attractive addition came in the form of a long, arcaded porch that swept around one side of the house, offering excellent views of the city below.

Kalman and his wife, Sarah, had four children, one of whom, Charles, was a friend of Scott and Zelda Fitzgerald and in 1909 founded the brokerage firm that evolved into today's RBC Dain Rauscher, Inc. The senior Kalman died in 1917, and his house was torn down a few years later to make way for the Park Court Apartments (1922), which remain on the site.

Although Charles Dickerman began investing in real estate in St. Paul in the 1860s, he did not move to the city until 1886,

when he began work on his $40,000 mansion, located on what was then known as Nelson Avenue but was later renamed Marshall. The avenue at that time extended a block east of its present termination at John Ireland Boulevard and formed the northern border of old Summit Park.

Born in Ohio, Dickerman ventured west to Iowa in the 1850s and first visited St. Paul in 1868, where by the late 1870s he had become a big player in the real estate market. "He bought large holdings, deliberately putting his whole faith in the ultimate success of the city's future," wrote one historian. "It is estimated that he bought millions of dollars worth of real estate, chiefly in what is now the wholesale district."[18]

To design his house, Dickerman called on German native Augustus Gauger, who had trained in Chicago before arriving

Arnold Kalman House, 192 Summit Avenue, about 1888. Built in 1870 for Osgood McFarland, the house was purchased twelve years later by Kalman, who remodeled and enlarged it.

Charles Dickerman House, 183 Marshall Avenue, 1936. The mansion's monumental front gable was unique in St. Paul.

Rufus Jefferson House (foreground) and Alpheus Stickney House, 276 and 288 Summit Avenue, about 1905. The neighboring mansions were both built in 1884 and demolished in 1930.

in St. Paul in the 1870s. Gauger's designs tended to be heavily ornamented and a bit overweening—qualities evident in Dickerman's brick and stone mansion.[19] The most curious feature of the busy front facade, which included a round side tower and small porch, was a tall gable encrusted with three Gothic-inspired columns and a pair of rocketlike turrets. Beneath this monumental gable were first- and second-floor picture windows, complete with balconies supported by massive brackets. Inside, there were about twenty-one rooms, counting those on the third floor. The major rooms were paneled in oak, cherry, baywood, gumwood, and redwood, and many fireplace mantels were said to be "richly carved after special designs."[20]

Dickerman died in 1905, and after that the house seems to have gone the usual route, eventually being subdivided into at least five apartments. It was torn down in 1955 as part of a massive urban renewal and highway building program that swept away the last remains of a once charming residential precinct.

Rufus C. Jefferson House, 276 Summit Avenue, George Wirth, 1884 to 1930 (razed)

Alpheus B. Stickney House, 288 Summit Avenue, J. Walter Stevens, 1884 to 1930 (razed)

These two houses, although built next door to each other in the same year (and razed in tandem forty-six years later) were quite different. Jefferson's was pure Victorian street theater, sprouting two towers along with an abundance of gables, dormers, chimneys, balconies, and porches. The Stickney mansion was more foursquare and businesslike, suggesting that its owner did not care much for Victorian fuss and bother.[21]

Rufus Jefferson, who hailed from New York, had already done well in the lumber business in Illinois by the time he moved to St. Paul in 1883 and built his mansion. Besides owning large tracts of pineland in northern Minnesota, Jefferson invested in local real estate, always a good bet in St. Paul in the booming 1880s.[22]

Jefferson's architect of choice was George Wirth, a German who had studied at Cornell University and worked in several architectural offices before arriving in St. Paul in 1879. Wirth designed seven mansions in all on Summit before moving away in 1890. Jefferson's red brick pile, generally Queen Anne in character, included a terra-cotta frieze and an entry porch wrapped around a front stair tower. Another porch to the side and rear folded around a second tower with a bell-shaped roof. The same sort of Queen Anne eclecticism prevailed within, where the main rooms opened off a long transverse hall. The decorating—frescoed ceilings, olive-green tapestries, gilded mirrors, heavy mahogany woodwork—was sufficient to suffocate a canary. Upstairs, there were eight bedrooms for Jefferson, his wife, Genevieve, and their seven children. It is not known how long Jefferson and his family occupied the house.[23]

Jefferson's neighbor, Alpheus Stickney, was a lawyer, builder, inventor, author, and entrepreneur who was allied with James J. Hill for many years before striking off on his own. Born in Maine, he studied law there and then made his way to Minnesota, where in 1872 he became general manager of the newly formed St. Paul, Stillwater and Taylor's Falls Railway. In 1879 he moved to St. Paul to superintend construction of Hill's St. Paul and Pacific Railroad. A year later, he began performing similar work for the Canadian Pacific Railway but resigned amid allegations that he had profited from speculation based on insider knowledge of the line's proposed route.

In 1885 Stickney founded his own railroad, which extended south from the Twin Cities and ultimately became known as the Chicago Great Western. Its tracks passed through a settlement called South Park just southeast of St. Paul. There, in 1886, Stickney and a partner established the St. Paul Union Stockyards in what would be renamed South St. Paul. That same year, Stickney also hatched a grand scheme to create a giant circle of rails in Chicago that would allow railroads passing through the city to exchange and sort their freight cars. Stickney bought four thousand acres in southwest Chicago to create the "clearing yard," as he called it, but his plan proved impractical.[24]

Jefferson House, about 1885. Rufus Jefferson was a prosperous lumberman from Illinois who moved to St. Paul in 1883, perhaps to be closer to pinelands he owned in northern Minnesota.

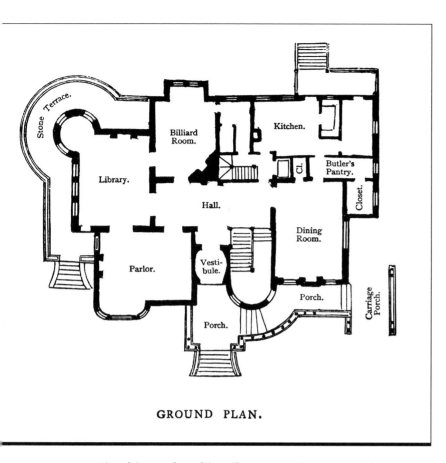

GROUND PLAN.

Plan of the main floor of the Jefferson House. The rooms were decorated with frescoed ceilings, tapestries, and gilded mirrors.

Stickney spent $40,000 to build his mansion on Summit. He and his wife, Katherine, had eight children, so a sizable home was needed. There was already a house on the property—Henry Rice's second mansion, built in 1857—and Stickney tore it down before constructing his residence. As designed by veteran St. Paul architect J. Walter Stevens, Stickney's stone mansion was plain for its time, with little exterior ornament, although a corner tower added a bit of a flourish to the proceedings.[25]

The house's most distinctive feature may have been its siting. Unlike virtually every other mansion on Summit, Stickney's had no front yard to speak of. Instead, the front steps, flanked by low stone walls, rose almost directly from the sidewalk to the home's entry porch. This proximity to the street gave the mansion the feel of a town house and also made it stand out from neighboring homes set farther back on their lots. Inside, the house consumed its share of forestry resources but was best known for its reception room ceiling, painted by

Stickney House, about 1890. Alpheus Stickney was an all-purpose entrepreneur who cofounded the union stockyards in South St. Paul in 1886.

Carl Gutherz. The Swiss-born Gutherz was a prominent artist in his day and later executed a mural at the Library of Congress.[26]

Stickney turned out to be the house's only owner. By the time he died a widower in 1916, his children were grown, and the house stood empty until its demolition fourteen years later. Its lot and that of the old Jefferson House to the north remained vacant until a condominium building filled in much of the site in 1996.

A child sits on the wall in front of the Stickney House, 1886. The mansion was built so far forward on its lot that the front steps began right at the sidewalk.

Russell Dorr House (left) and Theodore Schurmeier House, 5 and 6 Crocus Hill, southwest across Grand (then Oakland) Avenue, about 1900. Schurmeier's house looked like a hilltop castle.

CROCUS HILL MANSIONS

Russell R. Dorr House, 5 Crocus Hill, Willcox and Johnston, 1887 to 1958 (razed)

Theodore Schurmeier House, 6 Crocus Hill, Willcox and Johnston, 1888 to 1927 (razed)

As Summit Avenue lots filled in with new mansions in the 1880s, a number of St. Paul's wealthiest businessmen looked for lofty perches elsewhere. Just south of where Summit turned away from the blufftops at Ramsey Street, sites with spectacular views became available in Crocus Hill. James B. Power built one of the first homes there in 1879. Designed by his nephew, Clarence Johnston, the house burned down just three years later. The construction in 1885 of a new section of Oakland

Dorr House, about 1888. The first floor was built of brick and sandstone, but wood shingles covered the walls above.

(now Grand) Avenue along the bluffs helped open the neighborhood to development by creating a relatively easy grade up the hill for horsecars and later trolleys.[27] A tangle of short, often dead-end streets provided access to the houses on the heights there, giving the area a secluded feel quite different from Summit Avenue's open display of wealth.

Some of the largest homes were built along a short section of Goodrich Avenue known simply as Crocus Hill. To this day the street has one charming, albeit confusing, feature, which is

that its addresses proceed in no particular order. Two outstanding houses, in quite different styles, were built at 5 and 6 Crocus Hill in 1887–88. Both were designed by Willcox and Johnston, then among the busiest architectural firms in St. Paul. Clarence Johnston himself lived for many years at 2 Crocus Hill.

Schurmeier House, 1890. The mansion, probably the largest ever built on Crocus Hill, stood for less than forty years.

The Russell Dorr House, at 5 Crocus Hill, was an intriguing hybrid. Its main floor, built with walls of brick and Kettle River sandstone quarried in Minnesota, featured a deep Richardsonian Romanesque-style entry arch set beneath an ornately carved panel. Above, however, the house was faced entirely in shingles, à la the fashionable East Coast style later named for its favored siding material. Dorr's house, by virtue of its size and dramatic location, was among the most significant Shingle-style homes in the Twin Cities.

Built up from the edge of the bluffs, which were bare of trees then, the house featured a bulbous side tower with an open-air observatory, a broad central gable, and rear porches on every level. There were dramatic views from virtually every room in the house, "it having been designed with particular reference to all the landscape round about," said one newspaper. Huge bay windows at the rear, along with the porches, helped exploit these views. The kitchen and dining room were in the walkout basement, as were servants' quarters. The main floor's most notable room was a library in the base of the tower.[28] Dorr, who founded what later became the Minnesota Mutual Insurance Company, lived in the house with his family until about 1900. A succession of owners followed until the house was razed in 1958.[29]

Adjacent to Dorr's house, on the site of James B. Power's short-lived home, was perhaps the biggest mansion ever built on Crocus Hill, for wholesaling magnate Theodore L. Schurmeier. Described as one of the "grandest and most interesting houses in the city," it was a rambling mass of stone, brick, and terra-cotta that made for quite a sight from the flatlands below.[30] The mansion's unabashedly eclectic design culminated in a Victorian carnival of gables, towers, chimneys, and dormers, in styles ranging from French Renaissance to English Tudor. Despite its vaguely medieval profile, the house was thoroughly modern, and it was among the first in St. Paul to be lit entirely by electricity. Inside, the house was organized around a great hall. The hall and its inevitable grand staircase were finished in English oak. Equally inevitable was the outsized fireplace, which stood "in full view of the visitor as he enters the house," wrote an admiring news reporter.[31]

Theodore Schurmeier was the son of G. T. Schurmeier,

who founded a clothing company in St. Paul in the 1860s. After attending college in Ohio, young Schurmeier worked for James J. Hill and became a lifelong friend. By the 1880s he was a partner in the dry goods wholesaling firm of Lindeke, Warner and Schurmeier, which had grown out of his father's business. Schurmeier and his wife, Caroline, lived briefly on Virginia Street in a house designed by Cass Gilbert before moving to their mansion.

Schurmeier apparently led a troubled life, and when he fell ill on the East Coast in 1914, no one from his immediate family, including his wife, went to see him. He died alone later that year, at age sixty-two. Mary Hill, James J.'s wife, wrote in her diary on June 6, 1914: "Theodore L. Schurmeier was buried this afternoon. A pathetic ending to an unhappy life."[32] She did not elaborate. Family members remained in the home for some years after Schurmeier's death. It stood until 1927, when it was razed to make way for a smaller house, which occupies the site today.

August L. Larpenteur House ("Anchorage"), 341 North Dale Street, Davidson and Barber, 1860; remodeled, C. R. Dewey, 1891 to 1959 (razed)

By 1900 August L. Larpenteur, then approaching eighty years of age, was indisputably St. Paul's grand old man, the last of its founding fathers. He had arrived in the city-to-be in 1843, at a time when it was home to fewer than one hundred people, and embarked on a long career as a merchant, fur trader, and, of course, speculator in real estate (he was one of downtown St. Paul's original landowners). He sired ten children, spoke three languages (English, French, and Dakota), served on the city council, helped build a new St. Paul Cathedral in 1858, and was known to love fine horses. One chronicler of St. Paul described him this way: "He has a nervous, sanguine temperament, possesses a black, piercing eye . . . talks quickly, acts quickly, figures quickly. Judging from what he is now, one would think he must have been 'chain lightning' when young."[33]

As befitting his status as a successful pioneer, Larpenteur in 1860 built a stone house on the equivalent of ten city lots at the northwest corner of Dale Street and Rondo (now Concordia) Avenue. He, his wife, Mary, and his older children had lived earlier in downtown St. Paul at Third and Jackson Streets, near Larpenteur's business. The new house was a country estate located just outside what were then the city limits.[34]

The *St. Paul Pioneer and Democrat* reported in November 1860 that the house was built in what it called "the mansion style" and that it had twenty rooms.[35] Larpenteur and his builders, the local firm of Davidson and Barber, had started work on the house in 1856, but as with several other mansions of the time, completion was delayed by the financial panic of 1857. The house in its original form was a two-story stone box with hints of Italianate ornament. Little is known about the interior, but there must have been quite a few bedrooms given the size of Larpenteur's family.

Early twentieth-century photographs suggest that the house may have been enlarged at least twice to the rear, so that it eventually reached a length of more than seventy feet. St. Paul architect C. R. Dewey was in charge of at least one remodeling in 1891, when an upper front porch was added and the home's mechanical, plumbing, and heating systems were upgraded. A wonderful photograph of Larpenteur from 1910 shows him, dressed in tails and a top hat, sitting by the home's front porch, one hand resting on a cane. He looks to be a still sprightly fellow, even though he was eighty-seven years old.

Larpenteur lived at Anchorage, as he called the house, until 1917, when he moved in with one of his daughters not far away on Hague Avenue. He died in 1919, at age ninety-five, and with him went some of the last memories of what St. Paul had been like at the beginning of its urban life. Anchorage itself stood for nearly a century. Its last occupant was the Hazelden Foundation, which vacated the house in 1959 just before it was demolished for the Interstate 94 right-of-way.[36] ◆

August Larpenteur House, 341 North Dale Street, about 1900. The grounds encompassed ten city lots along Rondo (later Concordia) Avenue in what is now the Interstate 94 right-of-way.

August L. Larpenteur, looking sprightly at age eighty-seven, outside his home in 1910. He moved from the house in 1917 and died two years later.

CHAPTER 4

RICE PARK, WEST SEVENTH, and THE WEST SIDE

◆

Rice Park was set aside in 1849 as part of Rice and Irvine's Addition, one of St. Paul's earliest plats, but the park took a while to develop. The first shade trees were planted in 1860 (with members of the police force, for some reason, being called on to do the work), and by the 1870s the park's amenities included a bandstand and a fountain. Far bigger improvements came in 1883, when the city staged a gigantic celebration to mark completion of the Northern Pacific Railway's transcontinental line. President Chester Alan Arthur traveled to St. Paul to add some oratorical heft to the proceedings, and in preparation for his visit the park received a thorough upgrading that included installation of new electric streetlights (the first in the city).[1]

Despite the park's manifest charms, it never became the focus of a mansion district. Most of the homes that ringed the park in its early days, including a pair of "Alpine" cottages built on Market Street in 1866, were of modest size. Just a block from the park, however, on Sixth Street near St. Peter Street, a very substantial stone mansion was built in 1860 as a residence for the Catholic bishop of St. Paul. Later, at least one mansion, a

five-unit row house, and several double houses appeared along the park's western edge on Washington Street, but commercial encroachment from the downtown core limited further residential development. The proximity of Irvine Park (also platted in 1849) probably served to draw away home builders as well. Photographer Charles Zimmerman's Moorish-style townhome, dating to the late 1880s, was the last—and most interesting—house built on Rice Park.[2]

A few other town houses, a type of home common on the East Coast but rare in the land-rich Twin Cities, cropped up elsewhere in the vicinity of the park. Among them was the Jacob Hammer House, a busy Victorian that stood on long-gone Franklin Street. By the early decades of the twentieth century the blocks around Rice Park had been largely cleared of houses and were dominated by government and civic monuments such as the U.S. Courthouse and Post Office (Landmark Center), the St. Paul Public Library–Hill Reference Library, and the old St. Paul Auditorium.

The West Seventh neighborhood, located just west of

Seven Corners, was settled in the earliest days of St. Paul, and it remains the largest repository of pre–Civil War era houses (at least two dozen) in the Twin Cities. Located on level ground close to downtown and served by one of St. Paul's earliest thoroughfares, the neighborhood was well positioned to attract pioneer home builders. Like Rice Park, however, West Seventh never supported an extensive mansion district, and the neighborhood's oldest surviving houses are almost all of the working-class variety.[3]

Even so, two of the city's earliest Greek Revival–style mansions were built there in about 1853. The George Swift (later Daniel Robertson) House was originally located on West Seventh near Sherman Street, not far from Seven Corners. Alpheus Fuller's mansion was next door on Seventh. Both of these homes included two-story-high columned entry porches and were among the most monumental of their day in St. Paul. A few sizable, if not especially grand, houses were also scattered around Irvine Park by the late 1850s.

Horse and buggy on Fourth Street at Rice Park, about 1885. The row houses lining Washington Street in the background were torn down in the early 1900s.

Gothic Revival-style "Alpine" cottages on Market Street, across from Rice Park, about 1890. Charles Zimmerman's Moorish town house is at right.

Irvine Park area, west across Chestnut Street, about 1863. Half a dozen or more of the houses in this early view of the neighborhood still stand.

As St. Paul continued to grow, more mansions were built along and near West Seventh in the 1870s. Among them was the Grace-Mannheimer-Goodkind House (1874), which is perhaps most notable for the long and tangled preservation battle that preceded its destruction in 1999. Fortunately, the neighborhood's most elaborate mansion from this period, the Alexander Ramsey House (1872), still stands on Exchange Street near Irvine Park. Mansion building in the Seven Corners area ended by about 1880 as commercial uses came to dominate the area.[4]

Perhaps the closest thing to a mansion district in the West Seventh neighborhood was along Pleasant Avenue, most of which has been destroyed by Interstate 35E. Pleasant ran parallel to Summit Avenue but at the bottom of the bluffs, and so the best views may have been upward, providing residents with visions of even greater wealth to aspire to. Among the first mansions on Pleasant was a columned Greek Revival house built in about 1857 for pioneer grocer Henry M. Dodge. It was later home for many years to an antiques dealer named Conrad Searle. Wagon builder George Mitsch had one of the biggest houses on the avenue, a full-throttled French Second Empire mansion completed in 1874. The Charles E. Flandrau House at 385 Pleasant was particularly significant, less for its Italianate architecture than for its rich family history as home to, first, a distinguished jurist and, later, two prominent authors.

Across the river from downtown, the cliffs and bluffs of the West Side would seem to have been a natural spot for mansions, but only a handful had appeared by the 1870s. Much of the West Side did not develop until the 1880s, and the neighborhood's separation from the rest of the city gave it a somewhat faraway air that made it difficult to attract the kind of merchant princes who built along Summit. With its easily mined sandstone cliffs perfect for caves where beer could be aged, the West Side did attract German-born brewers, who built a number of mansions, including the Anthony Yeorg House (1875), still a fixture of West Isabel Street. Other mansions, built in the 1880s and 1890s by families with business interests on the

An unidentified man stands in the yard across from the George Mitsch House, 237 Pleasant Avenue, about 1895. People's Church (1889–1940) is next door to the house at right of photograph, and Summit Avenue mansions rise in the background.

West Side, dot the high ground along and just back from the blufftops.

Two of the West Side's most impressive Victorian mansions, the Paul Martin and Adolph Rosen houses, are gone. The Martin House was on Prescott Street and featured an exceptionally tall tower. Rosen's stone mansion occupied one of the finest view sites in St. Paul, near the top of the Smith Avenue High Bridge on Cherokee Avenue.

The third St. Paul Cathedral and the bishop's residence, Sixth and St. Peter Streets, about 1860; the Hamm Building now occupies this site. The second cathedral, built in 1851, is at far right.

Bishop's Residence, 19 West Sixth Street, Joseph W. Smyth, 1860 to 1914 (razed)

It was good to be bishop of the Catholic Diocese of St. Paul in 1860, since the office came with the right to live in this mansion, which may have been the city's largest house of the time, although its plumbing apparently was less than divine. The residence was completed two years after the opening of a new cathedral next door, and it is interesting to compare the two buildings. The cathedral, an underwhelming Romanesque-inspired design, was built on a tight budget that prevented construction of a planned 250-foot-high tower. The bishop's residence, on the other hand, was described by the *St. Paul*

The bishop's residence, one of the largest houses of its time in St. Paul, about 1865. The bishop occasionally delivered blessings from the balcony.

Pioneer and Democrat as "perhaps ahead of any other building in Minnesota, and will compare favorably with the palatial residences of our Merchant Princes in the Atlantic Cities."[5] The house cost $15,000, fully half as much as the far larger cathedral.

The home's builder and first occupant was Bishop Thomas Grace, who was installed in St. Paul in 1859, two years after the death of the diocese's first bishop, Joseph Cretin. Grace was a South Carolinian who had been ordained in 1839, studied in Italy for five years, and served churches in Kentucky and Tennessee before coming to St. Paul. He was to remain bishop until retiring in 1884.[6]

His residence was the work of local master builder Joseph

Smyth, whose only surviving work in St. Paul is a stone house constructed in 1862 on Stewart Avenue. For the bishop, Smyth designed a 7,500-square-foot Italianate mansion marked by formal Renaissance-derived elements, including a Palladian entry with modified Corinthian columns. The mansion consisted of a three-story main block crowned by a cupola, two-story side wings, and another wing to the rear. Above the entrance was a second Palladian arch, through which a doorway opened out onto a small balcony where the bishop could speak to his flock and offer blessings. Like the cathedral, the house was built of local Platteville limestone.

Inside, the mansion included a reception room, "an audience chamber," a drawing room, a library, and a dining room on the first floor, as well as a bedroom and dressing room. There were six more bedrooms upstairs. The kitchen and servants quarters were in the rear. Not much is known about the layout of these rooms or the interior finishes, although the woodwork was said to be "grained in imitation of English oak." The house was lighted with gas, but other utilities were woefully deficient by modern standards. A church historian reported that the mansion "lacked even the facilities of an ordinary bathroom until 1896; and it was heated by wood or coal burners in each room until 1910, when a steam heating plant was installed."[7]

The steam heat proved to be a short-term investment. In 1914, a year before dedication of the present St. Paul Cathedral on Summit Avenue, both the residence and old cathedral were torn down. They were replaced by the Hamm Building, which opened on the site in 1920.[8]

Rice Park Area Town Houses

Charles Zimmerman House, 342 Market Street, Hodgson and Stem, 1887 to 1926 (razed)

Jacob Hammer House, 380 Auditorium (Franklin) Street, Hamilton, Zschocke and Turner, 1887 to ca. 1959 (razed)

Charles Zimmerman—a photographer, painter, magazine writer, and entrepreneur—was among the best-known men of his day in the Twin Cities. Born in France in 1844, he emigrated with his parents to the United States at age four. By 1856 the family was in St. Paul. Not long thereafter, Zimmerman built his own camera and landed a job with pioneer St. Paul photographer Joel Whitney. After serving in the Civil War, Zimmerman returned to St. Paul and eventually bought Whitney's photo studio. In 1880 he branched out into the steamboat business on Lake Minnetonka, where he owned a summer home.[9] His fleet eventually included six steamers, earning him the sobriquet of "Commodore." One writer described him as "a bright, quick, courteous, gentlemanly-looking man, with dark hair, black eyes and dark whiskers."[10]

The brick and stone town house Zimmerman and his wife, Ida, built on Rice Park in 1887 was in keeping with his artistic sensibility. It was not especially large, but it was intricately detailed. The home's horseshoe-arched picture window (infilled with stained glass), framed geometric ornament, and third-floor loggia all evoked the Moorish architecture of Spain. Buildings with a Moorish cast enjoyed some popularity in the United States in the 1880s (and again in the 1920s) but were never common, and Zimmerman's house certainly qualified as an exotic specimen in downtown St. Paul.[11]

The home's designer, Allen Stem, was one of St. Paul's most successful architects. Initially in partnership with Edgar Hodgson, he later teamed up with engineer Charles Reed. Known for their expertise with railroad stations, Reed and Stem won the initial commission for Grand Central Terminal in New York

Charles Zimmerman House, 342 Market Street, 1890. Zimmerman, a well-known St. Paul photographer, also owned a fleet of boats on Lake Minnetonka.

City in the early 1900s, although other architects completed the project.[12]

Zimmerman resided in his Moorish confection until his sudden death aboard a streetcar near Lake Minnetonka in 1909. By then, the new St. Paul Hotel, also a Reed and Stem design, had begun to loom up behind the town house, which was the only private residence left on Rice Park. In 1922 it became a clubhouse for young working women. This new use did not last for long, and in 1926 the house was demolished.[13]

A more conventional Victorian town house also stood in

Jacob Hammer House, 380 Auditorium Street, 1890. Like this house, Auditorium Street (originally Franklin) has disappeared.

the Rice Park area, on now vanished Franklin (later Auditorium) Street. Built of red brick and brownstone for a man named Jacob Hammer, it was Romanesque Revival in character, with a busy roofline sporting a steep front gable and a delightful little dormer. Few other town houses of comparable size (about five thousand square feet) or finish were ever built in downtown St. Paul. The house's history is obscure, but it was demolished in about 1959, and the Travelers Insurance Company complex now occupies the site.[14]

George K. Swift (later Daniel A. Robertson) House, 287 West Seventh Street (moved to 344 Sherman Street in 1883), ca. 1853 to 1956 (razed)

The Greek Revival style, with its links to the earliest democracy, was thought to represent American ideals, and it was so popular in the United States from the 1820s through the 1850s that it came to be called the National Style. It was most commonly used for domestic architecture, and much of the Twin Cities' pioneer housing stock fell into the Greek Revival camp, although of a simple kind. This house, a full-dress Greek Revival mansion with a two-storied columned portico and side wings, was among the finest homes of its day in the Twin Cities.

The house was built for George Swift, who arrived in Minnesota in the early 1850s to invest in real estate but soon returned to his native Ohio. In 1855 the property was acquired by Daniel A. Robertson, whose career included stints as a newspaperman, lawyer, politician, honorary colonel, horticulturist, farm activist, real estate speculator, historian, and writer.[15] Born in Canada, Robertson moved to Ohio and then on to St. Paul, where in 1850 he established a newspaper, the *Minnesota Democrat*, and promptly took on two of the state's most powerful men—Henry Sibley and Alexander Ramsey—by accusing them of fraud in negotiating Indian treaties. Later, he veered off into politics, serving as mayor of St. Paul and then as Ramsey County sheriff.[16] He also found time to help found the Minne-

sota Historical and Horticultural societies, all the while wielding a sharp pen that made him, in the words of one biographer, "a most dangerous antagonist in a controversy."[17]

His clapboard house, occupying an oversized lot at the corner of West Seventh and Sherman Streets, featured a full-height portico supported by four fluted Doric columns. The main portion of the house was a two-story box, but there were wings to either side, which may have been later additions. No interior images have been found, and nothing is known about the size, arrangement, or number of rooms. It is likely, however, that the home had an impressive library, since Robertson over his long life amassed at least two thousand books, many of which he bequeathed to public collections.

Robertson and his wife, Julia, to whom he was married for fifty-one years, raised six children in the house, where they lived until 1883. In that year, Robertson moved the house around the corner to 344 Sherman and built a three-story business block on its former site. By then, the Seven Corners area was increasingly given over to commercial uses, and many of the neighborhood's houses became rental properties. Robertson and his wife apparently spent much of their time in Europe until his death in 1895.

Their old house was subdivided into apartments in the early 1900s, and by the 1950s had become something of a dive, many of its tenants "better known in the police files than the blue book," according to a newspaper columnist. The house was probably the last of its kind in St. Paul when it came down in 1956.[18] A medical office building now occupies the site.

John Grace (Mannheimer-Goodkind) Double House, 270–72 West Seventh Street, Monroe Sheire?, 1874 to 1999 (razed)

The many names associated with this house reflect its long and complicated history. Built by a Ramsey County sheriff, the house's tenants included a mayor of St. Paul, two prominent

Daniel Robertson House, after its move to 344 Sherman Street, about 1888.
Built for George Swift in 1853, it was among the most prominent Greek
Revival-style homes in St. Paul.

John Grace (Mannheimer–Goodkind) double house, 270–72 West Seventh Street, about 1930. The house had to be moved back on the lot in 1933 when Seventh Street was widened.

merchant families, and several generations of roomers. In 1980 it briefly became the city's first bed-and-breakfast inn, only to be plunged a few years later into a bitter preservation feud that ultimately led to its destruction.

The French Second Empire–style brick double house, possibly the work of master builder Monroe Sheire, was constructed in 1874 as an investment property for John Grace, who was retiring as Ramsey County sheriff after six years in office. The house stood across West Seventh from the home of former sheriff Daniel Robertson, whom Grace had succeeded. Unlike Alexander Ramsey's fulsome mansion (also built by Sheire) on the same block, Grace's rental house was modestly detailed, although it included a full-length front porch. The house looks to have been divided down the middle, with mirrored but otherwise identical floor plans.

Among the initial renters in 1874 was Dr. Jacob H. Stewart, then mayor of St. Paul. Stewart had gained a measure of renown in 1861 by becoming the first physician to volunteer for service with the Union Army as part of the First Minnesota Regiment. Captured by Confederates at the First Battle of Bull Run, he was freed in a prisoner exchange. Stewart moved from the house in 1876 after being elected to Congress.[19]

By 1877, two prominent, interrelated merchant families, the Mannheimers and Goodkinds, occupied the entire property. Brothers Robert, Emil, and Jacob Mannheimer owned a large downtown department store that bore their name. Their sister Mina's husband, Louis Goodkind, was also involved in the business. The Goodkinds and their five children lived on one side of the house, while the Mannheimer brothers—along with Jacob's wife, children, and mother-in-law—were on the other.[20]

The mercantile clan moved away in 1890, and for the next ninety years the home was a boarding house and later apartments. The house, which in 1933 was moved back on its lot to accommodate widening of West Seventh, gradually settled into a state of genteel shabbiness. When new owners transformed it into the Bleick House in 1980, it looked to have a bright future, but the bed-and-breakfast folded after only three years.[21]

The owners of a neighboring structural steel company bought the property, by then part of the Irvine Park Historic District, with the idea of turning it into corporate offices. Their plans ran afoul of preservation guidelines, however, and a protracted battle ensued. By late 1980s one of the owners had resorted to scrawling derogatory messages (sample: "St. Paul preserves another eyesore") on the home's boarded-up windows. The situation went downhill from there. In 1999 the city finally approved demolition of the vacant, all but ruined house.[22]

Charles E. (later Charles M., Grace) Flandrau House, 385 Pleasant Avenue, 1871 to 1955 (razed)

St. Paul has long been home to more than its share of writers, but why the city spawns so much literary talent remains a matter of guesswork. Perhaps the presence of so many old moneyed families, a rich source of fictional material, has something to do with it. Then, too, there is the vaguely melancholic arc of the city's history. It burst to life with phenomenal promise in the nineteenth century only to lag behind its flashier cross-river rival, settling in on itself like a collapsed star, dense with its own peculiar gravity. F. Scott Fitzgerald is—and probably always will be—the city's most famous literary presence, but there were many others.

Among them were the Flandraus, a family of writers that included jurist and historian Charles E. Flandrau, his son Charles Macomb Flandrau (usually called Charlie), and his daughter-in-law, Grace Flandrau. All of them lived at one time or another in the family home, and few other St. Paul mansions have had such a long association—more than eight decades—with a single family. The Italianate-style house, which in its later years became a rather spooky old place, was well known to Fitzgerald (a friend and admirer of the younger Flandrau). Sinclair Lewis also visited from time to time.[23]

The elder Flandrau, who arrived in St. Paul in 1853 from New York, was an Indian agent, lawyer, politician, and ultimately an associate justice of the Minnesota Supreme Court. He was especially renowned for leading the defense of New Ulm, Minnesota, during the 1862 Dakota War. Adventurous, self-possessed, and charming, he also had a lethal streak, displayed in New Ulm when he laced a barrel of whisky with strychnine to poison Indians at random (he ultimately abandoned the plan, fearing soldiers might drink the liquor). Before his death in 1903, he wrote several books, including *Encyclopedia of Biography of Minnesota*, still a valuable reference work.

Although Flandrau was well off, he was not among St. Paul's

Flandrau House, 385 Pleasant Avenue, 1950. Charles E. Flandrau built the house in 1871, and it stayed in the family until it was razed in 1955.

richest men, and so he chose to build his new house on Pleasant Avenue, literally a step below Summit Avenue. Located along what is today the north side of Interstate 35E just east of Grand Avenue, the house was set on a five-acre bluffside lot offering a mix of gardens, woods, and ravines, which Charlie called "our little Paradise." The house, sided in clapboard, was broad and plain, with an expansive front porch. Inside, an entry hall with a mahogany parquet floor and redwood paneling led to a winding staircase. Two libraries, one redecorated in the fashionable Moorish style, were among the most prominent rooms.

The house sheltered a blended family that by 1875 included five children. Charles E. Flandrau had two daughters by his first wife. After her death, he remarried and sired two sons—Charlie and William (who went by his middle name, Blair)—with his second wife, Rebecca. She in turn had a son from her first marriage, John W. Riddle. He became a career diplomat and served as U.S. ambassador to Russia under President Theodore Roosevelt, who also happened to be a friend of Charles E. Flandrau and an occasional dinner guest at the house on Pleasant. It was indeed a small world in those days.

Charlie Flandrau was born in 1871, the same year as the house was built, and he was to spend his entire life there, although he traveled widely and lived for long stretches in Mexico and France. By the time he went off to Harvard in 1891, young Flandrau was already an accomplished writer. In 1897 he made a name for himself with the publication of a series of stories about his college life called *Harvard Episodes*. Tart and lively, the book was widely reviewed, and before long Flandrau was writing stories for the *Saturday Evening Post* (where Fitzgerald would later become a star).

There was soon talk that Flandrau might well might become a leading literary figure. It never happened. He lacked the passion and ambition that drove Fitzgerald, perhaps in part because he had no need to earn a living (family stock investments made him well off his entire life). He was also an alcoholic and probably a closeted gay, both of which did not make his life any easier. Although he went on to produce one highly regarded travel book, *Viva Mexico!* (1908), the promise of his youth was never fulfilled. He died, at home, in 1938, and today his work is little remembered.[24]

Grace Hodgson Flandrau, who married Charlie's brother, Blair, in 1909, lived in the family house for the next few years and again after her husband's death, also in 1938. She was a fascinating character—a brilliant observer, a clever social satirist, a piquant writer, and the life of every party. Her first three novels, which appeared between 1917 and 1924, were crisp social

Charles E. Flandrau (right), with sons Blair (left) and Charlie (standing) and stepson John W. Riddle, about 1895. Charlie was a popular writer and a friend of F. Scott Fitzgerald.

Grace Flandrau and canine friend, about 1917. She was the last member of the family to live in the house on Pleasant Avenue.

satires of high society, and one of them, *Being Respectable*, was made into a movie. Like her brother-in-law, she also wrote a popular travel book, *Then I Saw the Congo* (1929), and was the author of many short stories, essays, and journalistic pieces.

Yet at the heart of her life was a dark family secret centering on her father, Edward J. Hodgson, a wealthy St. Paul banker. After his death in 1903, Flandrau learned that she was in fact the daughter of his longtime mistress, not his wife, who nonetheless had raised Grace as if she were her own child. It was a devastating revelation—there may have been sexual abuse as well—one that Flandrau finally explored in her last novel, *Indeed This Flesh* (1934).[25]

As the years went on, her literary career tailed off into obscurity. In 1950, she left St. Paul for good after specifying, as Charlie had insisted in his will, that the family house be demolished rather than sold or moved. For some reason, it took five years before the house, where the greatest Flandrau stories of all had played out, was finally torn down. No other house was ever built on the property, which is today a small parcel of wild woodland.

West Side Mansions

Paul Martin House, 225 Prescott Street, Edward P. Bassford, 1887 to 1970s (razed)

Adolph T. Rosen House, 334 Cherokee Avenue, 1899 to 1963 (razed)

Although neither of these houses was as grand as those on Summit Avenue, both exploited sites with superb views. As with other West Side mansions, they were built by men with businesses in the neighborhood. Originally an independent community in Dakota County, the West Side area was annexed to St. Paul in 1874. Many of its residents—Germans predominated—also worked in the neighborhood, in the breweries and factories that occupied the river flats.

Paul Martin was a prominent West Side real estate dealer and developer who built at least two business blocks bearing his name (on South Robert and Wabasha Streets). In 1887 he also built one of the neighborhood's biggest houses, on a blufftop lot on Prescott Street. Designed by longtime St. Paul architect Edward P. Bassford, the house was an Eastlake–Queen Anne blend with a tinge of the North Germanic in its banded white stone and red brick window arches. What really made the house stand out was an angled four-story-high rear tower that culminated in a tall, steep roof. Inside, there was a fine open staircase and a fireplace in every room.[26]

Martin was not in the house for long. Charles H. Lienau, publisher of a German-language newspaper in St. Paul, bought the house in 1890. He, too, had a short stay, moving to California five years later. The house went through a variety of owners and tenants (it served briefly as a drug treatment center) over the next decade. Then, in about 1908, it became the St. Paul German Hospital, where surgery was perfumed in the tower's top floor to take advantage of the good light there. Renamed West Side General in 1913, the hospital was enlarged in 1928 with the addition of a wing to the south side of the old house. The mansion's last incarnation was as part of Riverview Memorial Hospital, which opened in 1949. Known as the "north wing," the old mansion remained in use as office, storage, and laboratory space until its demolition in the 1970s. Riverview Hospital operated until 1980, when it, too, was torn down.[27]

The Adolph T. Rosen House, perched near the top of the Smith Avenue High Bridge, was built for a Swedish immigrant who found success in the fur business in St. Paul. Born in 1856, Rosen went off to sea at age fourteen, neglecting to tell his parents of his plan, and they thought he was dead until he suddenly returned home four years later. He soon married and, for reasons unknown, adopted his wife's last name (his birth surname remains a mystery). In 1880 he made his way to St. Paul, where his wife soon died. He remarried, and by 1885 he had established his own fur company, specializing in buffalo robes, on the West Side flats.[28]

Paul Martin House, 225 Prescott Street, 1888. The exceptionally tall tower offered a panoramic view of the Mississippi River valley and downtown St. Paul.

Rosen's brownstone mansion, from which he could literally look down on his business, was completed in 1899 as a very late example of the Romanesque Revival style. The architect is unknown but was almost surely from St. Paul.[29] To enhance his views, Rosen purchased and tore down two small homes on the bluff side of Cherokee Avenue, then donated the land to the city as a park (it remains so to this day).

Considered a showpiece, Rosen's house was pictured in at least two souvenir albums of St. Paul published around 1900. The broad, high-gabled house featured a wraparound front porch with unusual stone, or possibly concrete, railings. A pair of stone lions, well known to neighborhood children, guarded the front steps, while a carefully tended garden adorned the yard. The interior, according to one frequent visitor, was "just lovely, with mahogany woodwork. You entered into a small hallway and then a parlor. On the south side was a living room and in the southwest portion a conservatory. . . . The Rosens had beautiful furniture throughout the house."[30]

Rosen, described as "a very jolly man devoted to his family," lived in the house until his death in 1930. His wife died shortly thereafter, and in the mid-1930s the house was converted into a nursing home known as the Cherokee Sanitarium. New owners acquired the home in the early 1960s and tore it down to make way for River Ridge Apartments, which remain on the site. ◆

Adolph Rosen House, 334 Cherokee Avenue, about 1902. The house was located on the blufftop just east of the Smith Avenue High Bridge.

CHAPTER 5

AROUND ST. PAUL

By 1900 St. Paul was a city of 163,000 people, the richest of whom tended to stick close to one another atop the bluffs of Summit Avenue and the Hill District. Summit, which ultimately became the site of more than four hundred houses, was like a great pool into which the city's wealth drained, and it only grew larger as some of the city's other historic mansion districts, such as Lowertown and Capitol Heights, began to dry up. Elsewhere across the city, mansions of the full-bodied type, with the kind of baronial swagger that only very deep pockets can muster, were a rarity. Summit's dominance was so pronounced, in fact, that only one new mansion district, along East River Road, emerged in St. Paul in the twentieth century.

Still, big houses did appear here and there around the city, sometimes in unexpected places. Among the oddest—a mini-mansion at best—was the Paul Ferodowill House, built around 1900 on long-vanished Indiana Street. The peculiarities began with its location. Instead of occupying high ground, the house stood on a large lot *below* the West Side cliffs a block or so

southeast of today's intersection of Plato Boulevard and Ohio Street. Ferodowill, a contractor, made the home even more unusual by encrusting portions of the walls with mosaics consisting of bits of broken glass and dishes. At least five porches dripping with gingerbread, some of it shaped like shower hooks, added to the property's festive, if rather bizarre, air. The house survived, its exotic details more or less intact, until wreckers finally got to it in 1966.[1]

On St. Paul's East Side, the hilly little neighborhood known as Railroad Island had a few houses that qualified as mansions in their day, beginning with the wonderfully weird Greek Revival-Alpine Chalet house built at 547 Beaumont Street in 1854 for Swiss immigrant Frederick de Freudenreich. One of the founders of Chaska, Minnesota, Freudenreich bore the honorary title of "baron," thereby exercising one of the great privileges of being a nineteenth-century gentleman. Perched on about ten acres atop a steep hillock, his house was tiny compared to Summit Avenue mansions, but when it was built, it would been

Paul Ferodowill House, near present-day Plato Boulevard and Ohio Street,
1890s. Mosaics were incorporated into its walls.

Frederick de Freudenreich House, 547 Beaumont Street, 1905. Built in 1854 for a Swiss immigrant, the house stood until the 1990s.

*Dr. Charles H. Alden House, 554 Holly Avenue, 1890. The house, which fea-
tured a curving, two-story porch, was razed in the 1950s. The porch was an
unusual feature.*

one of the neighborhood's most prominent homes. The baron's chalet, which later became the home of pioneer photographer Edward Bromley, was finally demolished in the 1990s.[2]

A few later mansions, such as the French Second Empire–style home (gone) of the Reverend Andrew Patterson on Minnehaha Avenue, were also built in Railroad Island. Overall, however, the East Side never developed anything like a true mansion district beyond the original one atop Dayton's Bluff, where the last big houses were built just after 1900. Not even Lake Phalen and its large park, which opened in 1899, proved to be a lure for mansion builders, perhaps because the East Side as a whole had come to be viewed by then as largely working-class territory.

St. Paul's other major lake, Como, also failed to attract many mansions despite its scenic appeal. One of the earliest, built as a hotel but later associated with the McKenty and Davidson families, was on the southeast corner of the lake. The most ambitious attempt to attract wealthy home builders to Como came in 1884, when developer Cary Warren laid out lots around the southwest side of the lake in hopes of creating an upscale commuter "suburb" served by the nearby Northern Pacific Railway. Warrendale, as it was called, never quite lived up to its expectations, although a handful of large Victorian-style homes were built overlooking the lake.[3]

Warrendale was one of several railroad suburbs created in what is now St. Paul in the 1880s. Macalester Park, Merriam Park, Union Park, Hazel Park, and St. Anthony Park were in this category. They all featured curving streets, large lots, and access via commuter trains (later replaced by streetcars) to downtown. Yet very few mansions sprouted up in these genteel neighborhoods, which instead became known for their stock of comfortable, upper-middle-class homes. In St. Anthony Park, the largest of these communities, there were a few mansions, including the John McMurran House, a shingle-style beauty designed by Allen Stern in 1888. Later owned by former Minnesota governor William Marshall, the house burned down in 1900.[4]

Allen Stem was the architect of another wonderful shingle-style house, for Dr. Charles H. Alden, at 554 Holly Avenue. It, too, is gone. The neighborhood around Union Park, now known as Iris Park, was much smaller than St. Anthony Park, but its winding streets harbored at least one impressive mansion: the John G. Hinkel House, built in 1886 at 1879 Feronia Avenue. An engraving shows the house, in full mansarded regalia, posed very nicely behind a circling wall of brick and stone. It was razed in 1963.

Farmsteads with sizable houses were scattered around what is now St. Paul well into the twentieth century. One of the largest belonged to Edwin A. C. Hatch, who in the early 1860s built an Italian Villa–style home at the southwest corner of what is today Lexington Parkway and Randolph Avenue. The home, later owned by William Nettleton, remained a farmstead for well over two decades.

The opening of the first segment of Mississippi River Boulevard in 1900 provided access to some of the most beautiful land in St. Paul, high above the river gorge, and the first mansions appeared a few years later. One estate here dwarfed all others. Built between 1913 and 1916 for Oliver Crosby, Stonebridge was a Xanadu of woods, water, and gardens, the likes of which will never be seen again in the Twin Cities.

Henry Clater (later John X. Davidson) House (Como House Hotel), southeast corner Como Lake, Fallis and Gates, 1858 to ca. 1900 (razed)

Several historic photographs of Como Lake depict a large brick building that is invariably identified as the home of real estate developer Henry McKenty. Trouble is, there is no evidence that McKenty ever lived in the house, although it is possible that he and his family used it briefly as a summer residence. McKenty, however, arranged the deal by which the building was constructed, initially as a resort hotel. Only later did it become

RESIDENCE OF J. G. HINKEL, ESQ., AT UNION PARK.

John G. Hinkel House, 1879 Feronia Avenue, 1886. The house was a nursing
home for many years before it was razed in 1963.

home to a prominent family of ice skaters headed by John X. Davidson.

McKenty was one of the most fascinating and tragic figures in the early history of St. Paul. For a few sweet years in the 1850s, riding high on a real estate bubble so big and buoyant that it must have felt immune to gravity, he was among the state's richest men. A wiry dynamo who had migrated to St. Paul from Pennsylvania in 1851, McKenty "seemed to be driven by a forty-horse steam power engine," wrote his friend Thomas Newson. "He came to St. Paul, just at a time when his genius as a real estate man had ample opportunity for free scope, and he led off in his special department as the great warrior of his profession. He was pre-eminently king!" At his peak, McKenty's land holdings statewide totaled fifty thousand acres or more. In St. Paul, he owned much of the land around Como Lake, which he had named (it was known earlier as Sandy Lake). He also had holdings north of St. Paul extending all the way to present-day Arden Hills, where Lakes Johanna and Josephine are named after his wife and oldest daughter.[5]

His sobriquet, "Broad Acres" McKenty, reflected his propensity for thinking big. In 1857, believing his Como property was destined to become one of the city's garden spots, McKenty spent $6,000 to build a road from downtown St. Paul to the lake. In that same year, he cut a deal with a wealthy Delaware farmer named John J. Henry, who had come to St. Paul in search of investment opportunities, to build a resort hotel overlooking the lake. McKenty sold (for $1,000) a lakeside lot to Henry, who in turn agreed to build a hotel on the site.[6]

Completed in November 1858, the foursquare, two-story brick hotel, near today's intersection of Como Boulevard and Gateway Drive, was impressive for its time and place, with bracketed eaves adding a bit of Italianate zest to what was otherwise a sedate Greek Revival design. It was built, and probably designed, by Fallis and Gates, "well-known contractors in our city," according to the *Pioneer Democrat Weekly* of St. Paul. As designed, the place had about twenty rooms.[7]

The hotel, as it turned out, did not open in 1858 or for several years to come. In 1857, a financial panic touched off by the failure of an insurance company in New York struck St. Paul and all of Minnesota with thunderous force. Credit dried up, loans were called in, and McKenty's real estate empire began to collapse. With the economy in desperate shape, there was no market for a new hotel, and the building stood vacant for a time, although it may have been rented out at some point for residential use. It finally opened as the Como House Hotel in 1866 after Henry sold it to new owners.[8]

Como House Hotel, southeast corner of Como Lake, late 1860s. After its construction, it stood vacant for several years and did not open as a hotel until 1866.

A young girl (possibly one of John X. Davidson's daughters) on a pony in front of Como House, about 1870. All of Davidson's children became professional skaters.

Meanwhile, McKenty slowly went broke. Wrote Newson: "McKenty kept his office on the corner of Cedar and Third Streets, but one could see that he was financially worried. The same old pleasant smile played about his features . . . yet to one who knew him well there was a tinge of sadness which elicited the secret sympathy of all his old and well-tried friends." In 1863 he returned to Pennsylvania in an unsuccessful attempt to rebuild his fortune in the oil regions there. Later, he tried his luck in California, again to no avail. In the summer of 1869 McKenty "returned to St. Paul . . . a broken-spirited man whose life had become a burden," in the words of the *Pioneer Press*. Late one August afternoon, while at the home of his brother-in-law Charles D. Gilfillan (founder of St. Paul's municipal water system), McKenty killed himself with a revolver shot to the temple. He was forty-eight years old.[9]

A year later, Johannah McKenty received a financial boost when Ramsey County issued $5,000 in bonds to her as payment for her husband's road, which became Como Avenue. The money helped Johannah lead a comfortable life, but it could not stave off troubles to come. In 1879 her youngest daughter, Emily, died at age sixteen, possibly a suicide like her father. Grief engulfed the widow, and a year later, in June 1880, she hung herself from a beam in the family home on Wabasha Street. The last remaining McKenty, twenty-two-year-old Josephine, found the body.[10] There has never been another family saga quite like it in the history of St. Paul.

A year after Henry McKenty's suicide, the Como House Hotel closed, and the property was purchased by John X. Davidson for use as a family home. Davidson was a printer and newspaperman who had owned the *St. Paul Pioneer* for a brief time, but his real passion was speed skating, and a lake house was just what he wanted. He and his wife, Susan, had three sons and three daughters, and the whole family skated on the frozen lake during the winter months. All six children went on to professional skating careers. Mable Davidson was the best known of the daughters and became a sensation in Europe as a figure skater before her untimely death from tuberculosis in 1897. Among the sons, Harley Davidson (no relation to the motorcycle company) was especially prominent, and won many titles in both ice and roller skating.[11]

In 1873, as the city of St. Paul acquired land for Como Park, yet another financial crash occurred, roiling the mortgage markets, and the Davidsons lost the house to foreclosure. By 1876 the brick building was again a hotel, called the Como Park, and it remained so until 1887. After that, the building's history is obscure, but it apparently was gone by 1906. The spot where the house stood is now parkland, and one of the city's beauty spots, just as Henry McKenty dreamed it would be.

John Royall McMurran (later William Marshall, Joseph Elsinger) House, 2268 Commonwealth Avenue, Hodgson and Stem, 1888 to 1900 (burned)

The first attempt to develop the St. Anthony Park neighborhood occurred in the early 1870s, when a group of investors hired Chicago landscape architect Horace Cleveland to design a "suburban" community aimed at attracting ultrawealthy home builders. Cleveland, best known for his park planning in the Twin Cities, responded with an elegant scheme that called for a picturesque ramble of streets set amid lots ranging from five to twenty-five acres. This vision of residential grandeur never materialized, in part because the recession of 1873 poisoned the real estate market. St. Anthony Park finally took off in the mid-1880s, when new investors formed an improvement company, replatted the entire neighborhood to accommodate smaller lots than those in Cleveland's plan, and began building homes intended largely for an upper-middle-class clientele.[12]

Real estate dealer John Royall McMurran headed the improvement company, a position that allowed him to set aside for his own use twelve lots atop a wooded ridge overlooking Langford Lake (now gone) and its park. It was perhaps the choicest site in all of St. Anthony Park, and there McMurran built an estate that included a barn, a water tower, and a Shingle-style house described by *Northwest Magazine* as "the most palatial residence to be found anywhere in the suburbs of St. Paul."[13]

Architect Allen Stem was, along with fellow St. Paulite Cass Gilbert, a master of the Shingle style, and the McMurran house showed him at the top of his form. Oriented toward what is today Hillside Avenue and the park, the house rose from a base of multicolored boulders that extended outward to create a massive, arched porte cochere. Above, greenish-brown shingles covered everything, wrapping around an assortment of bays, porches, gables, and dormers. Stem's composition culminated in a six-sided tower with inward sloping walls and a glassed-in lookout beneath a copper roof.

The home had fifteen or more rooms—finished in ebony, cherry, mahogany, and oak, among other woods—arrayed around a two-story-high hall. A stained-glass skylight illuminated the hall, which was ringed by galleries leading to the upstairs bedrooms. The main floor included reception, dining, and breakfast rooms, parlors, and a library.[14]

McMurran lived in the home for only two years. Its next owner was William Marshall, who fought in the Civil War, served as governor of Minnesota in the late 1860s, and was among the early investors in St. Anthony Park. A speculator at heart, Marshall apparently took a big financial hit in the depression

John McMurran House, 2268 Commonwealth Avenue, shortly after its completion in 1888. Governor William Marshall later bought the fifteen-room mansion.

Remains of the McMurran House after fire, 1900. Joseph Elsinger of the Golden Rule Department Store in St. Paul was its last owner.

that began in 1893, and died in California three years later. The home's last occupant was Joseph Elsinger, co-owner of the Golden Rule Department Store in St. Paul, who lived in the house long enough to see it burn to the ground in 1900. Smaller homes, three of which use portions of boulder foundations that survived the fire, now occupy the site.

Edwin A . C. Hatch (later William Nettleton) House, 1100 Randolph Avenue, Augustus Knight, 1863 to 1876 (burned)

Edwin A. C. Hatch arrived in Minnesota from New York in the 1840s to begin an uncommonly adventurous career. He worked as a trader and later as a government agent to the Blackfeet Indians in Montana. Possessing what one writer described as a "peculiar and striking" presence, Hatch formed his own cavalry battalion following the 1862 Dakota War in the Minnesota

Edwin A. C. Hatch (later William Nettleton) House, 1100 Randolph Avenue, 1874. The mansion, which occupied a twenty-five-acre estate, burned down in 1876.

River valley.[15] Two year later he devised an audacious scheme to kidnap two Dakota leaders, Shakopee (also known as Little Six) and Medicine Bottle, who had fled to Canada after the war. Hatch tracked down the Indians in Canada, drugged them, and brought them back to Fort Snelling, violating international law in the process. Shakopee and Medicine Bottle were hanged after a less than punctilious war crimes trial in 1865, while Hatch became a local hero.

By then, Hatch had profited sufficiently from his not always savory dealings in Indian country to build a stone mansion on twenty-five acres southwest of today's intersection of Lexington Parkway and Randolph Avenue. Only one image of the house, from an 1874 atlas, survives.[16] It shows an Italian Villa–style home with a front tower, a wraparound porch, and long wings extending to either side. A cupola, or possibly a second tower, lurks to the rear. Inside, there were thirteen rooms, many finished in white or black walnut, and the house was said to offer "all the modern improvements," including attic tanks that supplied water (piped in from springs on the property) to the bathrooms and kitchen. The mansion cost $12,000, making it a very expensive home for its day. The architect, Augustus Knight of St. Paul, probably drew on pattern books for the design.[17]

Hatch and his family, which then included four children, lived in the house until 1871, when it was sold to William Nettleton, who had recently arrived from Duluth, a city he had helped to found in the 1850s. Nettleton had worked in the Indian trade and as a farmer before settling in Duluth, where he became active in politics and railroading. In addition to Hatch's house, Nettleton bought 130 acres of land around it to establish a dairy farm. The farm apparently prospered, but the mansion did not fare as well. In May 1876 fire raced through the house, and only the ruined walls were left standing.[18]

Nettleton and his wife, Helen, built a new twenty-two-room, wood-frame house after the fire, but it was not as monumental as the old stone mansion. Nettleton moved in 1883 to Spokane, Washington (where he fell to his death from a railroad bridge under rather mysterious circumstances in 1905), but his son, George, stayed on in the house until the 1890s. The property was then bought by John Wardell, who established a bottling business using the spring. In 1951 the Wardell family sold much of the property to a developer, who built what are now known as the Lexington Park Apartments. The rest of the property was sold, for another apartment building, in 1965, and the second Nettleton house was razed. A low limestone wall along Randolph and Lexington is all that remains of the old estate.[19]

Oliver Crosby Estate ("Stonebridge"), 302 Mississippi River Boulevard South, Clarence Johnston, 1916 to 1953 (razed)

On twenty-eight acres overlooking the Mississippi River gorge, inventor and entrepreneur Oliver Crosby in the early 1900s presided over the greatest estate ever built in St. Paul. Stonebridge, as he called it, was a vast and beautiful folly, doomed from the start by its size and the cost of maintaining it. Crosby's life there, amid gorgeous gardens and waterfalls tumbling down from the hills, must have seemed like an intense and splendid dream, made all the more so by the knowledge that it could not last.

Born in the textile milling town of Dexter, Maine, Crosby was a classic Yankee tinkerer, with the sharp, clean mind of an engineer and a knack for machinery of all kinds. "As a small boy of ten or twelve years," one biographer reported, "he often surprised full-fledged mechanics with his knowledge. . . . Journeymen at the bench allowed him to use their tools once seeing how well he knew their use." After obtaining a degree in mechanical engineering from the University of Maine, where he was also class poet, he ventured west in 1876 to St. Paul, which was the home of an old family friend, Alpheus B. Stickney, who had also been born in Dexter and who later built a mansion on Summit Avenue.[20]

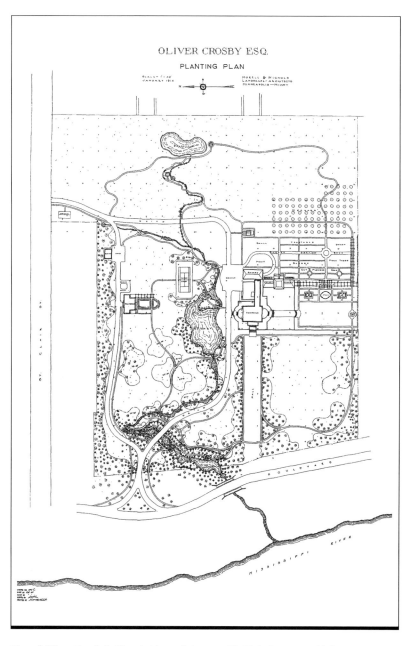

Plan of Oliver Crosby's Stonebridge estate, near St. Clair Avenue and Mississippi River Boulevard, about 1910. It was the most magnificent estate in St. Paul's history.

Crosby lived with Stickney and his family and took on a variety of jobs, including a stint as a cook in a lumber camp and another as a railroad fireman. Six years later, at age twenty-seven, Crosby cofounded what became the American Hoist and Derrick Company (later Amhoist Corp., now gone), located for many years on St. Paul's West Side flats. Crosby's inventive genius—he devised a clip for holding wire cable that still bears his name and also developed cranes for railroads and

shipyards—helped propel the company to success, and by the turn of the century he was a very wealthy man.

He built his first mansion, which still stands, at 804 Lincoln Avenue in St. Paul in 1900, but it was too small a container for his dreams. Seven years later he purchased a tract of hilly, forested land between present-day St. Clair and Jefferson Avenues and began creating his estate. He hired Clarence Johnston, the architect of his first house, to be his designer-in-chief,

Oliver Crosby House, north side from Lake Elizabeth, about 1920. A reservoir near Mt. Curve Boulevard fed water to the lake via a small stream.

Living room in the Crosby House, about 1925. Oliver Crosby died in 1922, just six years after moving into the mansion.

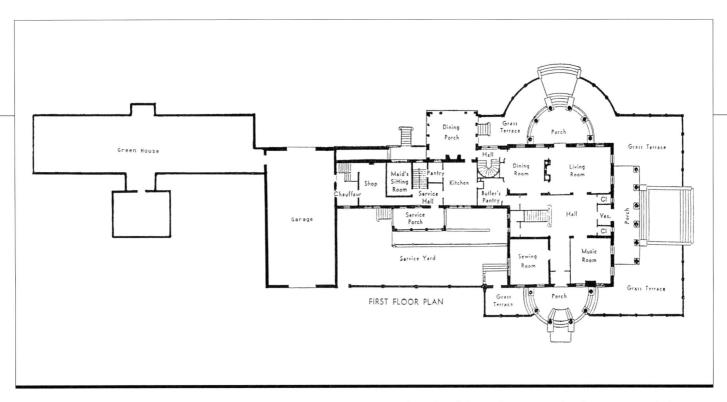

FIRST FLOOR PLAN

First-floor plan of the Crosby House. With its long east wing, the house was shaped like one of the cranes built by Crosby's firm, American Hoist and Derrick Company.

and also brought in landscape architects Anthony Morell and Arthur Nichols, who had established an office in Minneapolis only a year earlier.

What resulted was an estate as extraordinary for its grounds as for its twenty-thousand-square-foot mansion. Morell and Nichols supervised the planting of hundreds of trees, laid out a garden with statuary, brick walkways, and a pergola, and created a mall extending to Mississippi River Boulevard. They also oversaw construction of two ponds, one acting as reservoir on the highest part of the estate and the other (named Lake Elizabeth, after Crosby's wife) located next to the mansion. A stream fed by the reservoir descended through the grounds in a series of rapids and waterfalls, then flowed beneath a stone arch bridge (which gave the estate its name) before emptying into the Mississippi.[21]

The mansion itself, completed in 1916, was a stately exer-cise in Georgian Revival, faced in red brick and sporting three colossal porticos. It was built almost entirely of concrete and hollow tile, fireproof materials designed to last for the ages. The twenty-four-room house was shaped very much like one of Crosby's cranes, its squarish main body connected to a long narrow wing that housed the kitchen, pantries, and servants' quarters. In the main section, all the rooms were reached from a central hall with a switchback staircase. The basement included a ballroom. Marble, exotic woods, and ornamental plaster were among the finishing materials. Johnston based the home's details on American Colonial models, but there was not much spark to his design, and in photographs the main rooms look as embalmed as a funeral chapel.[22]

Garden party at Stonebridge estate, about 1920. The party era was short-lived, and the house stood vacant for more than a decade before its demolition in 1953.

Attached to the house was a nine-car garage. An early and enthusiastic motorist, Crosby owned a Stutz Bearcat and a least one electric vehicle, which his wife sometimes drove. One other major building on the property was a hundred-foot-long greenhouse, where Crosby pursued his interest in horticulture.

Crosby and his wife were the mansion's only occupants (not counting eleven servants and a chauffeur), since two of their children were grown and the third was at college. The Crosbys enjoyed entertaining, and photographs show garden parties with women in white dresses and men in dark suits wandering amid the flowers and statues and whispering trees.

The parties were soon over. Crosby was sixty-one when he moved into Stonebridge, and he died just six years later, in 1922. Elizabeth stayed on in the house, a palace for one, until her own death in 1928, after which the couple's only son, Frederic, lived in the house with his family for the next seven years. Plans for subdividing the estate were prepared as early as 1923, but nothing was done until after Elizabeth's death. In 1928, most

of the estate was sold, with only the mansion and three acres remaining in the family's hands. New streets, like Woodlawn Avenue, were cut through the grounds, and ninety or so residential lots were offered for sale. Fewer than ten houses were built, however, before the Great Depression intervened. By the mid-1930s many of the lots had been forfeited because of unpaid taxes, and redevelopment came to a standstill.

The mansion also fell on hard times. After Frederic Crosby moved away, the house was finally tax-forfeited to the state in 1944. Ramsey County, which administered the property, tried to sell the mansion without success. In 1952 the city of St. Paul suggested that the house be used as a governor's mansion, but a bill to that effect failed in the state legislature, and in 1953 Stonebridge was demolished.[23] Today, about seventy homes occupy the grounds of the old estate. The eponymous stone bridge and one of the estate's waterfalls can still be found in the yards of two of those homes, but otherwise little remains of Oliver Crosby's dream. ◆

CHAPTER 6

SUBURBAN ST. PAUL

In 1886–87 George W. Sheldon, a prolific author of what today would be called coffee-table books, produced a hefty two-volume tome called *Artistic Country-Seats* that offered photographs, plans, and lengthy descriptions of more than ninety American mansions thought to be among the best suburban homes of the day. Most of the featured homes were in the Northeast, where great constellations of outsized estates could be found in the tony suburbs ringing Boston, New York City, and Philadelphia and in seaside resorts like Newport, Rhode Island.[1]

Sheldon also cast his eye to the west, however, and included four St. Paul homes and two from Minneapolis in his salute to wealth on the urban fringes. Trouble was, none of the six qualified in any sense as a country house. The St. Paul mansions were all on Summit Avenue, hardly a bucolic environment in the 1880s, while the Minneapolis homes were in the Washburn–Fair Oaks neighborhood just a mile or so from downtown. It is possible Sheldon knew so little about the Twin Cities that he assumed the mansions, with their big yards, must be in the suburbs. A more likely explanation is that Sheldon was simply unable to find the kind of estate-quality homes he was looking for in suburban areas of the Twin Cities.

This dearth of big country mansions was especially evident near St. Paul, although the situation was not all that different around Minneapolis until the 1890s, when great estates began to blossom on the shores of Lake Minnetonka. For some reason, however, few Minnetonka-sized estates took hold around White Bear Lake, the largest body of water in suburban St. Paul. Even so, many summer homes sizable enough to be considered mansions were built at White Bear during the Victorian era and later. Some of the finest, on Manitou Island in the village of White Bear Lake and in the resort community of Dellwood, have been lost.

Connected by rail to St. Paul in 1868, the village of White Bear Lake by the 1880s was a bustling little community where resorts, pavilions, and hotels flourished during the summer months. Many of the early lakeside homes there were simple affairs, but a far different class of housing soon appeared on

Manitou Island, which was long, narrow, nicely wooded, and well away from the noisy hotel crowds. Its development as an exclusive residential enclave began in 1881, when a group of fourteen businessmen led by William Merriam purchased the fifty-acre island.

The group hired landscape architect Horace Cleveland to lay out a series of loop roads on the island, then built a clubhouse. By 1883 the island's first three summer homes, usually referred to as "cottages," were under construction. All three were designed by Clarence Johnston, the architect of Merriam's 1882 Capitol Heights mansion in St. Paul. By 1886 a total of eleven houses had been constructed on the island. More big homes were built in the 1890s and later, including several designed by Cass Gilbert.[2]

Henry Boardman House, off Dellwood Avenue near Meadow Lane, Dellwood, 1887. It was replaced in the early 1900s by a larger home.

On the other side of the lake, where a spur line built in 1870 provided rail access to St. Paul, a real estate promoter named Augustus Kirby Barnum developed the resort community of Dellwood at about the same time Manitou Island acquired its first houses. Barnum, whose personal real estate holdings included a mansion on Summit Avenue, kicked off the development at Dellwood by building his own lake home (now mostly gone), designed by Gilbert and completed in 1884. A number of intriguing Shingle-style "cottages" were built over the next few years. One of the best, designed by St. Paul architect Allen Stem in 1887, was the Henry Boardman House, which stood for less than twenty years before being replaced by a larger home. Dellwood's biggest estates, however, were not built until the twentieth century. Most still stand, but a few have been lost, including Stem's own summer home, built in 1914.[3]

A few miles west of White Bear, James J. Hill began creating his enormous North Oaks estate in the 1880s. Yet Hill's

Henry C. James House, near Highway 61 and Glen Road, Newport, 1888. James was a lawyer who had offices in St. Paul.

Roscoe Hersey House, 416 South Fourth Street, Stillwater, about 1880. This house still stands, but the tower is gone.

five thousand acres, which included a large, but hardly ostentatious, residence overlooking Pleasant Lake, were much more of a working farm than a true country estate and so would never have found a place in a book like Sheldon's *Artistic Country-Seats*.

Elsewhere around St. Paul, a smattering of suburban mansions appeared in the late nineteenth and early twentieth centuries. Perhaps the biggest of them all, the twelve-thousand-square-foot Cordenio Severance House ("Cedarhurst"), enlarged to its present form by Cass Gilbert between 1911 and 1917, still stands in Cottage Grove. The Henry C. James House, built about 1888 in Newport, featured a three-story porch and an impressive hexagonal tower. Smaller but equally interesting was the Fred H. and Electa Snyder House ("Crossroads") in Falcon Heights. Built in the early 1900s at the southwest corner of Snelling and Larpenteur Avenues, it was one of only a handful of houses in the Twin Cities designed by Emmanuel Masqueray, architect of the St. Paul Cathedral and the Basilica of St. Mary in Minneapolis.

Fifteen miles east of downtown St. Paul, the old St. Croix River town of Stillwater could also boast of a sizable collection of mansions by the late nineteenth century. Like St. Paul, Stillwater offered steep bluffs perfect for mansion builders seeking the primal satisfaction of looking down on everyone else in town. Founded in the 1840s and home to many lumber barons, Stillwater never developed a Summit Avenue–style mansion row, but some of its big houses from the 1860s and 1870s, such as the much modified Roscoe Hersey House (1878) at 416 South Fourth Street, were as imposing as any of their time in the Twin Cities.

Many of Stillwater's showpiece homes were in the North Hill neighborhood, which offered superb vistas of the St. Croix valley and the town below. Isaac Staples's mansion (ca. 1867) was by far the most prominent of these homes, but other lumbermen, like Martin A. Torinus, also built impressive homes that are now gone.[4]

Around White Bear Lake

Augustus Kirby Barnum (later Allie Hewitt) House, 48 Dellwood Avenue, Dellwood, Cass Gilbert, 1884 to ca. 1935 (partially razed)

Allen H. Stem House, 56 Dellwood Avenue, Dellwood, Allen H. Stem, 1914 to 1940 (burned)

Manitou Island "cottages," Cass Gilbert, Clarence Johnston, 1880s and later to ca. 1950s and later (razed)

The 1880s were the ultimate boom time in the Twin Cities. Minneapolis gained 118,000 people during the decade, while St. Paul added 92,000, tripling its population. This influx of people led to a superheated real estate market that attracted all manner of speculators. Among them was Augustus Kirby Barnum of St. Paul. Like all of his breed, Barnum was a plunger, ready to assume big risks for the prospect of big gains. So it was when in 1881 he acquired 250 acres along the undeveloped northeast shore of White Bear Lake and platted it, in lots ranging up to five acres in size, as Dellwood.[5]

Barnum promoted his new holdings as a fine spot for summer homes protected from what he called "the desecration of the rowdy, shanty-building element," but it was not until the St. Paul and Duluth Railroad opened a small station in Dellwood in 1883 that the development gained momentum. To prime the pump, Barnum built a clubhouse in 1884 and a large cottage for himself. The cottage was designed by twenty-six-year-old Cass Gilbert, then beginning what would prove to be a spectacular career.[6]

The Barnum house, one of Gilbert's first essays in the Shingle style, was sited on a small knoll above the lake. It rose from a boulder base to a broad projecting gable, with a small bedroom wing to one side topped by a promenade. Porches, including one sheltering the entry, all but surrounded the house. Far bigger and costlier homes would be built around Dellwood in the years to come, but none excelled Gilbert's cottage in capturing the breezy spirit of summer life at the lake.

Drawings and plan of the Augustus K. Barnum (later Allie Hewitt) House, 48 Dellwood Avenue, Dellwood, 1884. This summerhouse was one of the earliest commissions of architect Cass Gilbert.

Barnum House, looking south toward White Bear Lake, 1888. The second floor was removed in the 1930s, when this building became a children's playhouse.

Allen Stem House, 56 Dellwood Avenue, Dellwood, 1914. Stem was a prominent St. Paul architect who designed several summer homes at White Bear Lake.

Barnum, who would lose his fortune in the depression of 1893 and die a pauper thirty years later, barely occupied his cottage before selling it to his mother, Allie Hewitt. She stayed on for many years and improved the grounds with gardens and pathways. In 1929 new owners bought the property for the purpose of building a large lakeside home. As part of that project, the second floor of the old cottage was lopped off and the remaining portion converted into a children's playhouse.

Another of Dellwood's most significant homes was designed for and by Allen H. Stem, a leading St. Paul architect. He won numerous commissions in Dellwood, designing his first home there in 1887. Stem's own summer place, completed in 1914 on the present site of the White Bear Yacht Club, was no cottage. The L-shaped, two-story house, done in a simplified version of the popular Renaissance Revival style, featured a charming arcaded porch and a living room outfitted with a marble fireplace, ornate mirrors, and fine chandeliers. The grounds included a garden set amid balustraded walls and terraces.

Stem and his wife, Lucy, had plenty of time to enjoy the good life on the lake after his retirement in 1920. Their retirement portfolio was enhanced by a $500,000 judgment Stem won that same year against a New York architect he had accused of stealing much of the Grand Central Terminal project in New York from his firm. The house survived Stem, who died in 1931, by only a few years. After the White Bear Yacht Club's building next door burned down in 1937, the club acquired the house. It was then sold to a new owner, who cut it in half so that he could move it to a site at nearby Pine Tree Lake. There, in about 1940, the house burned down.[7]

Across the lake on Manitou Island, most of the major nineteenth-century "cottages" were designed by either Gilbert or his chief St. Paul rival, Clarence Johnston. Beginning in about 1884, Johnston designed half a dozen summer homes on the island. Some remain, but others—including the Queen Anne-style Sylvester M. Cary House—are gone.[8] Gilbert came to the island a bit later. Among his first Manitou projects was a delight-

Sylvester Cary House, Manitou Island, White Bear Lake, about 1890. Development of the island began in 1881 after it was purchased by a group of fourteen St. Paul businessmen.

ful Shingle-style house for Jasper Tarbox, designed in 1889. Although the house featured a polygonal tower, it had a strong horizontal feel overall, with bands of windows tucked under the eaves and long post-and-beam porches.[9] Gilbert's Colonial Revival manor for St. Paul hardware wholesaler William Dean, completed in 1892 and substantially remodeled seven years later, ranks as perhaps the greatest of Manitou's lost mansions. It was demolished in about 2005, one of many early homes on the island torn down to make way for more modern dwellings.[10]

James J. Hill House and Farm ("North Oaks Farm"), north of Highway 96 and east of Hodgson Road, North Oaks, James Brodie, 1883 and later to ca. 1950s (subdivided and redeveloped for housing)

James J. Hill was not a man to do things on a small scale. None of the other great men of his era in Minnesota could match his sweeping continental vision or his broad range of interests, and unlike many of the slick, fancy-suited railroad barons of the time, he built to last. His house on Summit Avenue remains the most massive work of domestic architecture in the history of St. Paul, while his Stone Arch Bridge in Minneapolis seems impervious to time. Not surprisingly, Hill—an Ontario farm boy by birth—also thought big when it came to pursuing his passionate interest in agriculture and fine livestock. North Oaks Farm was the place where Hill felt most at home, and he and

Barn and shorthorn cows at James J. Hill's North Oaks Farm, north of Highway 96 and east of Hodgson Road, North Oaks, about 1910.

his family spent much of every year there, arriving in late spring and sometimes staying all the way into November.

When he bought his first three thousand acres in North Oaks, Hill already owned a 160-acre stock farm with seventy-five pedigreed cattle (including the prized bulls Lord Chancellor and Berkeley-Duke of Oxford) near Lake Minnetonka.[11] Hill's interest in farming was strategic. Better livestock, he believed, would make for more prosperous farmers, who in turn would use his railroads to ship their bounty. Over the years, he distributed thousands of his animals, free of charge, to farmers, all with the idea of improving their herds. Hill had hoped to expand his Lake Minnetonka farm but found land prices there too steep for his liking. When the North Oaks property became available, he snapped it up for $50,000.

Hill acquired the property from Charles Gilfillan, who had bought the land in 1876 to secure its four pristine lakes, which

Greenhouse, North Oaks Farm, 1915. At its peak, the farm encompassed about five thousand acres.

still provide part of St. Paul's water supply. A lawyer by profession, Gilfillan was the moving force behind the St. Paul Water Company, which had constructed the city's first water system in 1868, initially using Phalen Creek as its source and later tapping into White Bear Lake as well. Neither source proved satisfactory, however, in part because of lawsuits brought by mill owners and others worried about low water levels. To avoid such problems in the future, Gilfillan not only bought the lakes in North Oaks but also, as a buffer, thousands of acres around them. In 1882 he sold the St. Paul Water Company to the city. Soon thereafter, he sold most of his North Oaks acreage to Hill, who agreed to various legal restrictions regarding use of the lakes' water.[12]

Hill set to work at once to build the farm of his dreams. By 1884 he had two dozen hands in his employ plus another 350 or so men working on construction projects. Cow, hog, horse, and sheep barns soon appeared (the 250-foot-long cow barn was the largest), along with a state-of-the-art creamery. A blacksmith's shop, granary, conservatory, farm office, boardinghouse, and several small single-family homes for farmworkers were built as well. Almost all of these buildings were near today's intersection of Red Barn and Evergreen Roads. Hill also wasted no time enlarging the property, adding another two thousand or so acres to his holdings within seven years. The result was a farm so big that it required twenty miles of perimeter fencing.

By 1900, the farm's superintendent reported quite a collection of livestock: more than 200 head of cattle, 750 hogs, 300 sheep, 160 horses, and 400 poultry. To add a wild note to the proceedings, Hill kept elk and buffalo on the farm as well. Although livestock were the heart of the operation, Hill also experimented with crops (Jim Hill corn was one of the varieties developed at the farm) and started a tree nursery.[13]

It is one measure of how important the work of the farm was to Hill that he never built a truly monumental home on the property, as did so many of the squires of Lake Minnetonka. For more than twenty years, Hill, his wife, Mary, and the children spent their time on the farm in a plain, wood-frame home that Gilfillan had built in the 1880s. It is likely Hill expanded the old farmhouse for his family, but he did not build a new home, on a hill on the west side of Pleasant Lake, until 1914. Although the family referred to it as "the bungalow," the brick house was actually an Arts and Crafts foursquare, sturdy and unpretentious, with large verandas to catch the summer breeze. Louis Hill, James J.'s second son and business successor, also had homes on the farm. The first one, near the old farm home, was completed in 1906. Later, he built a chalet-style house, which still stands on Pleasant Lake's southeastern shore.

Besides his mansion in St. Paul, Hill owned homes on the East Coast and in Europe, but the farm at North Oaks was clearly his favorite place of all. When he died in 1916, he was buried on the farm, although his and Mary's bodies were later moved to a cemetery. Mary continued to summer at the farm until her own death in 1921. Louis then assumed control, although he did not really share his father's interest in agriculture and animal husbandry. The farm's operations were curtailed as Louis rented out land to other farmers and also set aside nineteen acres for a Fresh Air children's camp run by the Volunteers of America.

Great estates tend inevitably toward subdivision when their original owners are gone, and so it was with North Oaks Farm after Louis Hill died in 1948. Two years later, Hill's heirs formed the North Oaks Corporation to develop high-end housing on the property. A golf course opened in 1951, the same year that the first new home was built on the old farm property. By 1956, when it was incorporated as a village, North Oaks counted 276 residents. The population now numbers close to 5,000.

James J. Hill's lakeside house was demolished in 1959, and all but three of the old farm buildings—the dairy, the blacksmith's shop, and the granary—have vanished as well. The three have been restored by the Hill Farm Historical Society and in 1999 were added to the National Register of Historic Places.

James J. (later Louis) Hill House, North Oaks Farm, about 1920. Hill built the house in 1914, two years before his death.

Fred H. and Electa Snyder House ("Crossroads"), south-west corner Snelling and Larpenteur Avenues, Falcon Heights, Emmanuel Masqueray, 1907 to 1947 (razed)

In the early 1900s this country house, designed by the French-born architect of the St. Paul Cathedral and the Basilica of St. Mary in Minneapolis, was the scene of extraordinary musical events. The fabled Italian tenor Enrico Caruso sang in the home's music room. Ignacy Jan Paderewski, the piano virtuoso who was to become prime minister of the short-lived Republic of Poland, also performed in the house, as did other musical luminaries who came through St. Paul on concert and opera tours.

The woman who hosted these events was Electa Annette Snyder, whose life was in many ways as dramatic and improbable as the grand operas she loved. Known as Nettie to her friends, she grew up in a small town in Wisconsin, went abroad as a child to study voice, became an acclaimed singer and voice teacher as well as the nation's leading female impresario, endured a scandalous divorce, and ended her days living in a villa in Florence, Italy, once owned by Galileo.

Fred and Electa Snyder House, southwest corner of Snelling and Larpenteur Avenues, Falcon Heights, about 1910. Enrico Caruso and Ignacy Jan Paderewski were among the musical luminaries who gave concerts at this house.

Living and dining rooms of the Snyder House, about 1910. The gracious home was designed by Emmanuel Masqueray, architect of the Cathedral of St. Paul.

Her second husband (the first died, probably of exhaustion) was Fred H. Snyder, also a native of Wisconsin. The couple married in 1889, a year after Nettie had taken up residence in St. Paul. The Snyders then moved to South Dakota and later Mankato, Minnesota, where Fred managed hotels. Nettie, meanwhile, gave voice lessons but also spent much time in Florence studying with a voice teacher. By 1905, the couple was back in St. Paul, where Fred built and owned the eponymous Frederic Hotel at Fifth and Cedar Streets.

The hotel, which burned down in 1961, was a favorite stopping place for touring stage actors and musicians, and Nettie established a popular studio there for singers. Soon, she began a new line of work as a concert promoter. She brought in prominent musicians and also managed to attract the Metropolitan and Chicago opera companies, which played to sold-out houses at the St. Paul Auditorium. Her activities as a promoter were duly noted in a 1910 book on the entertainment business, which pronounced her "the most successful woman manager in America."[14]

At the height of her career, in 1907, she and Fred built a summerhouse near the State Fairgrounds in Falcon Heights. Dubbed Crossroads, it was likely the first house in the Twin Cities designed by Emmanuel Masqueray, then in the midst of his two great church projects.[15] The limestone and stucco home was not especially large—probably three thousand or so square feet—but it was unusual, combining typical Tudor Revival elements such as half-timbering with a distinctively high French roof. An array of French doors leading out to the front porch added another uncommon touch to the design.

Inside, a living room, dining room, and small lounge extended across the entire front of the house beneath a continuous beamed ceiling. Only a pair of pillars separated the living and dining rooms, which together served as a mini-concert hall for the Snyders' weekly music salons.[16] A magazine article described the house as "one of the pleasantest places possible in the cool northern summers, when artists and managers who pass that way never fail to stop, if only for a whiff of the hayfields near Mr. and Mrs. Snyder's Italian garden and a chance to try the acoustics of her great music room with its seating capacity of a hundred persons."[17]

Despite its charms, the house eventually struck a discordant note with the Snyders. Fred turned out to be something of a playboy, using the place for assignations while Nettie was away in Italy or otherwise engaged. In 1922, three years after Fred sold the hotel and was living in California, Nettie filed for divorce, claiming her husband had taken up with a "prominent St. Paul married woman." Scenting the rich loam of scandal, the

St. Paul Dispatch and other local dailies gave prominent play to the story, which included allegations that Fred had served his companion "intoxicating liquors" at Crossroads while engaging in what were politely called "improper relations." Fred was also accused of having illicit fun in the California sun by partying with Hollywood types not known for their devotion to marital fidelity.[18]

The newspapers attended to the Snyders' divorce saga through 1922, periodically reassuring readers that the identity of the "prominent married woman" would be revealed once the case went to trial. It never did. The prospect of so much dirty laundry flapping in the public breeze led the Snyders to agree on the terms of a divorce in 1923, just before their scheduled confrontation in court. The newspapers, it can be surmised, were deeply disappointed.[19]

Nettie, already living part-time in New York City, received title to Crossroads as part of the settlement but did not spend much time there. In 1924 she moved to Galileo's old villa in Florence (the poet John Milton had also occupied it for a time), where she continued as a voice teacher. Even so, she returned to St. Paul occasionally during the summer months to stay in the home where she had staged so many grand parties and concerts. In 1928 she left Italy for good, visited St. Paul for the last time, then moved to California, where she died the next year at about age seventy.[20]

She willed Crossroads to her only child (a son by her first marriage), but it does not appear he ever lived there. In 1930 the house was converted into a restaurant. Two years later, it became The Brook, a supper club describing itself as "exquisite in its appointments" and "continental in its atmosphere." The club had only a short run, however, and by the late 1930s the house stood empty. After a brief stint as a nursing home, the house was torn down in 1947 to make way for the new headquarters of the Farmers' Union Grain Terminal Association. That building, now the TIES Education Center, remains on the site.[21]

Isaac Staples House, 509 North Second Street, Stillwater, Abraham Radcliffe, 1871 to ca. 1917 (razed)

Isaac Staples, who arrived in Minnesota in 1853, was among the most successful of the Maine lumbermen who came to the St. Croix valley when it was an Eden of white pine. Described as "restless, alert, far-seeking, systematic and persistent," Staples—known as "Ike" to his friends—was a rugged character who was as comfortable in north-woods logging camps (where it is said he left behind a trail of illegitimate children) as he was among the East Coast capitalists who financed many of his ventures. He and his backers at one point owned forty thousand acres of pine land in the valley, more than anyone else, much of it secured for little more than $1 an acre through the purchase of government land warrants issued to military veterans. In 1854 Staples and a partner, Samuel Hersey, built the largest sawmill

Isaac Staples House, 509 North Second Street, Stillwater, about 1870, above his sawmill. Staples was among the wealthiest of the St. Croix valley's lumbermen.

Staples House, 1880. Terra-cotta imported from Italy was used to create the distinctive window hoods.

yet seen in Stillwater. Two years later, he bought a controlling interest in the St. Croix Boom Company, which sorted logs coming into Stillwater and turned out to be hugely profitable.[22]

Possessed of enormous drive and an eye for detail powered by a photographic memory (he could return to a remote logging camp at the beginning of a new season and tell workers where every piece of equipment had been left the year before), Staples by 1870 was among Minnesota's richest men and largest landowners. His business interests went well beyond logging. He owned nine farms, most of which grew food for his lumber camps. The largest, known as the Maple Island Farm, was eleven miles northwest of Stillwater and had its own gristmill as well as two lakes stocked with fish. He also built several business blocks in downtown Stillwater, ran a general store there for many years, dealt in real estate, owned steamboats that plied the Mississippi River all the way to St. Louis, and was president of the Lumberman's National Bank.[23]

As the money poured in, Staples decided to build a mansion that would provide the ultimate visual proof of his role as Stillwater's reigning merchant prince. He chose a superb site with panoramic views on a promontory in the North Hill neighborhood, directly above a sawmill he had recently acquired. St. Paul architect Abraham Radcliffe was hired to design the yellow brick and brownstone mansion, which upon its completion in 1871 ranked among the state's largest and most lavish homes. The overall design was conventional French Second Empire, with a front tower, a lower octagonal tower to one side, and the usual mansard roof. More distinctive were the arched window hoods made of terra-cotta reputedly imported from Italy.

Not a great deal is known about the home's undoubtedly sumptuous interior, but descriptions mention a grand staircase with bronze handrails, ash and walnut woodwork on the main floor, a huge third-floor ballroom, and walls adorned with numerous paintings of Staples and his family. Staples was fifty-five years old, his children mostly grown, by the time he and his wife, Olivia, moved into the house. The ballroom suggests that they entertained with some frequency. Staples also occupied himself with a conservatory on the east side of the house, where he grew fruit trees and other specimens. Just past the conservatory were vineyards, planted on terraces that stepped down the bluff.[24]

Staples was not in the best of health for much of the time he lived in his mansion. He was diagnosed with diabetes in 1880, and in 1893—the same year Olivia died—he suffered a stroke. Five years later, at age eighty-one, he followed her to the grave, and the mansion more or less succumbed with him, as did the great St. Croix pineries from which his mills alone consumed as many as 550,000 trees a year. None of Staples's five surviving children wanted the mansion, which stood vacant and deteriorating while the family spent six years squabbling in court over his multimillion-dollar estate. Later, vandals and then a fire in 1910 further damaged the old house. The date of its demolition is something of a mystery, but it was gone by about 1917. Today, Pioneer Park occupies the site.[25] ◆

MINNEAPOLIS

CHAPTER 7

CENTRAL DOWNTOWN

"Sometimes when I turn into Tenth Street from Hennepin Avenue I rub my eyes and pinch myself to make sure that I am awake," an old-time resident of downtown Minneapolis wrote in the 1930s, "for it does not seem possible that fifty years could wipe out one of the prettiest 'home' centers so completely."[1] The writer's nostalgia arose from a hard core of fact. From the 1860s to the early 1900s, mansions belonging to the city's most prominent families took up entire downtown blocks, forming a lost residential world of towered houses and green lawns that is hard to visualize today.

In the late nineteenth century visitors to Minneapolis, as well as local boosters ever ready to dip their pens into the bottomless pool of Victorian hyperbole, often remarked upon the city's bounty of fine homes. Yet all of this residential grandeur, at least in the downtown area, never quite coalesced into a clearly defined mansion district, as E. V. Smalley, editor of *Northwest Magazine*, noted in 1895. He wrote that "Minneapolis has hundreds of handsome houses but it can show no one street sacred to wealth and aristocracy, like Summit Avenue in

St. Paul. . . . The fine mansions are scattered here and there . . . [and] up to this date it is not essential for people who aspire to positions on the crest of the wave of fashion to live in any particular street or ward."[2] Smalley's claim was true enough, although the city's mansions were not as randomly dispersed as he made them out to be, and a few streets, like Mount Curve Avenue on Lowry Hill, were already well on their way to becoming "sacred to wealth."

Once Minneapolis was opened to settlement in the 1850s, it did not take long before big houses began to appear just beyond the commercial core, initially concentrated in the Gateway District near Hennepin and Washington Avenues. No particular place stood out, however, since the downtown area was wide-open prairie that offered none of the topographical drama found in St. Paul. There was, of course, one extraordinary physical feature in central Minneapolis: St. Anthony Falls. But it was quickly hemmed in by industry, leaving no room for an upscale residential district.

With little scenic ground on which to build mansions, the

Demolition of the Charles Prior House, 306 Seventh Street South, and surrounding shops and office building, southeast across Third Avenue South, 1941. The Hennepin County Government Center now occupies the entire block.

Hugh G. Harrison House, 1112 Nicollet Avenue, south from Eleventh Street, about 1920. The mansion, built in the 1860s on a lot the size of a half block, was razed in 1922.

first generation of wealth in Minneapolis did indeed scatter here and there, as Smalley pointed out. A handful of the city's elite, most notably flour miller Dorilus Morrison, established country estates well away from downtown as early as the 1850s. Others, like Hugh G. Harrison, who built a mansion at Twelfth Street and Nicollet Avenue in 1867, ventured to the distant downtown fringes. Most of the city's moneyed class, however, preferred to locate closer to the center of commerce. As late as 1875, half of Minneapolis's thirty thousand or so people still lived within a one-mile radius of the downtown core.[3]

Some of downtown's earliest mansions, including Samuel Gale's imposing stone home of 1864, were built along and near

Cricket players at the Curtis Pettit House, 1001 Second Avenue South, probably about 1880. The house, one of the largest of its day in Minneapolis, was torn down in 1926.

Fourth Street, which was just far enough back from the river to be clear of its industrial activity. Alfred E. Ames, father of the man who would turn out to be the most spectacularly corrupt mayor in Minneapolis history, built an even earlier Greek Revival–style home on Fourth near Chicago Avenue.

By the 1870s, however, most of downtown's big houses could be found south and east of Nicollet Avenue and Fifth Street, in an area where significant commercial encroachment had not yet occurred. Seventh Street, where Alonzo C. Rand built his mansion, was especially popular. A handful of luxurious homes, such as Thomas Walker's, also took root on Hennepin Avenue before it assumed its more permanent character as a theater strip. Many of these nouveau riche monuments belonged to men who had made at least some of their money in flour milling. In 1871 Curtis H. Pettit, owner of a mill bearing his name at St. Anthony Falls, built the grandest French Second Empire pile yet seen in Minneapolis at 1001 Second Avenue South. William Judd's mansion (1873) at Fifth and Chicago was nearly as large, occupying an entire square block.

As commercial development marched steadily south along streets like Hennepin and Nicollet, mansions followed suit. By the late 1880s, new mansions were being built primarily along or near Tenth, Eleventh, and Twelfth Streets. The ultra-charming Frederick A. Dunsmoor House (ca. 1885) at 224 Tenth Street South was among the notable homes here. Perhaps the outstanding downtown mansion from this period, also on Tenth, belonged to Frederick Pillsbury. His father, George, had a home nearby, as did other flour millers, including John Crosby, whose Elizabethan-style house (1898) at 414 Eighth Street South appears to have been the last mansion built in the central part of downtown.

After 1900, the story of the downtown mansions is one of decay and demolition. New upscale residential areas—along Park Avenue, around Loring Park, on Lowry Hill, and in the Lake District—lured away downtown mansion owners, who were not averse to selling out for a profit. Once deprived of their owners,

Children's parade outside the Frederick A. Dunsmoor House, 224 Tenth Street South, 1880s. This picturesque house, built of red sandstone, came down in the 1950s.

*William Judd House, Fifth Street and Chicago Avenue, ringed by parked cars,
about 1925. Once known as Evergreen, the mansion was demolished a year
later.*

the houses rarely thrived. "For the most part, the handsome old residences of early days are now cheap lodging and boarding houses," a newspaper wrote in 1921. "Some have been turned into carpenter shops and garages; most of them are shabby, run down and decrepit, awaiting the inevitable day when the wreckers will pull them down for new business blocks."[4]

The wreckers were in fact very busy in the years from about 1910 to 1930, when stores, offices, hotels, and theaters replaced the bulk of downtown's Victorian mansions. Both of the Pillsbury mansions, for example, were razed by 1916 to make way for new hotels (the Curtis and the Leamington, both now gone as well), while the Rand, Judd, and Pettit houses all came down in the 1920s. By the 1950s, the central part of downtown Minneapolis was all but scoured of mansions, just as was the case in St. Paul and most other American cities.

Alfred E. and Albert A. Ames House, 721 Fourth Street South, 1857 to 1906 (razed)

Municipal corruption has erupted only twice on a grand scale in the Twin Cities. One episode occurred in the 1920s and 1930s in St. Paul, when police-protected gangsterism ran amok. The other great outbreak was in Minneapolis from 1900 to 1902, when Mayor Albert Alonzo ("Doc") Ames presided over scandals so numerous and ripe that the muckraker Lincoln Steffens featured them in one of a famous series of magazine articles later published in book form as *The Shame of the Cities*.[5]

Ames was an unlikely scoundrel, since his father, Alfred Elisha Ames, also a physician, was one of the pillars of pioneer Minneapolis, who began his career in St. Anthony before buying land in the new city across the river. Trained in the law as well as medicine, Alfred helped draw up Minneapolis's incorporation papers and served as the village's first postmaster. In 1857, presumably before the financial panic hit, he built one of the young city's largest Greek Revival homes. It stood (on the site of today's Metrodome Plaza) in a part of the city then considered quite distant from downtown. Government, however, was much closer at hand, since the mansion—occupying a lot that initially encompassed four square blocks—was just across Chicago Avenue from the first Hennepin County Courthouse, also built in 1857, on land donated by Ames.[6]

Ames's two-story clapboard house, like so many of its era in the Twin Cities, is poorly documented, but photographs convey a good sense of its general appearance. The house consisted of a projecting central pavilion flanked by symmetrical wings, all sporting low-pitched gable roofs in imitation of the pediments of Greek temples. A small porch, set rather awkwardly to one side of the central section, sheltered the front door and its sidelights. The porch roof, which doubled as a balcony, had ornate iron railings. Among the home's distinctive features were toothed window heads, an uncommon feature on provincial examples of the Greek Revival style. Ames also built what was reputed to be the city's first greenhouse on his property and put a German gardener in charge of it. It appears that Ames and his wife, Martha, who had eight children, the last born in 1858, lived in the house until at least 1874, when Alfred died.

The fourth of the couple's seven sons, Albert was fifteen when his parents moved into the house, but its chaste styling, designed to reflect republican ideals, apparently did not rub off on him. After graduating from medical school in 1862 at age twenty, he signed up for military duty and served with two Minnesota regiments that saw action during the Dakota War and the Civil War. Later, he drifted off to California, but returned to Minneapolis following his father's death and assumed his medical practice. Albert was by then the married father of three children, and it is not clear whether he or any other Ames family members lived in the house after 1874. By the early 1880s, the home was a boardinghouse, suggesting that the family had sold it.

Albert, meanwhile, went into politics. Handsome, well-liked, and known for his sympathy toward the poor, Ames won the

Alfred E. Ames House, 721 Fourth Street South, about 1900. Ames was one of Minneapolis's first physicians.

first of six terms as mayor of Minneapolis in 1876. A decade later, he ran as the Democratic Party candidate for governor of Minnesota and lost by only 2,600 votes. In 1900, Ames was elected to his final term as mayor, and for reasons unknown—

he may simply have needed the money—he immediately launched the most crooked administration in the city's history. He installed his brother Fred as police chief, had him fire any officers suspected of honesty, then used the department as a roving shakedown squad devoted to the acquisition of boodle. Some of the schemes, such as forcing prostitutes to purchase illustrated biographies of city officials, reached a lunatic level of inspiration. Most infamous were so-called big mitt poker games, organized by the police, in which stacked decks were used to fleece the unwary.

It was all very lucrative, but it did not last for long. Hovey C. Clarke, a reformer who had opposed Ames in the mayoral election, took over a grand jury in 1902. Indictments quickly followed. Ames was forced to resign and then watched as brother Fred and other associates went to prison. The slippery doctor eluded a similar fate. He won an appeal after being convicted in 1903 of taking a bribe, and two retrials ended in hung juries.

Albert "Doc" Ames, the boodle king of Minneapolis, about 1905. Many of his associates (including his brother) went to prison, but Ames eluded that fate.

He lived out his last years on the Near North Side of Minneapolis, dying at age sixty-nine in 1911. By then, the old family house where he had grown up in the shadows of the county courthouse was already gone, lost to the ceaseless push of progress.[7]

Samuel C. Gale House, 115 Fourth Street South, 1864 to 1903 (razed)

Samuel Gale arrived in Minneapolis in 1857, not an auspicious year for beginning a career in real estate. The speculative bubble that burst that year left debt and misery in its wake, but Gale weathered the disaster and later established a successful company specializing in real estate development, loans, and insurance. Two of Gale's brothers—Amory, a Baptist missionary, and Harlow, also a businessman—preceded him to Minnesota. Like so many of the New Englanders who migrated to Minneapolis (Gale was from Massachusetts), he became involved in civic, cultural, and charitable activities. He served on the school board and was a strong supporter of the Minneapolis Society of Fine Arts, which later evolved into the Minneapolis Institute of Arts.[8]

Gale's first mansion, located at the southeast corner of Fourth and Marquette (then called Minnetonka Avenue), was a measure of how quickly he had made his fortune. Built of local gray limestone reputedly quarried from an island near St. Anthony Falls, the house was an early Minneapolis example of the fashionable Italian Villa style. Even so, its mansard roof, said to be among the first in the city, was decidedly French. The home's most charming feature was a pagoda-like front tower adorned with two little balconies and crowned by an upswept roof terminating in a pinnacle. Nothing is known about the interior, nor has the home's designer been identified, although he was probably local, since out-of-town architects in those days were rarely hired for residential work in Minneapolis.[9]

Samuel C. Gale House, 115 Fourth Street South, 1890, with an unidentified couple sitting on the front steps. This house was perhaps the first in the city with a mansard roof.

Gale House about 1900, a few years before it was razed. After the Gale family moved out, the building was used for various commercial purposes.

A new bank rises on the former site of the Gale House (next to Boutell Brothers Furniture), 1903, northwest along Fourth Street. Commercial expansion eventually claimed almost all of downtown Minneapolis's nineteenth-century mansions.

Gale and his wife, Susan, with the aid of two Bohemian servants and a nanny, ultimately raised five children in the house, which was just a few blocks from Gale's offices at 229 Nicollet Avenue. He was also close to his brother, Harlow, who lived next door on Fourth in another large home. Other housing on the block was more modest, however, and it was only later that the city's wealthiest residents sought to secrete themselves in exclusive enclaves.

Gale's stone mansion proved to be one of only a few built in the immediate neighborhood, which by the early 1880s began to lose its residential character. In 1885 the *Minneapolis Tribune* constructed a seven-story office building (which burned down four years later) catty-corner from Gale's mansion, signaling the commercial onslaught to come. As a real estate man, Gale needed no help in reading the tea leaves, and in 1889 he and his family decamped to a magnificent new mansion near Loring Park.[10]

Sometime before then, it is likely Gale sold off the front portion of his property on Fourth, where in 1889 a new building was completed for the National Bank of Commerce. The old mansion, its tower now overlooking the back of a six-story building only yards away, soldiered on for a few more years. It may have been apartments for a while and also appears to have been used as a bicycle shop before it finally came down in 1903 to make way for yet another bank building.[11]

Alonzo C. Rand House, 525 Seventh Street South, Joseph Haley, 1874 to 1923 (razed)

By the early 1870s, Seventh Street between about Nicollet and Chicago Avenues was perhaps the closest thing in Minneapolis to a mansion row. A dozen or more big houses could be found along this stretch of the street. Railroad executive Charles H. Prior lived at 306 Seventh, all-purpose entrepreneur William Washburn was at 503, and miller Rufus Stevens had a towered Italianate home near Portland Avenue. Of all the houses along

Seventh, the most curious belonged to Alonzo C. Rand, an owner of the Minneapolis Gas Light Company.[12]

Rand's mansion, at first glance, appeared to be a conventional foray into the fustian realm of the French Second Empire. Broad and boxy, the house included the usual mansard roof decorated with a metal balustrade, a small front porch supported by clusters of more-or-less Corinthian columns, and a variety of bay windows bumping out from the first floor. The exterior walls, however, were highly unusual, made of blocks formed out of an asbestos-like mineral compound known as Asbestine.[13]

Presumably, Rand chose the faux stone to save money, but it is also likely that he liked the idea of using what was at the time a novel material. An inventor as well as an astute businessman, Rand was a pioneer in the process of making gas from coal. He moved to Minneapolis in 1874 and took over the local gas company three years later, at a time when its product was so expensive that only the well-do-to could afford it. Rand was soon able to bring down the price by perfecting a new method for manufacturing the gas, and by the 1880s his business was booming. He was a success in other fields as well, serving as mayor of Minneapolis from 1878 to 1882.

Rand and his wife, Celina, had just eleven years to enjoy their mansion. On July 12, 1885, the Rands, two of their four children—Mary, eighteen, and Harvey, fifteen—along with their ten-year-old nephew and four members of another family, chartered the thirty-five-foot-steamer *Minnie Cook* for a pleasure excursion on Lake Minnetonka. A storm came up, the boat swamped off Lookout Point, and all ten people aboard, including the pilot, drowned. That night, the *Minneapolis Tribune* reported, "crowds of people of all classes strode quietly by the house of the late A. C. Rand. . . . Words of sympathy were spoken in whispers, and questions concerning the finding of the bodies were asked and answered in the same manner."[14] The funerals were held a few days later, and thousands stood along the route of the procession to Lakewood Cemetery.

A year later, surviving family members, including sons

Alonzo Rand House, 525 Seventh Street South, about 1880. The house was clad in a faux stone material called Asbestine.

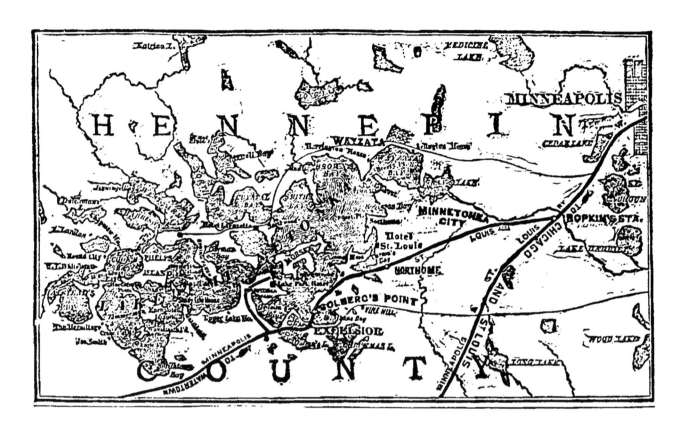

A SAD SEARCH.

The Work of Diving and Dragging for the Victims of Sunday's Disaster.

The Long, Painful Task Finally Completed at 7:15 O'clock Last Evening.

Harvey Rand and His Sister, Mrs. Coykendall, Clasped in Each Other's Arms.

Details of the Search as It Proceeded Through the Gloomy Day.

Affecting Scenes as the Bodies One by One Are Brought to the Surface.

Expressions of Grief and Sympathy Heard on Every Hand from All Classes.

Appropriate Resolutions Passed by the City Council at a Special Meeting.

Telegrams of Condolence Received from Many Quarters—Funeral Arrangements.

The drownings of Alonzo Rand and four members of his family at Lake Minnetonka were big news in the Minneapolis Tribune on July 13, 1885. Ten people died when their boat capsized during a sudden storm.

Rand House about 1905, with employees of Northwestern Agriculturist maga-zine gathered outside. The mansion was previously home to the Minneapolis Club.

Alonzo T. and Rufus Rand, sold the house to the Minneapolis Club, which occupied it until 1892.[15] After that, the mansion housed several tenants, including an agricultural magazine, before it was torn down in 1923 to make way for the Sexton Building, which remains on the site.[16]

Pillsbury Mansions

Charles A. Pillsbury House, 927 Second Avenue South, Leroy Buffington?, ca. 1875 to ca. 1920 (razed)

George A. Pillsbury House, 225 Tenth Street South, Leroy Buffington, 1879 to ca. 1910 (razed)

Frederick C. Pillsbury House, 303 Tenth Street South, Leroy Buffington, 1888 to 1916 (razed)

Three members of the Pillsbury flour-milling family once had homes along Tenth Street, although the arrangement did not last for long. Charles A. Pillsbury, who led the way in establishing the family's milling empire, built the earliest of the homes, at the northeast corner of Tenth Street and Second Avenue South, in the 1870s. He arrived in Minneapolis in 1869 (his brother, Frederick, soon followed), bought a stake in a flour mill, then set up his own firm three years later. Adopting the latest in milling technology, the company was an immediate success, and by 1881 its giant A Mill on the east bank of St. Anthony Falls was the largest in the world.

Very little is known about Charles's house, but its outline on old maps suggests that it was an averaged-size mansion of its day, probably in the five-thousand-square-foot range. Like several other owners of early downtown mansions, Charles moved away in the 1880s to the Washburn–Fair Oaks neighborhood. Even so, another Pillsbury—his father, George A.—remained on Tenth Street. Although George was a ground-floor investor in the family's flour-milling business, he did not move to Minneapolis until 1878. His younger brother, John S. Pillsbury (also

an important investor in the flour company), was the family's pioneer in Minnesota, settling in St. Anthony in 1855. George, meanwhile, remained in his native New Hampshire, where he was a banker.[17]

George was sixty-two by the time he decided to join his brother and two sons in Minneapolis, hiring architect Leroy Buffington to design a mansion. John S. Pillsbury by this time had also commissioned Buffington to build a mansion near the University of Minnesota campus. The homes, both completed in about 1879, turned out to be remarkably similar, at least on the outside, raising the possibility that the brothers may have worked out some sort of two-for-one deal with Buffington.

George's house, at the southwest corner of Tenth Street and Third Avenue South, was among the earliest downtown mansions to abandon the Italianate and French Second Empire styles in favor of the Queen Anne or something heading in that direction. The red brick house sported steep gables with ornamental wood trusses, porches awash in gingerbread trim, decorative window hoods, front and side bays, and a romantic little balcony hung from the third floor. The mansion drew some of its inspiration from the Gothic-tinged work of the English designer Charles Eastlake.[18]

Pillsbury made himself at home in Minneapolis so quickly that by 1884 he was elected mayor. He later became president of the Northwestern National Bank as well as a director of several other companies. He and his wife, Margaret, were also active in the Baptist Church and became known for their charitable endeavors. By the time Pillsbury died in 1898, the neighborhood around his mansion was changing rapidly as commercial development oozed south from the downtown core. In 1912, the Leamington Hotel filled in the block where the mansion once stood. The Leamington itself came down in 1990, and a parking ramp now occupies the site.

The finest of the Pillsbury houses belonged to Frederick, the younger of George's two sons. Only eighteen when he joined brother Charles in Minneapolis in 1870, he became a

George A. Pillsbury House, 225 Tenth Street South, about 1893. George's son, Charles A. Pillsbury, was a founder of the family's flour-milling empire.

Frederick C. Pillsbury mansion and carriage house, 303 Tenth Street South, about 1890. The massive brick and stone house stood for only twenty-eight years.

partner in the milling business six years later. By the 1880s he had helped organize another milling company and had also gone into banking and railroading. He was interested in agri-

culture as well and owned a farm near Lake Minnetonka, where, one biographer reported, he "surrounds himself with cattle, like himself, of ample girth."

In 1888 Fred continued the family tradition by hiring Buffington to design a new home for himself, his wife, Alice, and their four children, in the Richardsonian Romanesque style, which

Within the drawing: Harvey Ellis del.

L·S·BUFFINGTON·ARCHITECT.
MINNEAPOLIS·MINN·1888

Drawing by Harvey Ellis of the front door of the Frederick C. Pillsbury House, 1888. Ellis was one of the finest draftsmen of his era and probably designed the spectacular door.

Sitting room of the Frederick C. Pillsbury House, about 1893. Pillsbury died at age forty in 1892, just four years after the mansion was completed.

was extremely popular in the Twin Cities and elsewhere in the Midwest from the late 1880s until about 1895. Dark, boldly scaled, and adamantine, Richardsonian buildings conveyed a sense of mass and power.[19]

For Fred Pillsbury's mansion, Buffington—who never let a design go to waste—all but duplicated a scheme he had prepared in 1885 for a new Minneapolis Public Library. The result was a house with a rather institutional look. Both the mansion and a stunning carriage house that adjoined it were built of red brick and brownstone. Essentially a two-story square, the mansion came with three corner towers of varying dimensions, a hefty porte cochere on Third Avenue, and a carved arched entry reached from a stone staircase along Tenth Street.

Set within the arch was the house's most astonishing detail: a front door of barbarian splendor featuring panels inlaid with colored glass, metal studs, and swirling wrought-iron ornament. One local publication, displaying a bit of provincialism, pronounced this door "one of the most elaborate . . . ever designed." Harvey Ellis, a much-traveled draftsman who had

wandered into Buffington's office sometime in 1886 or 1887, may have designed the door, which he depicted in a marvelous drawing that shows a fashionably dressed woman and two alert dogs posing in front of it.[20]

The door led to the home's opulent main floor, which was arranged around a central hall and included a morning room with a semicircular bay, a library, a drawing room, and a dining room outfitted with an enormous fireplace surrounded by Mexican onyx and Tiffany tiles. Patterned plaster and stencil work provided much of the decorative program, while the mill-work lineup included mahogany, sycamore, satinwood, and oak, among other prime species.

In 1892, while on a business trip, Pillsbury became ill with what turned out to be diphtheria, and died a few days later, at age forty. His mansion had an even shorter life, falling to the wrecker in 1916 to make way for an addition to the Curtis Hotel. The Ameriprise Operations Center now takes up the entire block. ◆

CHAPTER 8

LORING PARK, HAWTHORNE PARK, and OAK LAKE

A newspaper writer in the 1930s toured the Loring Park neighborhood—then an architectural stew of car dealerships, hotels, apartments, and crumbling old mansions—and recalled the time when it was "one of the most socially exclusive sections of the city." The remains of that lost age were still evident in "some of the aristocratic dwellings of early days, among them a number of fine old houses at whose imposing fronts ornate Corinthian pillars, once the height of architectural style, still stand guard beside unrepaired and weather-beaten doors." It was a familiar complaint, but in the case of Loring Park change occurred with particular ferocity, leaving behind a mansion district that was spectacular but short-lived.

Mansions began appearing in the neighborhood by 1870, about the same time that pioneer farmer Allen Harmon, namesake of Harmon Place, platted his first addition. Lumberman Charles Bovey's Italianate mansion at Thirteenth Street and Harmon was especially prominent. A block or so to the south, the man who gave Yale Place its name, Washington Yale, owned forty acres of wooded land and in the early 1870s built what was described as a "pleasant residence" in the middle of his private forest.[1]

It was not until the 1880s that bona fide mansion districts developed along Harmon and south of Fifteenth Street West. The impetus for this influx of wealth was the park itself, known as Central Park when it opened in 1883 but later renamed in honor of park board president Charles Loring. With its pond (deepened and reshaped to make it more appealing) and well-tended lawn, the park became an instant attraction in a downtown that otherwise offered little in the way of green space, and it did not take long for a number of the city's elite families to establish themselves in new homes nearby.

Harmon Place proved especially fertile ground for mansions. By the early 1890s, two dozen or more lined Harmon from Eleventh Street westward. Many of the grandest, dating to the late 1880s, were on the north side of the park between Willow Street and Hennepin Avenue. Samuel Gale's quartzite

Harmon Place, looking northeast from Willow Street, 1915. Only one historic mansion remains on Harmon today.

castle at 1600 Harmon Place headlined the show. Rufus Rand's nearby Classical Revival–style mansion, completed in 1891, was among the last built on Harmon.[2]

The area south of the park also drew well-heeled residents, including Jacob Tourtellotte, who occupied a twin-towered Victorian home on Fifteenth Street West. To the south, Oak Grove Street and later Clifton and Groveland Avenues were once thick with mansions. One notable house, on Oak Grove, belonged to William D. Hale, a partner in William Washburn's

William K. Morison double house, 1506–8 Harmon Place, about 1915. The rambling Queen Anne-style residence, which overlooked Loring Park, was razed in the 1960s.

milling operation. Known as Crest Wood, it stood amid grounds that extended all the way south to Groveland. Although some mansions remain here, many more have been lost, including the picturesque Asa Bowers Barton House (later the home of Charles Loring) and the Francis B. Hart House, both from the 1880s and both on Clifton. Mansions were built here into the early decades of the twentieth century. Two of the largest from this later era were the Frederic W. Clifford House at 325 Clifton and the Charles D. Velie House at 225 Clifton.

Well before much of the Loring Park area developed, the blocks across Hennepin Avenue to the north had already filled in with houses. Among them were a sprinkling of mansions near Hawthorne Park, which once formed a wedge of greenery between Twelfth and Thirteenth Streets on Hawthorne Avenue. Two of the largest houses, one belonging to Eugene M. Wilson and the other to William W. McNair, overlooked the park.

To the north and west of Hawthorne was the Oak Lake neighborhood, which Samuel Gale platted in 1880. It was east

Francis B. Hart House, 436 (later 1720) Clifton Place, about 1890. Built in 1887, the house was torn down about 1930.

Oak Lake neighborhood, 1898, with Lyndale Avenue at the lower edge and Sixth Avenue North (Olson Highway) at far left. All of the neighborhood's historic homes were cleared away by redevelopment in the 1930s.

of Lyndale Avenue where the Minneapolis Farmers Market and a variety of industrial buildings now stand. Hilly and wooded in its original form, Oak Lake was laid out with curving streets that meandered around two small ponds, and initially it attracted a colony of more than 150 mostly upper-middle-class families. Fashionable Minneapolis architect Leroy Buffington designed some of the development's first homes, and although they were not quite mansions, they were large and substantial. Oak Lake's appeal to the "better" classes proved short-lived, and in the early 1900s it began a long slide from which it never recovered.

Loring Park's decline was less precipitous than Oak Lake's, but in the end Harmon Place in particular proved just as susceptible to commercial encroachment as earlier downtown mansion districts. The automobile industry drove much of the transformation. Between 1905 and 1920 more than one hundred auto-related businesses established themselves along Harmon and nearby portions of Hennepin. New apartment buildings shouldered their way in as well, and by the 1920s many of the old mansions began coming down. Rufus Rand's house was among the last to fall in the 1970s, as the neighborhood underwent yet another wave of change and renewal centered around the Loring Park Greenway. Today, Harmon Place is the site of only one historic mansion, the Alden Smith House (1888), no longer a private residence.[3]

South of Loring Park, where commercial pressures were less intense, the pleasant streets along Lowry Hill continued to harbor a sizable number of mansions until the 1960s, when Interstate 94 chewed away parts of Clifton, Groveland, and Ridgewood Avenues. Apartment buildings, some dating to the early 1900s, had by then infiltrated much of the area as far south as Oak Grove, and the freeway opened the way for a new round of construction, including the neighborhood's first residential high-rises. Today, only a dozen or so mansions remain there, mostly along Clifton and Oak Grove, with the bulk of them now used for institutional or business purposes.

HOMES ON HARMON

Frank E. Little (Edward W. Decker) House, 1414 Harmon Place, Leroy Buffington, 1888 to 1936 (razed)

Samuel C. Gale House, 1600 Harmon Place, Leroy Buffington, 1888 to 1933 (razed)

Rufus Rand House, 1526 Harmon Place, William Channing Whitney, 1891 to 1975 (razed)

These homes offer a representative sampling of the mansions that once lined Harmon Place near and along the north side of Loring Park. Gale's mansion was by far the most prominent of the trio—it qualified as one of the architectural wonders of the city—but the Little and Rand houses were also of considerable interest as designs. Although they were built within a span of just six years, the three mansions presented decisively different looks, reflecting how rapidly architectural style evolved in the Twin Cities in the late 1880s.

The Frank E. Little House was the first to be completed, on a midblock site between Spruce Place and Willow Street, just east of the park. A partner in a downtown real estate firm, Little is an obscure figure who left no deep footprints behind, but he must have been doing well in the late 1880s, when according to one newspaper he paid $160 a front foot for the lot on which he built his mansion. The house, known only through a pair of photographs and a drawing or two, came from the busy office of Leroy Buffington, an architect whose career encompassed the full range of Victorian design. Mixing Queen Anne and Shingle-style elements, among others inspirations, the house offered such curiosities as a beehive tower, a front overhang shaped rather like a railroad lounge car, checkerboard trim, and tiled upper walls. Then and now, it could not have been mistaken for any other home in Minneapolis. No descriptions of the interior have been found, but the house undoubtedly came fully loaded with all the finery Buffington could muster.[4]

Little's tenure in the house was short-lived, and it went

Frank E. Little (later Edward W. Decker) House, 1414 Harmon Place, about 1889. The curving front overhang was one of the home's many peculiar features.

L·S·BUFFINGTON ARCHITECT
MINNEAPOLIS MINN AD·1888·

Drawing by Harvey Ellis of the Samuel Gale House, 1600 Harmon Place, 1888. The castlelike house was built of ultra-hard Sioux quartzite from southwestern Minnesota.

Gale House, west across Maple Street, about 1900. Its tower was a stone bullet aimed at the heavens.

through two more owners until banker Edward W. Decker, who would later go on to commission a magnificent Prairie School house at Lake Minnetonka, bought the place in 1903 for $10,000. Not long after he and his family moved in, Decker acquired a lot next door, on which he promptly built an "automobile sales building," as he described it. Then, no doubt con-

templating the impact of his handiwork, he moved away. By the time the mansion was finally demolished in 1936, it was owned by the Luther Ford Company.[5]

Three years before the demise of the Little-Decker House, the far larger and costlier mansion built a block and half away by Samuel C. Gale in 1888 had come down, its passing much mourned by the *Minneapolis Journal*, which claimed the home had once been "the showplace of the northwest." Although Gale's mansion—the second one he had built downtown—was

Entrance hall and oak-paneled staircase of the Gale House, about 1893. Samuel Gale and his family lived in the house for only six years.

not the biggest or costliest of its era in Minneapolis, it was indeed extraordinary by virtue of its design and the quality of its detailing.[6]

After deciding to sell his 1860s mansion at Fourth Street and Marquette Avenue, Gale secured a prime lot overlooking Loring Park at the northwest corner of Sixteenth (Maple) Street and Harmon, then hired Leroy Buffington to design a new home. Gale's timing could not have been better. Harvey Ellis, an exceptionally gifted designer and renderer, had just signed on

as a draftsman in Buffington's office. He took Gale's project in hand, transforming what had been an uninspired initial design into an intense, romantic, and highly sculptural Romanesque fantasy. With its sweeping roofline, dramatic half-arched front entry, circular tower topped by a cone of solid stone, and rock-solid attached carriage house, the mansion was an improbable architectural fairy tale from the Middle Ages as filtered through Ellis's distinctive imagination.[7]

Costing at least $100,000, the mansion was also an unmatched local exercise in the might of masonry. The walls were built entirely of ultra-hard Sioux quartzite, a reddish granite quarried near Pipestone, Minnesota. Because it was so difficult to dress or carve, the stone was laid up in random rough-faced blocks, forming walls as rugged as cliffs. "No cut [drawing] can give a true idea of the extreme massiveness of the building," said the *St. Paul Pioneer Press*, adding that the house "bids fair to withstand the tooth of time for centuries."[8] This prediction proved to be badly mistaken.

Gale, a real estate broker whose fortune had swollen during the 1880s when land prices in the Twin Cities rode a seemingly endless upward spiral, spared no expense inside the house, where a huge central hall on the main floor provided much of the architectural drama. Paneled in oak stained "a pale amber green," according to one account, the hall was the setting for an elaborate staircase with as many switchbacks as a mountain highway. The hall led to a sequence of ornate rooms, among them a library that opened onto a porch with views of the park and a drawing room "finished in white and gold with a ceiling of pale yellow silk with a pattern in plush of a pale blue appliqued thereon, the pattern emphasized with silver-headed nails of hemispherical shape." It can be assumed that Gale's wife, Susan, took charge of the decorating, which does not seem to have lacked for color or completeness.[9]

Upstairs, there were six bedrooms (the Gales had five children, at least three of whom were young enough to be living with them when the mansion was built). The master bedroom offered a novel feature in the form of apple wood taken from the orchard on the Massachusetts farm where Gale had been raised. The attic included the usual servants' quarters plus a gymnasium, an uncommon domestic amenity at a time when wealthy men, judging by their girths, did not go overboard about working out.

Despite its splendors, the mansion was home to the Gales for only six years. It is not known why they moved out. Perhaps the place was simply too much to maintain, or perhaps Samuel Gale, savvy real estate man that he was, saw the neighborhood's commercial future and decided to leave before housing values declined. The new owner was Martin B. Koon, a onetime district court judge and successful corporate lawyer who later helped found the Minneapolis Institute of Arts.[10] Koon and his family soon vacated as well, however, and the house was no longer used as a private residence after about 1915, by which time the blocks around it were thick with auto dealers and other businesses. After a tour of duty as a nursing home, the mansion was razed at the height of the Great Depression. Its destruction led the *Journal* to recall that Gale had once stated the house would "live 100 years. Minneapolis will never crowd it out in that time." Instead, the mansion built for the ages disappeared into the dust only forty-five years after its massive stone walls began to rise above Loring Park.

In 1891 Rufus R. Rand built a large house in a far more restrained style at 1526 Harmon, directly across Maple Street from Gale's mansion. Rand—whose parents and two siblings had drowned six years earlier at Lake Minnetonka—was secretary-treasurer of the Minneapolis Gas Light Company (later Minnegasco), founded by his late father, Alonzo. Rufus's three-story brick and stone house, designed by William Channing Whitney, was a relatively early example of the sedate Classical Revival style that by 1890 had begun to succeed the old, wild varieties of Victoriana. A local champion of the style, Whitney was well on his way to becoming the favored architect of Minneapolis's social and financial elite by the time he designed Rand's handsome but understated mansion. Looking much like the clubhouse it would later become, the mansion, with its four-square massing, symmetrically arranged windows, and chaste classical detailing, was quite a contrast to Gale's rock-bound fantasy. The mansion's interior is poorly documented, but a photograph from 1930 suggests that the rooms were arranged

Rufus Rand House, 1526 Harmon Place, about 1898. The Classical Revival styling of the house was quite a departure from the rock-ribbed Romanesque look of Samuel Gale's mansion across the street.

Parlor in the Rand House after it became a women's shelter, about 1930.
Minneapolis Community and Technical College now occupies the site.

in simple fashion along a central hall and were treated in the same subdued manner as the exterior.[11]

Rand and his wife, Susan, who also owned a large summer home near Monticello, Minnesota, raised two children in the mansion. Their son, Rufus Rand Jr., went on to renown as a World War I aviator and also built the Rand Tower in downtown Minneapolis as well as a Lake Minnetonka estate, which now serves as the headquarters of Cargill, Inc.

Like other residents of Harmon's mansion row, the Rands soon felt the hot breath of commercial encroachment, and they moved elsewhere around 1900. The house then served a succession of institutional occupants, beginning in 1906 with the Women's City Club of Minneapolis, which stayed for twenty years. A woman's shelter and the First Unitarian Society were among the later tenants. These institutional uses kept the mansion going until 1975, when it was razed for construction of what is now Minneapolis Community and Technical College.[12]

Clifton Avenue Mansions

Asa B. Barton (later Charles M. Loring) House, 100–102 Clifton Avenue, William Channing Whitney, 1887 to 1962 (razed)

Charles D. Velie House, 225 Clifton Avenue, William Channing Whitney, 1906 to 1962 (razed)

Frederic W. Clifford House, 325 Clifton Avenue, Harry Jones, 1905 to 1968 (razed)

Asa Barton, from Maine, was one of the earliest settlers in the Loring Park area, arriving in the 1850s with his wife, Olive, and their daughter, Florence. In 1862 he bought a button-cute Carpenter Gothic–style cottage at Spruce Place and Oak Grove Street. Barton expanded the house with a series of additions, including an octagonal tower with mini-battlements, and lived there with his family for the next twenty-five years.

By 1887, when he served as treasurer of the Minnesota Brush Electric Company and secretary of the Island Power Company, Barton was able to build a bigger mansion on Clifton Avenue a block or so from his old cottage. The new house, a fourteen-room Queen Anne finished in brick and patterned shingles, was in the vanguard of a wave of mansion building that transformed Clifton between 1885 and 1910. Featuring a polygonal corner tower, a broad front porch, and numerous bays, balconies, gables, and undulations, the house was an unusually colorful specimen from the drafting table of architect William Channing Whitney, whose later work would be nothing if not sober.[13]

In 1895 Florence Barton, then thirty-six years old, married sixty-two-year-old Charles Loring, whose first wife had died a year earlier. Well known as the Minneapolis Park Board's first president (and the namesake of Loring Park), he was a successful businessman involved in flour milling, real estate, and railroading. He was as well a founder of the brush electric company that employed his father-in-law.[14]

Asa Barton died in 1904, and his widow a year later. The Lorings then moved into the house, where they lived for the next two decades. Charles died in 1922, and Florence in 1924. In her will, Florence donated the mansion to the Women's Welfare League, which turned it into a convalescent home. Like its immediate neighbors, it ended up in the path of progress and was razed in the early 1960s for the Interstate 94 right-of-way.

Some of Clifton's largest mansions were not built until the early 1900s, a period when fortunes consolidated and wealthy families sought to ensconce themselves in the grandest dwellings possible. Among those who built new homes on Clifton was Charles Deere Velie, whose middle name suggests the source of his fortune. His father, Stephen H. Velie, married the daughter of John Deere, founder of the farm implement company. After Deere died in the 1880s, Stephen Velie became the company's biggest stockholder. Charles, Stephen's oldest son, worked in the company's Minneapolis offices and was also involved in the automobile business and other ventures.[15]

Asa B. Barton's first house, Spruce Place and Oak Grove Street, 1862. The Gothic Revival–style home was a cottage aspiring to be a castle.

The mansion he and his wife, Louise, built at 225 Clifton reflected the growing popularity of the Tudor Revival style. Exploiting a range of forms based on English models from the Medieval period and later, the style was worked for everything from tract houses to mansions. Designed by William Channing Whitney, Velie's house featured walls of rough-faced limestone, a triple-arched entry porch, and sculpted Flemish gables. Inside, a great hall extending across the front of the house opened out to a suite of rear-facing rooms. The richly paneled hall had a central fireplace and a staircase at one end. Unlike busily decorated Victorian interiors, the hall was understated, its ornament limited to moldings and plasterwork on the ceiling.

Charles Velie died in 1929, but Louise stayed on in the house for a number of years (she died in 1962). In 1950 the mansion was donated to the local council of the Boy Scouts of America for use as its headquarters. The end came in the 1960s, when the mansion, like the nearby Barton House, was razed to make way for Interstate 94.[16]

The largest Clifton Avenue mansion belonged to Frederic W. Clifford. Built at a reputed cost of $725,000, it offered a more lively and complex version of the Tudor Revival style than Velie's home. Harry Jones's design for Clifford was a picturesque ramble of brick, stone, stucco, and half-timbering beneath a series of steep gabled roofs. The entry portal, crowned by a split pediment, was monumental in scale. To the rear, a rounded, castlelike protrusion harbored a screened porch. It opened out onto a circling terrace that overlooked the grounds, which extended south to Groveland Avenue, where brick walls with cast-stone balusters marked the estate's boundaries.

As with so many other English-inspired mansions of the time, Clifford's was oriented around a great hall. On one side a stairway with carved railings led past stained-glass windows to the second floor. On the other side was a huge fireplace flanked by doors leading out through the screened porch to the rear terrace. The home's other big rooms were also impeccably detailed in wood, plaster, and glass.

Asa B. Barton (later Charles M. Loring) House, 100–102 Clifton Avenue, 1924. The tower with small dormers was very picturesque.

Breakfast cereal—Clifford was a founder of the Cream of Wheat Company—paid for this grandeur. In 1904 Clifford, who was deeply interested in art and architecture, staged a design competition for a new factory and office building for Cream of Wheat. Jones won, designing a Classical Revival–style building that stood in downtown Minneapolis until 1939. By then, Clifford had left the company to "devote full time to private investments," as one account put it.[17]

Clifford and his wife, Grace, who had five children, lived out their lives in the mansion. He was a widower by the time he died, in 1947. Citing his work on numerous civic commissions

*Charles D. Velie House, 225 Clifton Avenue, about 1910. The sculpted gables
were an unusual feature sometimes found on Tudor Revival-style mansions.*

Main hall of the Velie House, 1926. This house was one of several Clifton Avenue mansions destroyed for the construction of Interstate 94 in the 1960s.

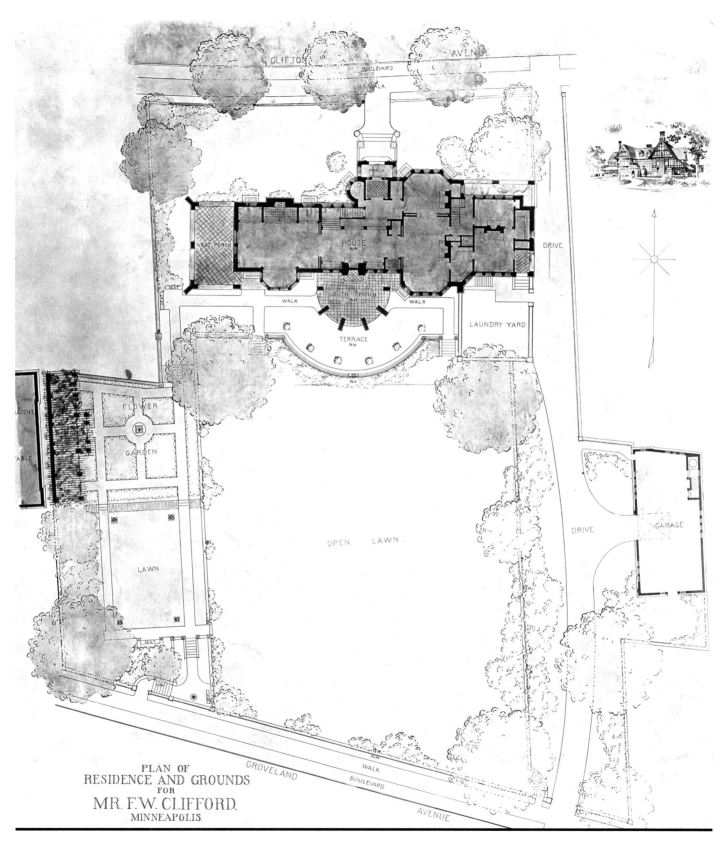

Plan of the Frederic W. Clifford House and its grounds, 325 Clifton Avenue,
about 1905. The backyard extended to Groveland Avenue.

and with the Minneapolis Institute of Arts, a newspaper described Clifford as "one of the last members of a group which played a leading role in development of the city."[18] After his death, the mansion become corporate headquarters for the Osborne McMillan Elevator Company. In 1968 the company sold the house to a developer, who tore it down to build an apartment tower.[19]

Front facade of the Clifford House on Clifton Avenue, 1940s. The cast-stone wall along the sidewalk featured an elaborate design.

Living room of the Clifford House, about 1905. Frederic W. Clifford, who lived in the house until his death in 1947, was a founder of the Cream of Wheat Company.

'WOODBURN.'
RESIDENCE OF HON. E. M. WILSON, COR. HAWTHORNE AV. & 13™ ST., MINNEAPOLIS, MINN.

Eugene M. Wilson House, Thirteenth Street and Hawthorne Avenue, 1874. Wilson was a lawyer and an original member of the Minneapolis Park Board.

PARTNERS ON THE PARK

Eugene M. Wilson House ("Woodburn"), Thirteenth Street and Hawthorne Avenue, 1872 to 1961 (razed)

William W. and Louise McNair House, 1301 Linden Avenue, F. B. Long and Co. (Edgar E. Joralemon), 1886 to 1961 (razed)

These two mansions overlooking Hawthorne Park led intertwined lives right up to the time they were demolished in 1961. William W. McNair and Eugene M. Wilson, known to their friends as "Mac and Gene," were from 1861 to 1869 partners in a Minneapolis law firm. Wilson, who hailed from what is today West Virginia, made his way to Minnesota in 1856 and became

the state's first U.S. Attorney two years later.[20] McNair was a New Yorker who had arrived in Minneapolis at about the same time. The two men were also in-laws: McNair married Wilson's sister, Louise. The law partnership ended when Wilson was elected to Congress. Soon thereafter, McNair was elected mayor of St. Anthony. In 1872, a year after his term ended, St. Anthony merged into Minneapolis, and Wilson was voted in as the first mayor of the newly combined communities.[21]

Wilson's brick mansion, dubbed Woodburn, was built fourteen years before McNair's and occupied a half-block lot when

William and Louise McNair House, 1886. William McNair (once a partner in a law firm with his neighbor Eugene Wilson) died a few months before the house was completed.

it was completed in 1872. The mansard-roofed, French Second Empire–style house stood in the midst of large grounds well planted with trees and crisscrossed by winding paths and driveways. An iron fence surrounded the estate, which included a substantial carriage house.

The estate's beautiful grounds were no surprise, given Wilson's interest in parks and landscaping. He lobbied for the creation of Hawthorne Park, established in 1882 and subsequently renamed in his honor. He was also an original member of the Minneapolis Park Board.[22] Wilson and his wife, Elizabeth, raised three daughters in the mansion, which was to be his last home in Minneapolis. After an unsuccessful bid for governor as the Democratic candidate in 1888, Wilson's health declined, and he died two years later, at age fifty-seven, while on a trip to the Bahamas.

Well after Wilson built his mansion, his old law partner outdid him with a larger and showier house next door to the north. William McNair, who had a broad range of business interests outside his law practice, reputedly spent $125,000 on his mansion. Planning began in 1883, when McNair—just forty-seven years old and newly retired—hired Franklin Long as his architect. Then in independent practice, Long would soon go on to join Frederick Kees in a partnership whose surviving work includes the Minneapolis City Hall. Among Long's draftsmen in the early 1880s was Edgar Joralemon, and he is generally credited with designing McNair's mansion, among the first houses in the Twin Cities to deploy elements of the Richardsonian Romanesque style.

Constructed of reddish Lake Superior sandstone, the house was big and burly, with a massive arched entry porch and an equally hefty porte cochere off to one side. Dominating the design was a tall front gable flanked by a projecting bay on one side and a column-mounted turret on the other. Overall, the house was a transitional work, mixing Queen Anne picturesqueness with stony Richardsonian discipline.

Inside, the mansion's twenty rooms were stuffed with all the finery a big budget could muster. The staircase consumed enough mahogany to reforest Honduras, the numerous fireplaces included mantels made of French onyx and other deluxe materials, and rich tapestries abounded. The mansion also had an elevator—said to be the first installed in a Minneapolis residence—that led up to the third-floor ballroom.[23]

McNair never made it to the dance. He died in September 1885, while the mansion was still under construction, and it was his widow, Louise, who finally occupied the house. She remained there until at least the time of her brother's death in 1890. By the mid-1890s, however, she was living on Lowry Hill. It is likely that her old mansion was vacant for a time before Archbishop John Ireland intervened.

Looking for a site for the new Basilica of St. Mary, Ireland bought both the McNair and Wilson mansions in 1904 for

Parlor of the McNair House, about 1893. The house was sold in 1904 and, with the Wilson House next door, became the home of St. Margaret's Academy for more than fifty years.

$30,000. A year later, however, he chose a site a few blocks away on Hennepin Avenue for the church. Ireland then sold the mansions to the Sisters of St. Joseph, who converted them into St. Margaret's Academy, a high school for girls.[24] Augmented by additions, the houses stood until 1961, when they were demolished after St. Margaret's moved to a new building. Hawthorne Park vanished a few years later to make way for feeder ramps to and from Interstate 394.

Multitowered Jacob Tourtellotte House (left), from across Loring Park pond, with St. Mark's Episcopal cathedral at center, about 1910. The Tourtellotte House was originally built for Frederick H. Boardman.

Frederick H. Boardman (later Dr. Jacob Tourtellotte) House, 505 (or 431) Fifteenth Street West, Edward S. Stebbins?, 1886 to 1922 (razed)

This distinctive and monumental house is among the most elusive of the Twin Cities' lost mansions. With its four-story, bell-roofed tower posing above the south end of Loring Park, the house was certainly a neighborhood landmark, yet it attracted only a modest amount of attention from either the general or architectural press of the time. The mansion's relative obscurity is surprising given that its owners—Frederick H. Boardman and, later, Dr. Jacob Tourtellotte—were both well known in Minneapolis.

Boardman was a real estate investor and lawyer. He served from 1901 to 1905 as Hennepin County Attorney and prosecuted the corruption cases involving Mayor Albert Ames. Boardman's mansion, built of red brick and light-colored stone,

Tourtellotte House, about 1900, with servants posed before it like statues. Jacob Tourtellotte was a physician by training but made his money in banking and real estate.

mixed Colonial Revival, Classical, and Victorian elements. The taller of its two towers culminated in an open belfry like those often found on schools of the time. It is likely the house was designed by Edward Stebbins, an architect who lived near Loring Park.[25]

In 1892 Dr. Jacob Tourtellotte and his wife, Harriet, who had just moved to Minneapolis, bought the house and remodeled

Harriet Tourtellotte, about 1919, some years after her husband's death.

it. One of their enhancements was a gracefully curved staircase with ornate iron railings that led down to the sidewalk on Fifteenth Street. Tourtellotte, born in Connecticut, served as a ship's surgeon during the Civil War.[26] In 1870 he and Harriet, a direct descendant of Benedict Arnold, moved to Winona, Minnesota, near where one of Tourtellotte's brothers lived. Tourtellotte never practiced medicine in Winona. Instead, he prospered in banking and real estate even as he and Harriet were stalked by tragedy. Their oldest daughter succumbed to scarlet fever as an infant, while their only other child, also a girl, died at age ten as a result of eating a tainted hot dog.[27]

In Minneapolis the Tourtellottes became active philanthropists, donating to many causes and staging benefits at their mansion.[28] Here is how the *Minneapolis Tribune* described an event at the house in 1895: "From the dining room table with its center piece of La France roses and ropes of smilax, and its decorations of pink ribbons and candles, coffee, ices and cakes were served. Frappes and bonbons were passed from small tables upstairs and down, where there were numerous assisting hostesses."[29]

When Tourtellotte died in 1912, the *Tribune* said he "never missed an opportunity to do a charitable act." A special funeral train took his body to Winona, where he was buried beside his lost daughters.[30] Two years later, Harriet donated $125,000 to build the Tourtellotte Memorial Deaconess Home at Asbury Hospital in Minneapolis. The building, now used as the library for North Central University, still stands. Harriet died in 1919.[31] The mansion was razed three years later to make way for what is now the Loring Park Office Building at 430 Oak Grove Street. ◆

CHAPTER 9

STEVENS SQUARE, WASHBURN-FAIR OAKS, and PARK AVENUE

By 1890 the era of mansion building in downtown Minneapolis was all but over as other parts of the city became favored ground for the conspicuous display of wealth. Two areas directly south of downtown, Washburn-Fair Oaks and Park Avenue, proved especially appealing to the moneyed crowd. Beginning in the mid-1880s and continuing well into the twentieth century, these two neighborhoods, along with Lowry Hill, were the city's most prestigious residential precincts. The roster of lost mansions here includes the palatial William Washburn House on the site of today's Fair Oaks Park.[1]

By the time Washburn began building his mansion in 1883, a scattering of country estates had already appeared south of downtown. One of the largest belonged to Richard J. Mendenhall, a banker turned horticulturist who in about 1874 built a limestone mansion near Eighteenth Street and First Avenue South, in today's Stevens Square neighborhood. The home, renowned for the "park like beauty" of its grounds, was part of twelve square blocks Mendenhall owned in the vicinity and

left largely undeveloped. After Mendenhall's death in 1906, his heirs sold the land, and over the next twenty years developers built the apartment house district that still dominates the neighborhood.[2]

An earlier estate, built in the 1850s where the Minneapolis Institute of Arts now stands, was just to the south of Washburn's property. It belonged to Dorilus Morrison, a lumberman (among many other pursuits) who was also the first mayor of Minneapolis. Morrison chose his ground well, siting his estate (which he dubbed Villa Rosa) on a small hill that offered views of the surrounding plains. At the time Morrison built, the area was mostly given over to farms, and his home was truly a place in the country. His son, Clinton, constructed a mansion of his own just across Third Avenue South, in 1873. It survived until the 1930s, when the Fair Oaks Apartments rose on the site.

Development did not really begin to crowd in on the Morrisons until the early 1880s, when Washburn's gigantic mansion and another of almost equal splendor built for John W.

Johnson (but soon sold to Charles Pillsbury) appeared nearby. Others quickly followed. In the early 1900s a second generation of mansions, some built on the sites of earlier homes, filled in most of the blocks around Washburn's estate and to the north toward Franklin Avenue. Flour milling families such as the Pillsburys, Crosbys, and Christians all built homes here during this period. George Christian's mansion at 2303 Third Avenue South, completed in 1919 and now home to the Hennepin History Museum, was the last to be built in the neighborhood.[3]

An even larger district of fine homes developed along Park Avenue, which for a time rivaled St. Paul's Summit Avenue as a mansion row. Park's "golden mile," as it was sometimes called, extended from about Eighteenth Street to Twenty-Eighth Street. Thirty-five or more mansions would eventually line this stretch of the avenue. Park's rise to prominence was quick. As late as the early 1880s, much of Park remained a dusty rural road of no great pretension, and it is said that millionaire miller William Dunwoody, who lived downtown, occasionally hired

Clinton Morrison (later John R. Van Derlip) House, 305 Twenty-Fourth Street East, 1920s. The house was torn down in the 1930s for the construction of the Fair Oaks Apartments.

boys to drive cows he owned to pasture land at Twenty-Sixth and Park. Within a few years, the cows gave way to mansions.

The crucial year in Park's transformation was 1885, when at least five big houses appeared along the avenue between Twenty-Second and Twenty-Sixth Streets. All of them were full-bore Victorians dressed to kill, and had they survived, Minneapolis would today have a Queen Anne enclave that could hold its own with any in the country. The James S. Bell House at 2215 Park, the Donald Kennedy House at 2314 Park, and the Edmund J. Phelps House at 2323 Park all offered plenty of Victorian eye candy. The two jewels here, however, were the festive Edward Barber House at 2313 Park and the John E. Bell House at 2401 Park. The Bell House was the magnum opus of the Queen Anne age in the Twin Cities, a mad piling up of parts that culminated in perhaps the most insanely complex roofline ever attempted in a northern climate. The place was so large and rambling that it reportedly required eighty tons of a coal a winter to keep the occupants from freezing.

The outbreak of Queen Anne delirium along Park was brief. By 1887, Romanesque Revival was the style of choice for the Frank W. and Frank B. Forman Double House at 2303–5 Park. Later, Tudor Revival and various classically inspired styles prevailed. Many of Park's most substantial mansions, such as the Frank Heffelfinger House, date to the early 1900s. Mansion building on the avenue ended in 1927 with the completion of the David Tenney House at 2318 Park.

Why Park—a straight, flat street no more scenic than others nearby—blossomed into a mansion row is not entirely clear, but once it did so home owners did their utmost to enhance its cachet. After forming an improvement association in 1890, residents established uniform setbacks for new houses, lobbied to have the avenue's width increased to one hundred feet, and chipped in money for various improvements, including asphalt paving (then a novelty) in 1892.[4]

Despite such efforts, Park's mansion row gradually faded away. Apartment buildings went up on parts of the "golden

Park Avenue, looking north from near Nineteenth Street, 1905. Mansions were first built along Park Avenue in the 1880s.

Donald Kennedy House, 2314 Park Avenue, about 1890. Originally this house was part of a group of Queen Anne–style mansions that lined the east side of Park Avenue between Twenty-Second and Twenty-Fourth Streets.

mile" as early as the 1890s, and by 1910 many mansions north of Twenty-Sixth Street had already been subdivided. Later, urban renewal, along with institutional and commercial encroachment, ate away at the avenue's stock of mansions. All of the great houses from the 1880s are gone, while the later mansions that remain are mostly used for corporate or institutional purposes.

Washburn–Fair Oaks has seen similar changes. Its two signature homes—the William Washburn and Charles Pillsbury mansions—are long gone. The neighborhood's surviving mansions, built in the early 1900s, have largely been given over to institutional uses, although a few private residences remain.

Richard J. Mendenhall House ("Guilford Place"), near First Avenue South and Eighteenth Street, ca. 1870 to 1922 (razed)

Life in the pioneer days of the Twin Cities, even for the wealthiest citizens, tended to be tumultuous. Fortunes were made and lost, careers undone only to be resurrected in some new form, families torn asunder by sudden death and then knit together again through remarriage. Contrary to F. Scott Fitzgerald's famous dictum, there often were second acts in American lives. So it was with Richard J. Mendenhall, a Quaker from North Carolina who settled in Minneapolis in 1856, found gold in real estate, lost much of it in banking, then rebuilt his life by making time to smell the flowers.

Soon after arriving in Minneapolis, Mendenhall and a friend established a bank and loan company that dealt primarily in real estate. A year later, Mendenhall married fellow Quaker Abby Swift, daughter of a Massachusetts sea captain. By 1870, when he and Abby built their country estate, Mendenhall was president of the State Bank of Minneapolis. His real estate holdings were also extensive, encompassing much of today's Stevens Square neighborhood as well as the southern reaches of Lowry Hill.[5]

Although banking was his business, horticulture was Mendenhall's love. His estate, named Guilford Place after his birthplace in North Carolina, was less renowned for its conventional French Second Empire–style limestone mansion than for its grounds, said to be "the most elaborate" in the city. "The house . . . stood in the center of wide lawns planted with rare shrubbery, trees and flowers," a newspaper wrote years later. "On each side it was flanked by great greenhouses in which Mr. Mendenhall dabbled with his horticultural experiments which he loved so well. . . . The old settlers remember the spicy fragrance of those greenhouse interiors, the hot moist atmosphere, and the proudly happy manner of their owner as he pointed out a new rose or some strange tropical plant which he had succeeded in making grow."[6]

Richard Mendenhall House and grounds, near First Avenue South and Eighteenth Street, 1874. Mendenhall made and lost a fortune in banking before turning to floristry.

Plants and flowers turned out to be Mendenhall's salvation. After the financial panic of 1873 shattered his banking business, Mendenhall became a florist. By 1893 he had "an entire city block . . . under glass," as one writer put it, and operated a retail flower shop downtown. Abby was equally busy with charitable endeavors and helped found the Bethany Home for unwed mothers. It appears that the Mendenhalls moved out of their mansion, probably in the 1880s, and either built or moved into a large brick house a block away at Eighteenth Street and Stevens Avenue.[7]

Abby died in 1900 (after contracting pneumonia while on a charitable visit). Richard lived until 1906. The couple had no children, and heirs sold off all of their property for its ultimate use as an apartment house district. Even so, the couple's stone mansion survived until 1922. It demolition, the *Minneapolis Tribune* reported, "meant the loss of another old landmark and started old settlers telling stories of the gentle but forceful old Quaker . . . whose home it was."

SOUTH SIDE MANSIONS

Dorilus Morrison House ("Villa Rosa"), Third Avenue South and Twenty-Fourth Street East, 1858 to 1910 (razed)

William D. Washburn House ("Fairoaks"), block bounded by Stevens Avenue, Third Avenue South, and Twenty-Second and Twenty-Fourth Streets East, E. Townsend Mix, 1884 to 1924 (razed)

Located within a block or so of each other, these very different houses demonstrated how within the span of a generation the accumulation of wealth transformed the Twin Cities. Morrison's home was an unprepossessing country estate. Washburn's forty-room mansion was a palace in a park, stuffed with luxuries. The builders of these disparate homes were cousins who hailed from the same town in Maine and who both reached Minneapolis in time to get in on the ground floor of almost every kind of business—lumbering, flour milling, railroading, and banking—by which fortunes could be made.

Morrison was the older of the two, born in 1814, and he had worked as a lumberman before he came west to inspect Minnesota's virgin pineries in 1854. He liked what he saw and settled in Minneapolis a year later. He quickly began making money in lumbering and other lines of work. In 1856 he was among ten original incorporators of the Minneapolis Mill Company, which controlled much of the waterpower at St. Anthony Falls. Later, he became involved in railroad construction, farm implement

manufacturing, banking, flour milling, and the production of coal gas. He also served as Minneapolis's first mayor after the city was officially incorporated in 1867.[8]

His house, completed in 1858 and probably expanded more than once thereafter, is not especially well documented, but photographs show that it was wood-frame and Italianate in style, with a squarish, projecting front tower flanked by arcaded porches. It was in essence a farmhouse—larger and fancier, to be sure, than most of its day but still in keeping with its rural setting at the time it was built. The house sat on ten landscaped acres that included the usual gardens and outbuildings. Morrison, who was married twice and had three children, never built another mansion, remaining at Villa Rosa, as the estate was called, until his death in 1898. The house was demolished in 1910, and Morrison's son, Clinton, later donated the property as a site for the new Minneapolis Institute of Arts. To this day, however, the land on which the institute stands is formally designated as Dorilus Morrison Park.

Morrison's house could fairly be described as modest. William Washburn's mansion, just to the north, was not. Like the man himself, it was flashy and outsized, as much gesture as substance, an architectural show designed to awe. There had never been anything quite like it before in Minneapolis.

Washburn hailed from a family of eleven children among whom brilliance and high achievement were the norm. One of his seven brothers, Cadwallader, built the Washburn A Mill in Minneapolis and was governor of Wisconsin. Another, Elihu, was a longtime congressman from Illinois and a confidant of Abraham Lincoln. A third, Israel, was governor of Maine. William was called "Young Rapid" as a child because of his mercurial temperament and fierce energy—qualities that were to propel him on a long but often controversial career in business and politics.

By the time he reached Minneapolis in 1857 at age twenty-six, he was tall, handsome, and well spoken, with piercing deep-set eyes and a commanding presence. His wife-to-be, Lizzie,

Dorilus Morrison House, Third Avenue South and Twenty-Fourth Street, 1898. This was the first mansion built in what later became known as the Washburn–Fair Oaks neighborhood.

wrote after first meeting him that she had never seen a man "so perfectly stunning." College-educated and trained as a lawyer, Washburn was soon appointed agent for the Minneapolis Mill Company, which his brother Cadwallader had a hand in

William Washburn House, southeast from Twenty-Second Street and Stevens Avenue, 1886. The mansion was the largest in Minneapolis at this time.

running. Over the next two decades, Washburn immersed himself in flour milling, banking, and railroading. He also waded into the political arena, serving as a U.S. congressman and senator.

His greatest achievement was the creation of the Minneapolis, Sault Ste. Marie and Atlantic Railway (the Soo Line), which provided a cost-saving route for shipping Minneapolis flour to the East Coast.[9]

Washburn and Lizzie were living in a fairly ordinary mansion

Carriage driver on duty in front of the Washburn House, about 1890. Washburn reputedly spent $1 million on the mansion and its grounds.

on Seventh Street in downtown Minneapolis when they decided in the early 1880s that the time had come to live very, very large. After acquiring a ten-acre site near Morrison's estate, Washburn hired E. Townsend Mix, a Milwaukee architect who was looking for work in Minneapolis, to design his mansion.

He reached farther east to bring in Frederick Law Olmsted, one of the designers of New York's Central Park, to landscape the grounds.

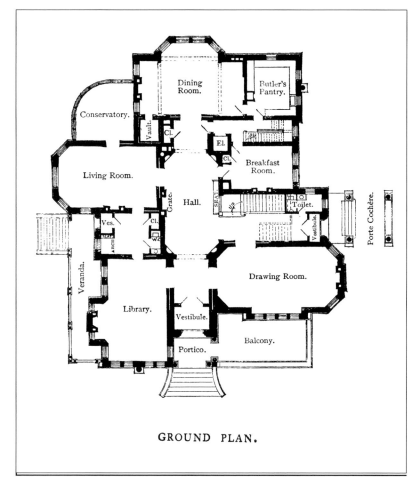

GROUND PLAN.

First-floor plan of the Washburn House, with the main entrance facing north toward Twenty-Second Street at bottom. All of the rooms were lavishly appointed.

By some accounts Washburn lavished $1 million on his new estate, which he called Fairoaks, and it was almost surely the most expensive ever built in Minneapolis up to that time. Mix, who would go on to design the Metropolitan Building in downtown Minneapolis, produced a rather odd house for Washburn. A mélange of Queen Anne, Tudor, Romanesque, and Gothic elements, the Kasota stone mansion made up in sheer size, thirty thousand or so square feet, what it lacked in cohesion.[10]

Situated near the northwestern corner of the grounds at Twenty-Second Street and Stevens Avenue, the mansion fea-

tured a projecting entry porch at the base of a ninety-foot tower, a porte cochere on the west side, and a collection of gables (some of the stepped variety), dormers, chimneys, and pinnacles animating the roofline. Inside, the plan was straightforward, with major rooms grouped around a central hall and staircase. Among the nicest features was a conservatory, which faced south to capture the winter sun, and could be reached from both the living and dining rooms.[11]

The interior was lush, dark, and densely furnished. Working with interior designer John Bradstreet, Lizzie supervised the decorations "to the minutest detail," according to one newspaper. The home drew favorable attention from the local press, with one magazine claiming "the Washburn residence . . . is an object of personal pride to every individual citizen of Minneapolis."[12]

The sumptuous wonders within began at the front vestibule, which offered mosaic floors, marble wainscoting, and frescoed ceilings. The central hall beyond was a mini-nave with a fourteen-foot-high vaulted ceiling and walls finished in stamped leather. Furnishings included "Indian chairs of scented wood and brass work from Benares; bedsteads of Japanese bamboo and bronzes brought from the banks of the Tiber; French pottery, huge vases from China and gems of English decorative woodwork." Bird's-eye maple, cherry, English oak, rosewood, Circassian walnut, Spanish mahogany, ebony, and other exotic woods abounded. The library included stained-glass windows depicting Dante, Shakespeare, Longfellow, and Bryant—four poets Washburn admired. An even grander window adorned the first landing of the main staircase. Marble floors (one inlaid with Washburn's initials), mosaic work, onyx fireplace mantles, solid brass fixtures, tapestries, oil paintings, and oriental carpets completed the decor of what may well have been the Twin Cities' ultimate Victorian interior.[13]

Upstairs, there were fourteen bedrooms, most of which had their own bathroom. The Washburns had eight children, six of whom survived to adulthood, and the youngest was just six years old when the couple moved into Fairoaks, which must have been quite a place to grow up in. Among the house's many amenities was an elevator that led to a billiard room, where Washburn and his friends could smoke after dinner. There were frequent parties—Lizzie was a renowned hostess—and the Washburns entertained many famous visitors, including Ulysses S. Grant. They also opened up the mansion once a year to the general public. For a donation of $1 (which went to charity), anyone could wander through the place and see how the other one-tenth of one percent lived.

The grounds offered pleasures of a more rustic nature, including a picturesque array of plantings, a small pond, and a tumbling little stream crossed by a wooden footbridge. There was also a domed greenhouse and a carriage house off Twenty-fourth Street.[14]

Despite his wealth, Washburn's last years proved trying,

Washburn House, library, about 1890. The room featured four stained-glass windows depicting famous poets.

Washburn House and grounds, west from Third Avenue South, about 1885. The ten-acre grounds, now Washburn–Fair Oaks Park, were beautifully landscaped.

Carriage house at the Washburn estate, off Twenty-Fourth Street, about 1890. Judging by the number of carriages, the Washburn family had plenty of transportation options.

mainly because of his role on the management committee of the Pillsbury-Washburn Flour Mills Company. The company collapsed in 1908 amid revelations that key executives had lost huge amounts of money speculating in wheat. Allegations of fraud and mismanagement followed. The company was eventually reorganized, but Washburn's reputation suffered serious damage in the process, as did his pocketbook.[15]

In 1910, Washburn donated Fairoaks to the city of Minneapolis for possible use as an art museum on the condition he and Lizzie be allowed to live out their lives in the house. The city accepted, although the art museum idea never worked out. Washburn died two years later, at age eighty-one. Lizzie moved away not long after to live with one of her sons. A caretaker occupied the mansion for a time, after which the Minneapolis Park Board assumed ownership. The mansion was used as a soldiers' recreation center during World War I and also as offices for charitable groups. The mansion proved too much to maintain, however, and it was razed in 1924. It was so large and well built that it cost $90,000 to bring it down. Fair Oaks Park now occupies the site.

John W. Johnson (later Charles A. Pillsbury) House, 2200 Stevens Avenue, Long and Kees, 1885 to 1937 (razed)

This stone mansion—a muscular mix of Romanesque, Gothic, and Tudor elements—was not as spectacular as Fairoaks, its neighbor across Stevens Avenue, but it was still among the largest homes of its time in Minneapolis. It was built for John W. Johnson, who prospered in the iron business after moving to Minneapolis in the 1860s. By 1874 he was sole owner of the North Star Iron Works, which had a large foundry along the Mississippi River near Second Avenue North.[16] Johnson sold the company in 1880, became involved in banking, and then built his mansion.[17] He does not seem to have fallen in love with the place; two years later he sold the property to Charles A.

Pillsbury, cofounder of the family flour milling company. Later, in the early 1900s, three other members of the Pillsbury clan would build mansions nearby, all of which still stand.

Built of Kasota stone, Johnson's mansion was among the earliest works of the partnership of Franklin Long and Frederick Kees, a firm that would soon became known for weighty Richardsonian Romanesque–style buildings. The mansion was decidedly eclectic. A pair of gables—one sculpted in late Tudor fashion, the other more regular but penetrated by an ornate chimney—dominated the mansion's front elevation along Stevens. A porch centered beneath the gables provided a grand entrance to the house. To the north, facing Twenty-Second Street above a porte cochere, was the home's most monumental feature: a four-story tower terminating in an outbreak of battlements. The image of home as castle was here expressed quite literally. The grounds, which were not nearly as impressive as those at Fairoaks, included a stone carriage house.[18]

Inside, a sitting room, library, parlor, and dining room were grouped around a wide hall. The staircase was placed to one side to accommodate an entrance via the porte cochere. Detailed descriptions of the interior are hard to come by (Washburn's mansion seems to have been of far greater interest to the press). The main rooms were finished with the standard array of fine woods, plus one more unusual choice: brown ash.

Charles A. Pillsbury died in 1899, after which one of his sons, Charles S., moved into the mansion. The house turned out to be a headache. Its stone had not been properly seasoned after quarrying, and the mansion's walls required extensive repair in 1912. At about the same time Charles moved to a new home just across Twenty-Second Street and sold the mansion to his twin brother, John S. After another costly round of repairs, John and his family moved away in the early 1930s. The mansion then stood vacant until it was demolished in 1937, although the carriage house stood for another six years. First Christian Church, built in 1954, now occupies the site.[19]

Charles A. Pillsbury House, 2200 Stevens Avenue, about 1890. The mansion was built for John W. Johnson, but he lived here for only two years.

First-floor plan for the Pillsbury House. A piazza sheltered the front door, which faced east toward Stevens Avenue.

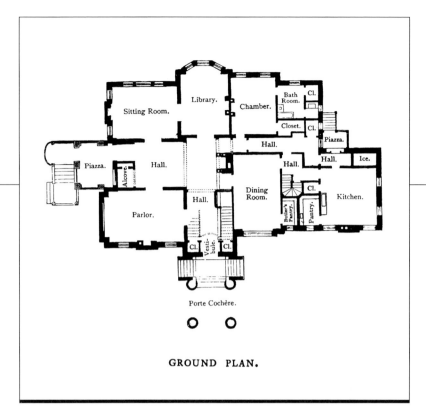

GROUND PLAN.

Pillsbury House in 1937, just before demolition. A castellated tower on the north side of the mansion was its most striking feature.

R. F. Hurlbert (later Edwin R. Barber) House, 2313 Park Avenue, about 1893.
This house was a festive example of the Queen Anne style.

Queen Anne Extravaganzas

R. F. Hurlbert (later Edwin R. Barber) House, 2313 Park Avenue, James K. Wilson, 1884 to 1930 (razed)

John E. Bell House, 2401 Park Avenue, Charles Sedgwick, 1885 to 1961 (razed)

The Queen Anne style came out of England, but it had nothing to do with the royal figure who reigned in the early 1700s. Its real source of inspiration went back to the Tudor and Elizabethan periods, as reinterpreted by Richard Norman Shaw and other English architects, who in the 1860s began designing houses featuring half-timbering and patterned brickwork. The style crossed the Atlantic, and in American hands it morphed into a kind of free-for-all, with architects and builders churning out an abundance of colorful "painted ladies" across the country. The style reached its apogee on the East and West Coasts, but Twin Cities architects produced their fair share of Queen Anne confections, the best of which date to the mid-1880s.

Park Avenue, which was developing just as the style peaked in the Twin Cities, became home to the city's finest group of Queen Annes. One of the most delightful was a mansion at 2313 Park built for R. F. Hurlbert but soon sold to Edwin Barber, who owned the oldest flour mill at St. Anthony Falls, the Cataract, built in 1859. Daniel Barber, Edwin's father, had arrived in Minneapolis in 1856, when Edwin was four years old, and bought the mill in the early 1870s. He operated it until his death in 1886, after which Edwin took over as sole proprietor. At about the same time, he moved into the house on Park with his wife, Hattie, and their children.[20]

The clapboard and shingle-clad house was a jolly affair with a vaguely Moorish cast, evident in its long front porch, which ended in a porte cochere on one side and a gazebo-like pavilion, topped by a fanciful pointed roof, on the other. Other features included a second-story oriel window, oval in shape and surrounded by intricate carvings, and a lookout emerging from the top of the roof. Unlike most Queen Annes, the house featured generally smooth wall surfaces and was restrained in its use of ornament.

The designer, James K. Wilson, had advocated just such an approach in a speech to his fellow Minneapolis architects in 1884. Wilson, who migrated to Minneapolis in the early 1880s, began his career in Cincinnati, where among many other works he designed the Plum Street Temple (1866), now a National Historic Landmark. In his speech Wilson complained that too many buildings were being "bedecked and bedizened with every manner of projections and gew-gaws, any kind of trash, so that it be a 'new style'—God save us!—and their little modest beauty be utterly extinguished and eclipsed forever. This is not a good way for any deserving and well constituted building to feel."[21]

The home's main floor included a parlor, library, den, and dining room centered around a thirty-seven-by-twenty-eight-foot hall. Oak trim was used throughout, another indication that Wilson strove for a unified design. Upstairs, the master bedroom had a fireplace and built-in seating in the oriel. The attic contained a billiard room along with the lookout. Barber and his wife lived in the house until the time of his death, or close to it, in 1920. The house was razed ten years later. The Phillips Eye Institute now occupies the site.

The John E. Bell House, a block south on Park, was perhaps the most madly energetic Queen Anne home ever built in the Twin Cites. Its owner, however, seems to have been the very image of a staid businessman. Born in New York State, Bell settled in Minnesota in 1857. He worked as a merchant in Minneapolis and later as a buyer for a St. Paul wholesaler. In 1870, he and a partner organized the Hennepin County Savings Bank in Minneapolis. Bell served as the bank's cashier and later as its president.[22]

His house was among the first local commissions for architect Charles Sedgwick, who had moved to Minneapolis in 1884. Sedgwick went on to a long career, designing such downtown monuments as Westminster Presbyterian Church (1898) and the original portion of the Dayton's (now Macy's) Department

John E. Bell House, 2401 Park Avenue, about 1948. Built for a banker, this building was the ultimate Queen Anne pile in the Twin Cities.

Store.[23] These later works were models of restraint compared to Bell's house.

From the very start, the house, which cost at least $20,000, captured the attention of the local press. Built of red St. Louis brick with white stone trim, its walls rose up behind a front porch decorated with no shortage of spindles and scrollwork. On one side the porch extended into a porte cochere that led to a brick carriage house. The house's glory was its roof: two steeply pitched stories interrupted by a scenic accumulation of front- and side-facing half-timbered gables, dormers, inset balconies, delicate oriels, and chimneys with patterned brickwork. The prospect of watery mischief amid all of these valleys, seams, and crossings must have been daunting, but the roofline seems to have survived more or less intact until the very end.

Within, the house offered more all-out Victorian bravado. The main hall, thirty-six feet long and eleven feet wide and lit by a stained-glass window, led through "a colonnade and arches in oak," as one publication described it, to the main staircase. Above the stairs was a dome "forming an ornamental ceiling, the dome being in turn lighted by windows opening above it from the front of the second story." Arrayed around the hall and stairway were a parlor, reception room, library, and dining room. Many of the home's interior walls were adorned with oil painting; water colors were used for the ceilings. All of the major rooms also included fireplaces with "massive and elegant" mantles and mirror frames. There were seven bedrooms on the second floor. The enormous attic featured a twenty-two-by-forty-two-foot "hall," which was probably used as ballroom.[24]

Bell, who was married twice and had four children, moved to Excelsior around 1900 but apparently owned the house until his death in 1909. Like many old mansions of its time, the house eventually became a nursing home. It survived in that capacity until 1961, when it was torn down and replaced by a parking ramp for the nearby Mt. Sinai Hospital.

Frank W. and Frank B. Forman Double House, 2303–5 Park Avenue, William H. Dennis, 1888 to 1953 (razed)

During the boom years of the 1880s and into the early 1890s, a number of deluxe double houses, in most cases occupied by members of the same family, were built in the Twin Cities. Unlike the generally more prosaic duplexes that became common by the early 1900s, these side-by-side Victorian houses rarely presented identical facades or floor plans. Some of them were very big, with each unit containing five thousand or more square feet, and they could be just as elaborately detailed as mansions of the period.

The Park Avenue double house built in 1887 for Frank W. Forman and his son, Frank B., was an especially luxurious example of its kind. The senior Forman hailed from New York State and ran a general merchandise business there before relocating to Minneapolis in the early 1880s, where he became a partner in Forman, Ford and Co., a wholesaler and manufacturer of glass and paint. Later, he and his son assumed full ownership of the company.[25]

Their stone veneer double house was designed by William H. Dennis, another transplanted New Yorker who began working as an architect in Minneapolis in 1878. Trained for two years in Paris, Dennis was primarily a commercial architect but also designed churches and residences, often favoring a French Renaissance look.[26] For the Formans, however, he turned to the then-fashionable Romanesque Revival style.

Both of the house's front doors were sheltered within a deep-set arch. Directly above was a bowed bay window surmounted by a small balcony emerging from another large arch set within a sculpted central gable. Another gable to one side screened a round corner tower with a third-floor porch. The elder Forman occupied the northerly unit, at 2303 Park, which was the larger of the two and included a side entry porch as well as a procession of gables, dormers, and chimneys along the roofline. By contrast, the south side of the house was quite plain and regular, suggesting that Frank junior may have had more modern architectural tastes than his father.

Like the Formans themselves, the double house was not widely publicized, and its interior arrangements remain a mystery. Frank W. lived in his side of the house until his death in 1910, although he spent much of his time traveling to and from Europe on ocean liners (his half brother, Justus Forman, a novelist and playwright of now forgotten works, was among more than nineteen hundred passengers who went down with the *Lusitania* after it was torpedoed off the Irish coast by a German U-boat in 1915).[27] Frank B. moved to a new mansion overlooking Lake Calhoun in 1902 but died soon after. The old family double house survived until 1953, when it was added to Park Avenue's long list of demolished mansions.

Frank W. and Frank B. Forman double house, 2303–5 Park Avenue, about 1910.
The Formans, father and son, owned a glass and paint company.

Frank T. Heffelfinger House, 2205 Park Avenue, William Channing Whitney, 1903 to 1983 (razed)

Five Victorian-era mansions once occupied the entire east side of Park Avenue on the long block between Twenty-Second and Twenty-Fourth Streets. The lineup included the Barber House, the Forman Double House, and homes owned by Edmund J. Phelps and James Ford Bell, all built in the 1880s. The fifth house, at 2205 Park, does not show up in any photographs, and little is known about it other than that it was torn down in about 1900 to make way for a new mansion for Frank T. Hef-

Frank T. Heffelfinger House, 2205 Park Avenue, and neighboring mansions, about 1905. The house stood until 1983.

felfinger and his family. Unlike the block's flamboyant Victorians, the Heffelfinger House was undemonstrative to the point of somnolence, reflecting how radically architectural taste had shifted in only fifteen years.

By the time Heffelfinger and his wife, Lucia, moved into their mansion in 1903, Park Avenue had solidified its reputation as one of the city's most prestigious addresses. All told, a dozen or so new mansions were built on Park after 1900, the last going up in 1927. The Heffelfingers' house was typical of the mansions of this era.

Heffelfinger, like others who built along Park in the early 1900s, represented the second generation of wealth in Minneapolis. His father, Christopher B. Heffelfinger, settled in the city in 1858, served in the First Minnesota Regiment in the Civil War, and went on to success manufacturing shoes. His home at 1838 Third Avenue South was just a few blocks from Frank's mansion. Frank's sister, Louise, the wife of James Ford Bell, was even closer, living next door at 2215 Park.

Born in 1869, Frank was schooled in New England and then worked for several years in the family shoe business. His career took a decisive turn in 1895 after he married Lucia Peavey, daughter of Frank H. Peavey, owner of the world's largest grain elevator company. Peavey died in 1901, and Heffelfinger became president of the grain firm six years later. He and Lucia also inherited ownership of Highcroft, the magnificent estate Peavey had built at Lake Minnetonka.[28]

Highcroft was the work of William Channing Whitney, the favored residential architect for Minneapolis's upper class, and it was no surprise that the Heffelfingers chose him to design their Park Avenue mansion. Not an apostle of novelty, Whitney tended to produce well made but not particularly inspired mansions, usually in the Tudor, Classical, or Colonial Revival styles fashionable at the time.[29] Whitney's design for the Heffelfingers was restrained even by his standards. The L-shaped mansion featured walls of rough-faced limestone, a calm roofline, regularly spaced windows, and an almost complete absence of ornament. Even the slightly projecting front entrance was understated. The overall style was Tudor Revival, albeit of a very mild sort.

The Heffelfingers, who had four children, lived in the house for only a decade or so. They later spent much of their time at Highcroft. Lumberman Thomas L. Shevlin and several later owners occupied the house, which was the last of the mansions on the block to be demolished, surviving until 1983. ◆

CHAPTER 10

LOWRY HILL

A. T. Andreas's *Illustrated Historical Atlas of the State of Minnesota*, which rarely shied away from civic boosterism, proclaimed in 1874 that "the beautiful Groveland Addition . . . is rapidly becoming a most charming village by itself. The wide Hennepin Avenue, which passes through it, is firmly macadamized, and the spacious lots are fertile and prolific. Here Thomas Lowery [sic], Esq., is erecting a residence which will cost $35,000. . . . Those seeking delightful residence property should view this favored spot."[1]

As it turned out, Andreas's glowing account of the "rapidly" developing Groveland Addition was, like his spelling of Lowry's name, inaccurate. The addition, platted by Lowry in 1872 and encompassing much of today's Lowry Hill neighborhood west of Lyndale Avenue, did indeed become a "favored spot," but it took quite a while. Lowry's mansion, completed in 1874, was the first big house on the hill that ultimately took his name. Another real estate developer, Henry Beard, graded what would become Mount Curve Avenue atop the crest of the hill

at about the same time. Later, around 1882, he built what may have been the first house on Mount Curve.[2]

Lowry's initial lack of neighbors came about in part because poor economic conditions in the 1870s retarded development throughout the city. The hill itself, a glacier-formed terminal moraine known as the Devil's Backbone on early maps, also presented problems. It was hard to reach from downtown, and much of its crest was too steep for homes to be built. In the late 1880s the top of the hill was finally leveled off. A few years later Lowry, who by then controlled the Twin City Rapid Transit Company, added a streetcar line along Douglas Avenue that made the hill readily accessible from downtown.

With these improvements in place, in the early 1890s Lowry set about developing an upscale residential district. He replatted the most desirable section of the hill, from Groveland Terrace up to Mount Curve, creating lots large enough to accommodate mansions. He also imposed a series of special zoning restrictions that, among other provisions, barred double

Lowry Hill, looking northeast toward what would become Loring Park, about 1875. The Thomas Lowry House (far left) had just been built.

houses and apartments, required new homes to cost at least $4,000, established a uniform setback of twenty-five feet, and specified that fences had to be of a "light and ornamental character." These restrictions were unusual at the time, when the city of Minneapolis was still years away from adopting a formal zoning code.

Next, Lowry hired the city's best-known architectural firm, Long and Kees, to design a trio of showcase homes along Groveland Terrace. One was sold to manufacturer William S. Nott, another to Long himself, and the third to department store magnate William Donaldson. The Nott and Long houses still stand, but Donaldson's mighty mansion at 21 Groveland is long gone.[3]

The depression of 1893 slowed development for a time, but as the economy picked up toward the end of the decade, a building boom occurred on the hill, not only along Groveland and Mount Curve but also on the streets extending south to Franklin Avenue. By 1920, most of Lowry Hill had filled in with

Excavating and leveling portions of Lowry Hill, 1886. The man in the foreground was probably an engineer supervising the work.

ENTRANCE TO LOWRY HILL, MINNEAPOLIS, MINN.
ORFF & JORALEMON, ARCHITECTS.

*Proposed Groveland Terrace entrance (never built) to Lowry Hill, 1893.
Thomas Lowry replatted portions of the hill in the early 1890s in hopes of
attracting wealthy residents.*

William Donaldson House (left), 21 Groveland Terrace, and other mansions, west from near Hennepin Avenue, about 1910. The Donaldson House was razed in 1933 when no one would purchase it for $10,000.

Franklin Long House, which anticipated the Moderne style of the 1930s, at 41 Groveland Terrace, 1893. It was razed in the 1930s, but another house designed and built by Long in 1894 still stands at 25 Groveland Terrace.

houses, including fifty or more that could fairly be called mansions. The majority still stand, but at least a dozen, among them some of the largest and most elaborate houses ever built in Minneapolis, are gone.

Groveland Terrace has suffered especially significant losses. Lowry's mansion, later owned by art collector Thomas Walker, was among the first to go, in the early 1930s.[4] As the Great

Depression deepened, other mansions began to fall. The Donaldson House, a rather forbidding Romanesque Revival hunk, came down in 1933 (it was offered for sale for a mere $10,000, but there were no takers). Two years later, one of the hill's most magnificent estates, the Lewis Gillette House at 40 Groveland Terrace, was demolished, less than a quarter of a century after it had been enlarged and refurbished at enormous expense.

Another casualty of the 1930s was a most peculiar house at 41 Groveland Terrace once owned by architect Franklin Long of the firm of Long and Kees. The house, dating to the 1870s, was among the oldest on the hill, but Long utterly transformed it around 1890 by giving it a proto-modern look that included a sweeping rounded corner and circular windows. A few years later, he moved down the street to one of the new houses he had designed for Lowry. By a certain irony, Long's original house was torn down just as the style it so presciently evoked—the so-called Streamlined Moderne—was becoming popular.

Mount Curve Avenue, Lowry Hill's other great repository of mansions, has also seen its share of demolitions over the years. Among the ranks of the departed is the Walter C. Tiffany House, a Shingle-style gem at 1612 Mount Curve designed by Harry Jones in 1889. It became a teardown only sixteen years later, when a larger mansion went up on the site. Also gone is the lovely Edmund G. Walton House, built at 802 Mount Curve in 1893 and demolished in 1959. Walton had been among Lowry's key associates when he replatted much of the hill in the 1890s.

Another great loss came in the 1960s, when William Dunwoody's Tudor Revival mansion was torn down. Built in 1905 for one of the city's wealthiest flour millers, the mansion occupied a gorgeous site extending all the way up the hill from Groveland to Mount Curve. Its demolition touched off a fight over plans to replace it with high-rise apartments. High-priced townhomes were eventually built instead, and to this day the sweeping views from Tom Lowry's hill are reserved for just the class of people he had in mind when he created his mansion district more than a century ago.

Thomas Lowry (later Thomas Walker) House, 2 Groveland Terrace, Leroy Buffington, 1874; remodeled and enlarged, Long and Kees, 1893 to 1932 (razed)

Thomas Lowry, the son of an Illinois farmer and once the undisputed transit king of the Twin Cities, arrived in Minneapolis in 1867 at age twenty-four to practice law and deal in real estate. Like his idol Abraham Lincoln (who in fact had been his parents' lawyer), Lowry was tall, slender, and articulate, and it did not take him long to make his mark. His career was greatly advanced by his choice of a wife, although there is some evidence he may have been wed, for barely more than a week, to a mysterious woman named Harriet not long before he made a far more propitious match with Beatrice Goodrich. His new bride was young (just sixteen), smart, and beautiful. She also happened to be the daughter of Dr. Calvin Goodrich, who, conveniently for Lowry, owned a 148-acre farm on the northern edges of what would eventually become known as Lowry Hill.

In 1872 Lowry bought half of his father-in-law's farm for $42,000. With a partner, he also bought land to the north along the face of the hill, platted it all as Groveland Addition, and then built his mansion on six prime acres just off Hennepin Avenue. It is likely that Lowry intended the mansion to function in part as a giant billboard extolling the good life that awaited future home builders on the hill.[5]

Designed by Leroy Buffington, the red brick mansion—located about where the newer and older portions of today's Walker Art Center connect—offered exceptional views to the south and east but was otherwise a conventional French Second Empire chestnut. Three stories high under a tiled mansard roof, the mansion was long and fairly narrow, with a porte cochere on the north side and a carriage house off Groveland.

Descriptions indicate that the mansion had a dozen or more rooms plus an attic ballroom and an art gallery. Furnishings included Gobelin tapestries and bronze Tiffany lamps, and there was also plenty of mahogany woodwork. There is a story

Thomas Lowry mansion and carriage house, north toward two grain elevators near Bassett's Creek, 1886. Lyndale Avenue is at the center of the photograph.

that Lowry, always ready to make a deal, once bartered away much of the home's furniture in exchange for a piece of real estate he coveted, a transaction that could not have pleased Beatrice, who was one of the city's most accomplished hostesses. The mansion received at least two major additions, the largest—over 2,500 square feet—coming in 1893.

A year or so before completing the addition, Lowry had created the Twin City Rapid Transit Company after years of complex financial maneuvering. The company's familiar yellow streetcars would become the workhorses of public transportation in St. Paul and Minneapolis for the next sixty years. Lowry, who later became president of the Soo Line Railroad in addition to overseeing the streetcar system, had to nurse the young transit company through the 1893 depression, which hit him so hard personally that he and Beatrice vacated their mansion

Lowry House after its purchase by Thomas Walker, about 1925. The lumber-man turned art collector lived in the home until his death in 1928.

Art gallery at Thomas Walker's first mansion, 803 Hennepin Avenue, 1905.
The State Theatre now occupies the site.

for a while and rented it out to save money. The company ultimately flourished under Lowry's leadership. At the time of his death in 1909, the Twin Cities' streetcar system was among the largest and best in the nation. Lowry, said one newspaper, was "probably the best known citizen in Minneapolis."[6]

Beatrice remained in the house until her death in 1915, after which it went up for sale. There was talk of a new public library on the site, but the idea did not take. Instead, Thomas B. Walker—multimillionaire lumberman, art collector, and a rather ornery character known to sleep with a pistol under his pillow—bought the place for himself, his wife, Harriet (who would die the next year), and his four hundred or so works of art. He was seventy-six years old, still wily and ambitious, and the house and its large lot were for him a means to an end.[7] Walker, who bought his first painting in New York City in 1874, had lived for years in a house at 803 Hennepin Avenue (on the site of today's State Theatre) that doubled as a quasi-public art gallery. Walker added onto the house eight times. By 1915 his art collection filled fourteen rooms. He was clearly a man in need of larger quarters.[8]

Lowry's mansion was only a temporary fix for Walker. In the mid-1920s, he began building a new stand-alone museum next to the mansion. It was completed in 1927, in a rather odd Moorish Revival style, which Walker apparently found fetching. A year after the museum opened, Walker died at age eighty-eight, having amassed an art collection worth an estimated $100 million, while the rest of his estate came to a relatively modest $1.62 million. Once the Great Depression set in, the old mansion became a liability, and in 1932 the house that Tom Lowry had built on the hill of his dreams was finally torn down.[9]

George H. Partridge House, 1 Groveland Terrace, Long and Kees, 1897; enlarged and remodeled, Kees and Colburn, 1904 to 1954 (razed)

Just to the north of Lowry's estate, off Hennepin Avenue, George H. Partridge built one of the largest of all the mansions on Lowry Hill in 1897. Completed just as the severe recession that had begun four years earlier was coming to an end, the mansion—easily fifteen thousand square feet or more—was among the first in Minneapolis to abandon all traces of Victorian foofaraw in favor of a deluxe, classically based style sometimes called the Second Renaissance Revival.

Born on a farm near Medford, Minnesota, Partridge did not seem likely to end up occupying a palatial estate. He was, however, smart and ambitious, and after graduating from the University of Minnesota in 1879 he went into civil engineering and railroad work. His trajectory to success received a rocket boost in 1882 when he married Sarah Wyman, daughter of Oliver C. Wyman, owner of a Minneapolis wholesaling firm. In 1890, he became a partner in Wyman, Partridge and Company, soon to be the city's largest dry goods wholesaler. Partridge also had other business interests and served as a director of Lowry's Twin City Rapid Transit Company.[10]

When the time came for Partridge to memorialize his success with a mansion, he hired Long and Kees—Lowry's favorite architects—to design it. What resulted was a thirty-room house, built with walls of grayish yellow brick, that drew its inspiration from the architecture of the Italian Renaissance. Deluxe and dignified, if a bit chilly, the mansion offered a kind of anti-picturesque antidote to the excesses of the Victorian era, and its style was to remain fashionable in the Twin Cities for the next twenty years.[11]

The mansion faced Groveland, where an arcaded porch sheltered the front door. A wide staircase led directly from the sidewalk up to the porch. Carefully enframed windows, a strong cornice, balustrades atop the porch and along the roofline,

George Partridge House, 1 Groveland Terrace, overlooking the "bottleneck"
at Hennepin and Lyndale Avenues, about 1904. The mansion was an early
example of the Classical Revival style in Minneapolis.

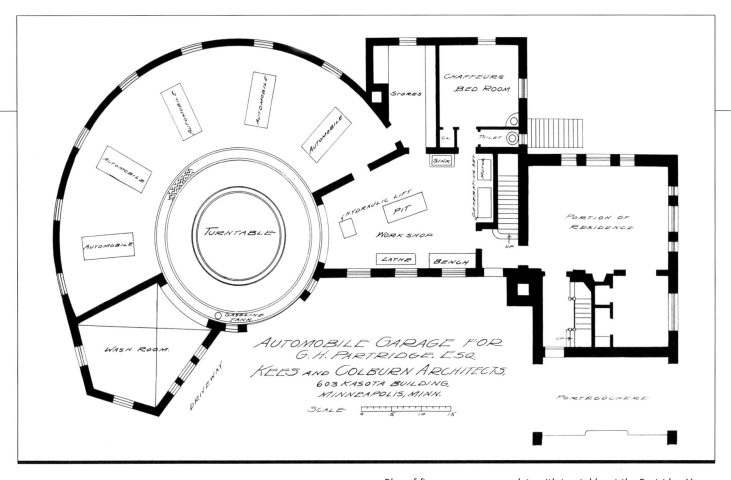

The labels on the plan read:

AUTOMOBILE · AUTOMOBILE · AUTOMOBILE · AUTOMOBILE · AUTOMOBILE · AUTOMOBILE

TURNTABLE

GASOLINE TANK

WASH ROOM.

DRIVEWAY

(HYDRAULIC LIFT) PIT

WORK SHOP

LATHE · BENCH

STORES

CHAFFEURS BED ROOM

CL · SINK

TOILET

GENERATING SET · MOTOR

UP · UP

PORTION OF RESIDENCE

PORTE COCHERE

AUTOMOBILE GARAGE FOR
G. H. PARTRIDGE, ESQ.
KEES AND COLBURN ARCHITECTS,
603 KASOTA BUILDING,
MINNEAPOLIS, MINN.

SCALE   0   5   10   15

Plan of five-car garage, complete with turntable, at the Partridge House, 1904. Partridge's fleet included three electric cars.

and corner quoins all contributed to the desired aura of classical respectability. The Hennepin Avenue facade included a rounded first-floor bay as well as a loggia accessed from the attic ballroom. A wing to the west contained servants' quarters, smoking and billiard rooms, and a covered porch extending above twin archways that led into a rear courtyard with a circular garage.[12] Enlarged in 1904, the garage had a turntable to make parking easier. At one point Partridge's personal fleet included three electric cars and another powered by steam. The garage's tile work was adorned by a concrete bas-relief sculpture depicting an automobile.[13]

A low wall that was eventually crowned by an iron fence surrounded the mansion and its grounds, which extended south to Douglas Avenue. Legend holds that Partridge was among the first Minneapolitans to light the trees on his property during the Christmas season, when thousands of cars traveling through the Hennepin-Lyndale Avenue "bottleneck" would have passed by every night.

The mansion was luxuriously appointed. First-floor rooms featured hand-painted tapestries, stencil work, tiled fireplaces, and beamed ceilings. The grand staircase was a vertical adventure, turning four times on its journey to the second floor's array

Partridge House, main hall and staircase, about 1905. Hand-painted tapestries and lush stencil work were among the decorative details.

Barrel-vaulted third-floor ballroom in the Partridge House, with lights built into the arches, about 1905. The family's four daughters made their social debuts here.

George H. Daggett (later Lewis S. Gillette) House, 40 Groveland Terrace, as originally built, about 1900. The tower with battlements contributed a medieval aura to the design.

of bedroom suites. A huge attic ballroom, its barrel-vaulted ceiling lit by rows of multicolored incandescent lights, was the scene of many dances and entertainments. It was also where the Partridges' four daughters, the youngest of whom was born in the house, made their society debuts. Two of them were later married in the mansion.[14]

Perhaps the largest gathering ever held in the house took place in 1932, when one thousand guests helped Partridge and his wife celebrate their fiftieth wedding anniversary. Partridge died later that year at age seventy-six. Sarah remained in the house until her own death in 1935. A newspaper article the next year suggested that the mansion would be torn down, but the daughters instead sold it to a religious organization known as the School of Psychology and Divine Science. The school stayed until 1954, when it in turn sold the mansion to an insurance company. Demolition soon followed. Before the great house came down, visitors were allowed to wander through and bid on its furnishings and fixtures, some of which are still scattered around the Twin Cities.[15] A small office building and the Kenwood Gables Apartments now occupy the site.

George H. Daggett (later Lewis S. Gillette) House ("Eldor Court"), 40 Groveland Terrace, McLeod and Lamoreaux, 1898; enlarged and remodeled, Harry Jones, ca. 1911 to 1935 (razed)

In its original form, the house dubbed Eldor Court by its first owner, grain dealer George Daggett, was a Tudor Revival mansion that, among the architectural gentry of Lowry Hill, fell somewhere in the middle ground in terms of size and splendor. Located well up the hill just west of Bryant Avenue, the L-shaped house rose from a rustic stone base past brick walls to a collection of half-timbered gables and dormers. Its signature feature, at the crook of the L, was an entry tower outfitted with battlements and a turret. The lord of this home-as-castle

stayed for only a few years, and it was the mansion's second owner, Lewis S. Gillette, who transformed it into one of the glories of the city.

Gillette is hardly known today, but in his time he was one of the Twin Cities' industrial titans. Born in Michigan in 1856, he headed west in his teens to attend the University of Minnesota. He was a brilliant student, obtaining degrees in both science and engineering. He married in 1877, after which he and his wife, Louesa, lived in Michigan. The couple, who eventually had five children, returned in 1881 to Minneapolis, where Gillette embarked on a lucrative career in railroading, manufacturing, construction, and real estate. He became especially prominent in the iron and steel business, heading a firm that specialized in structural frames for mining and industrial buildings. Gillette was also a founder of the American Bridge Company, later absorbed by the U.S. Steel Corporation. An inveterate traveler, his favored destinations included Europe and South America.[16]

After purchasing Daggett's house in about 1910, Gillette and his wife remodeled and enlarged it on a grand scale, hiring Minneapolis architect Harry Jones to take charge of the work. Jones had drawn up plans for Daggett back in 1898, although the house as built is usually attributed to another architectural firm, McLeod and Lamoreaux. To accommodate Gillette's desires, Jones expanded the home upward (by enlarging the second floor and adding an attic ballroom) and outward (by designing a stone-walled rear addition that included garages, a rooftop garden, and a courtyard built above a recreation room). By the time the project was completed in 1911, the mansion resembled a great stone fort posing above Kenwood Parkway.

The ornate interior—decorated by Minneapolis's resident apostle of good taste, John Bradstreet—included an expansive library, an oval-shaped music room, a beamed reception hall, and much intricately carved woodwork. The house was best known for its spectacular Moorish ballroom, a fantasy in plaster, tile, and wood modeled on the fourteenth-century Court of the Lions at the Alhambra in Granada, Spain. It was not the

Daggett House after Lewis Gillette transformed it into a walled estate, west across Bryant Avenue, 1912. Gillette died in 1924, and the mansion was torn down eleven years later.

Rear of the Gillette estate, south from Kenwood Parkway, 1911. The grounds included walkways, sculptures, and a Japanese shrine.

Moorish-style ballroom in the Gillette House, shortly after its completion, 1912. The ballroom was Gillette's private Alhambra in wood and plaster.

Gillette House, reception room, 1912. Minneapolis interior designer John Bradstreet oversaw the decorating.

first Moorish ballroom in the Twin Cities (Stillwater lumberman William Sauntry had built one on his property in 1902), but it must have wowed the Lowry Hill social set.

Gillette ordered up his Alhambra in the attic after a visit to Spain, commissioning Bradstreet and a team of artisans to re-create the famous monument's intricate ornament. At its unveiling in November 1911 (the occasion being the debut of Gillette's daughter, Louise) the ballroom won plaudits from the *Minneapolis Journal*, which pronounced it "a perfect and correct reproduction," although the real Alhambra probably never hosted cotillions.[17]

The mansion's grounds, which ran all the way down to Kenwood Parkway, were also extraordinary, offering walkways, pergolas, gardens, sculptures, benches, and even a Japanese shrine nestled beneath one of the high retaining walls. No other estate before or since on Lowry Hill was so complete a testament to one man's vision, and Gillette—when he was not away on his travels—must have reveled in his creation.

Edmund G. Walton House, 802 Mount Curve Avenue, about 1895. Walton was a real estate specialist who worked with Thomas Lowry to develop Lowry Hill.

Mansions of exceptional size that evoke a highly personal dream often do not last long once their moving spirit dies, and so it was with Gillette's estate. He died in 1924 in Mississippi at age sixty-nine. His wife died a few years later, and in 1935 the mansion—too much to maintain during the depths of the Depression—was torn down.[18] The Groveland Terrace Apartments, built in the 1960s, now occupy the site.

Edmund G. Walton House ("Grey Court"), 802 Mount Curve Avenue, Orff and Joralemon, 1893 to 1959 (razed)

In early 1959, as wreckers tore away at Edmund G. Walton's old house on Lowry Hill, one of his daughters, Dorothy, was on hand to mourn its destruction. "When I passed by recently I could see the sky through the stripped roof," she wrote. "Windows had been yanked out and stared vacantly while bricks had been dumped helter-skelter in my mother's garden where, long ago, passersby used to stop and hang over the gate refreshing themselves with its colorful charm. Memories came rushing into my mind of our life in that home as I watched the walls come tumbling down."[19]

The house, an early example of the Tudor Revival style in the Twin Cities, had been the Walton family's home for nearly thirty years, and like its longtime owner it was both charming and a little odd. Among Lowry Hill's early aristocracy, the English-born Walton stood out like a bright flower in a field of straw. Photographs often show him dressed in a white suit and panama hat, an outfit he wore even when everyone else in the scene was fitted out in far more sober attire. That Walton was something of a character became evident in 1885 when, at age twenty-one, he left his native London and relocated to, of all places, North Dakota, to manage a ranch, not a job for which he would seem to have been especially well qualified. He stayed on as North Dakota's resident English rancher for three years, then moved to Minneapolis, where an uncle lived, and went into real estate.[20]

Edmund G. Walton (in white) takes the reins in front of his house, about 1910.
The girl on horseback is probably one of his daughters.

One of many busily decorated rooms in the Walton House, about 1900. The mansion ended its days as a rooming house and was razed in 1959.

In 1892 Walton attracted the attention of Thomas Lowry, who was preparing to market his upscale Groveland Addition. Walton was put in charge of the job, and a year later made his own contribution to Lowry's budding development by building a house on Mount Curve Avenue just west of George Partridge's mansion. The house Walton built for himself, his wife, Nell, and their family (which ultimately included three daughters) was far smaller than the Partridge estate but much homier.

Designed by Minneapolis architect Edgar Joralemon, then in partnership with brothers George and Fremont Orff, the brick and shingle-clad house featured a steep roof rising above half-timbered side gables, a corner tower, and a broad front terrace set behind rugged stonework.[21] The terrace included an arched entryway flanked by tapering stone columns that supported a small balcony above. The overall effect was quaint in an English sort of way, just as Walton must have wanted.

The interior, designed by John Bradstreet, offered all the usual late Victorian theatrics: walls and ceilings adorned with oil paintings, overstuffed chairs and couches, oriental carpets, enough drapery to disguise a battleship, a basement ballroom, and an entry hall culminating in an elaborate, wood-paneled staircase. The grounds, which extended north to Groveland Terrace, incorporated a formal garden, where Walton sometimes posed for photographs.

Walton lived in the house until 1919, when he was struck down at age fifty-five in the influenza pandemic. His will was unusual. It specified that a single piece of music, a funeral march by Charles Gounod, be played at his funeral, with "a full wind orchestra" doing the honors. The will went on to say: "I desire that a lot be bought [at Lakewood Cemetery] near Lake Harriet facing east on a down-hill slope; also I wish to be buried in my own clothes. I also desire some memento, a bit of jewelry, to be given my friends and the boys at the office."[22]

A year or so after Walton's death, the house was sold to the newly created University Club of Minneapolis, but it was being used as a rooming house by the time of its demolition. There is now a condominium building on the site.

William H. Dunwoody (later Frederick G. Atkinson) House ("Overlook"), 104 Groveland Terrace (also 1200 Mount Curve Avenue), William Channing Whitney, 1905 to 1967 (razed)

None of Lowry's Hill historic mansions was more prominent than the forty-two-room Tudor Revival home built in 1905 by William Dunwoody and his wife, Kate. The house itself was no great work of architecture, but its five-acre lot, bordered by stone balustrades, was magnificent, offering unsurpassed views of the downtown skyline. The estate also had at least one feature unique in the Twin Cities: a private railway that ran through a short tunnel and was used to deliver coal to the mansion's huge subbasement boiler.

Dunwoody earned his fortune as a flour milling executive who excelled at seeing the big picture. An 1893 biographical sketch described him as a man "whose thought, elaborated in the quiet seclusion of his office, sets the machinery of business into ceaseless revolution, and achieves results by the unfailing success of well laid plans." Born in Pennsylvania, he worked in the grain business in Philadelphia before moving to Minneapolis in 1869. Two years later, at age thirty, Dunwoody became co-owner and manager of two flour mills at St. Anthony Falls. His visionary qualities quickly became apparent. He organized his fellow millers into a grain-buying association and also traveled to Europe to develop new markets for Minneapolis wheat. Later, as a partner in Washburn, Crosby and Company, he oversaw development of the so-called new process by which hard winter wheat could be ground into pure white flour.[23]

Dunwoody and his wife, who became well known in Minneapolis for her charitable endeavors, built their first mansion downtown on Tenth Street in 1883 (the house was later converted into a women's boarding home called Kate Dunwoody Hall). As commercial development encroached, the Dunwoodys made the move to Lowry Hill, hiring William Channing Whitney (who had also done the house on Tenth) to design what would become one of the neighborhood's—and city's—largest mansions.[24]

Built of red brick with stone trim, Dunwoody's mansion did not break from the conventional Tudor Revival mold. Its front elevation featured a triple-arched entry bay flanked by symmetrically arranged windows, a pair of tall front gables, a flared central dormer, and a modest amount of classically derived ornament. The grounds, where a curving balustrade followed the main driveway up from an iron gate on Groveland, were more lively and included terraces, gardens, and lookouts. The estate's name, Overlook, reflected its gorgeous site. Down the hill there was also a garage, which, like the one at George Partridge's nearby mansion, had a turntable.

The mansion's interior was well endowed with the usual emblems of wealth: hand-carved woodwork (including a superb staircase lit by leaded and stained-glass windows), stone and

William H. Dunwoody (later Frederick G. Atkinson) House, 104 Groveland Terrace, 1908. Dunwoody was among the most far-sighted of Minneapolis's wealthy millers.

Dunwoody House, looking east, 1908. Its site offered sweeping views and was perhaps the most magnificent on Lowry Hill.

copper fireplaces teeming with decorative detail, and a succession of grand rooms decked out with lush furnishings. The ballroom—an all but required feature in mansions of the time—was in the basement, while the second floor was given over to bedroom suites and numerous white-tiled bathrooms. The Dunwoodys had no children, and the mansion must have felt rather empty and echoing with so few occupants.[25]

Dunwoody died in 1914 and his wife a year later. Their wills included $3 million to endow what is now known as the Dunwoody College of Technology, located within eyeshot of the old mansion. Frederick G. Atkinson, another milling executive and one of Dunwoody's partners, bought the mansion in 1916 and lived there with his wife, Dorothy, until his death in 1940.

Another family occupied the house until 1967, when it was sold to developers, who promptly proposed tearing it down and erecting a twelve-story apartment building. In a letter to Lowry Hill home owners, one of the developers said the house was "obsolete" and, if left to deteriorate, would "take the neighborhood down with it." It was not a convincing argument, but even so the mansion was slated for demolition. Before it came down in October 1967, more than four thousand people paid a quarter to tour the mansion and bid on its many treasures. One couple bought the library (the room, not the books) for a mere $200 with the idea of incorporating it into a new house. As it turned out, the developers who razed the mansion never managed to build a high-rise, losing their bid to rezone the property after a legal battle that dragged on for twenty years. In the early 1980s a new developer finally filled in the long-vacant site with townhomes.[26] ◆

Living room of the Dunwoody House, 1908. After the home was demolished in 1967, an attempt to build high-rise apartments on the site was not successful.

CHAPTER 11

THE LAKE DISTRICT

◆

The Lake District—a beloved realm of water, parks, and handsome homes—is Minneapolis's defining place, an urban environment like none other in the nation. Yet for the first half century or so of the city's existence, the hilly, wooded land around the lakes was hardly considered an ideal residential precinct, for mansions or any other kind of housing.

Part of the problem was location. The lakes were a long carriage ride or walk from the downtown core in the pre-streetcar era, and so closer-in neighborhoods developed first. The lakes themselves also had shortcomings. Some of them, like the future Isles and Nokomis, were little more than marshes, while the deeper ones—Calhoun, Harriet, and Cedar—had swampy shorelines where mosquitoes swarmed in riotous abundance. No less an authority on the outdoor life than Henry David Thoreau, who tramped around the lakes on a visit to Minnesota in 1861, was moved to write in his journal: "Myriads of mosquitoes. Wood ticks." It took much dredging and shoreline rearranging by the Minneapolis Park Board, beginning in the late 1880s and continuing for more than twenty years, to create the lakes as they exist today.[1]

Once that work was done, the lakes, especially Harriet and Isles, finally began attracting mansion builders in the early decades of the twentieth century. Most of the big houses built at that time still stand—a testament to their quality and to the Lake District's enduring appeal as a place to live. Even so, a substantial number of mansions in this part of the city have been lost, including the Charles G. Gates House, the largest private residence ever built in Minneapolis.[2]

Long before Gates commenced his folly, a few mansions, usually built as part of large farmsteads, had appeared around the lakes. One of the earliest, on Lake Harriet, belonged to Charles McCormick Reeve and served as the centerpiece of a stock and dairy farm. To the north, between Lakes Calhoun and Harriet, was the enormous Lyndale Farm owned by William King. Encompassing 1,400 acres, it was the largest individually owned property in the history of Minneapolis. King was one of

Charles G. Gates mansion, 2501 Lake of the Isles Parkway East, looking south toward the lake, 1916. One of the home's two sunrooms is at right.

Roswell Russell House, Hennepin Avenue and Twenty-Eighth Street, 1890s. Built in 1873, the house was demolished around 1900 to make way for West High School, now also gone.

Charles A. Smith House, 2324 Emerson Avenue South, 1880s. The house was razed in the 1920s when Temple Israel was built on the site.

the city's indelible characters, a promoter and dreamer of the first order, and in 1870 he built a huge ramble of a house, along with barns and other outbuildings, at Bryant Avenue South and Thirty-Ninth Street near the eastern edge of the farm. A decade later, he also built a resort hotel and pavilion on the eastern shore of Calhoun, which by then had become accessible from downtown via the so-called Steam Motor Line. The line went on to the northwestern corner of Lake Harriet, paving the way for homes to be built there.

Another large farm, east of Lake of the Isles, belonged to Roswell P. Russell, who had begun his life in Minnesota as an Indian trader at Fort Snelling before opening what was reputed to be the first store in the village of St. Anthony in 1847. In the early 1850s Russell built a small farmhouse on his property at today's intersection of Hennepin Avenue and Twenty-Eighth Street. Russell later moved the house (which still stands at Twenty-Sixth Street and Bryant Avenue South) and replaced it in 1873 with a much larger French Second Empire–style mansion that was in its day a prominent Hennepin Avenue landmark. It was razed in the early 1900s to make way for what would become another neighborhood landmark, West High School, now gone as well.[3]

For much of the 1880s, development in the Lake District concentrated along and near Hennepin as it angled its way south of Franklin Avenue. Today, this portion of Hennepin is a busy commercial thoroughfare, but it was not always so. From 1884 to 1905, Hennepin south of downtown was an officially designated city parkway that was home to quite a few mansions. Near Twenty-Fourth Street and Hennepin, the Charles A. Smith House (on the current site of Temple Israel) was typical of the large wood-frame Victorians built in parts of the Lake District in the 1880s.[4]

Development quickened by the early 1900s, when Frank B. Forman and his wife built one of the grandest of all the city's lakeside mansions on the eastern shore of Calhoun. The Forman mansion, a stately exercise in the Classical Revival style set amid immaculately tended grounds, lorded over the lake for half a century before being demolished. When Forman built his Tara on Calhoun, Lake of the Isles was still a mix of swampland and open water that could not be counted among the city's beauty spots. The park board's dredgers were soon at work, however, and by 1911, when the lake was connected via canals to Calhoun and Cedar, it had been transformed into a charming body of water with two wooded islands and a long finger reaching up to Franklin Avenue. Although a handful of houses had been built in the vicinity in the 1880s, the mansions that now ring the lake almost all date to the first three decades of the twentieth century.

Not long after the dredging work came to an end, Charles G. Gates—a speed-obsessed playboy who had inherited a fortune from his father—married a Minneapolis woman and then set about building a mansion along the eastern side of the lake on a more magnificent scale than Minneapolis had ever seen before or is likely to ever see again. Finished in 1914, the mansion was of a size only equaled of late by the homes of computer billionaires, hedge fund managers, and the occasional Hollywood producer. Despite the millions spent on it, the Gates House turned out to be a chimera, gone in a flash, and it remains by far the greatest of all the lost mansions of the Twin Cities.

Charles McC. Reeve House and farm ("Sunnyside"), Lake Harriet Parkway and Forty-Eighth Street West, ca. 1870 to ca. 1915

Perhaps what is most remarkable about this house is that its early owner was still alive in 1946, when he gave an interview to the *St. Paul Dispatch* on the occasion of his ninety-ninth birthday. By that time Charles McCormick Reeve, who liked to abbreviate his middle name as McC., was the oldest living graduate of Yale University, and when he was asked to explain

Charles McC. Reeve in his military uniform, about 1900. He led the Thirteenth Minnesota Regiment during the Spanish-American War.

A summer gathering at Reeve's house, Lake Harriet Parkway and Forty-eighth Street West, 1900. The house was built as part of a three-hundred-acre stock and dairy farm.

his longevity, he replied tartly, "I used to drink and smoke occasionally, but I gave it up because I felt like it."[5]

Born in Danville, New York, Reeve was the son of a U.S. Army general who served in the Civil War. After graduating from Yale in 1870, he settled in Minneapolis, where an uncle was already established in business. Reeve became involved in banking, owned a flour mill, and was also active in choral and musical societies.[6] By the mid-1870s he and his wife, Christine, had taken up residence in a brick house overlooking Lake Harriet, in what was then Richfield Township. It is likely that the house was built by his uncle, Budd Reeve, who owned a three-hundred-acre stock and dairy farm on the southwestern side of the lake. Budd moved to North Dakota in 1880, and it appears Charles then took possession of the farm, called Sunnyside. He also operated a concession on the lake during the summer months, selling refreshments and renting out a fleet of sixty-eight rowboats, which the Minneapolis Park Board bought in 1889 when it took over the operation.[7]

Reeve's house, a Greek Revival–Italianate mix, was not especially large or fancy as mansions go, but its beautiful site and spacious grounds made it well known in the city at a time when there were few other homes on Lake Harriet. The house included a broad front porch and a hexagonal cupola, from which the Reeves enjoyed fine views of the lake and surrounding countryside.

The only known photograph of the house shows a gathering of well-dressed people in the front yard. It was taken around 1900, possibly at an anniversary celebration of the Battle of Manila during the Spanish-American War of 1898, when Reeve led the Thirteenth Minnesota Regiment. One such celebration at the house, in August 1902, included a revolver shooting contest, which must have made for a lively afternoon by the lake. Reeve and the thirteen hundred or so men of the Thirteenth Minnesota spent a year in the Philippines, fighting the Spanish and later native insurgents. A brigadier general, Reeve also served as Manila's police chief during the American occupation.[8]

After the war, Reeve was appointed warden of Stillwater State Prison but soon returned to his business interests. The house at Lake Harriet seems to have been largely a summer place, since Reeve and his wife usually wintered in California. The house was probably torn down sometime in the early 1900s, when Reeve subdivided his farm into housing lots. He moved to a new summer home at Lake Minnetonka in about 1915. He was still living there in 1947, when he died just six weeks shy of his one hundredth birthday.

William S. King House ("Lyndale Farm"), 3900 Bryant Avenue South, 1870 to 1920 (razed)

In 1920 a writer for the Minneapolis Tribune toured the old farmhouse where William S. King had spent a good part of his eventful life. The house, a multi-porched Italianate affair with symmetrical wings and a cupola, was about to be razed. Perhaps writing from personal familiarity, the reporter recalled how in the old days the house, "painted buff, with brown trimmings and gay awnings shading its windows . . . sat proudly in the center of a wide, beautifully kept lawn, on whose velvet surface young men in tight trousers and girls with lace mitts on their slender hands, played leisurely, mirthful games of croquet."[9] Completed in 1870, the twenty-two-room house was part of a complex of buildings, including several superb barns that made King's 1,400-acre Lyndale Farm one of the wonders of the young city. He was something of a wonder himself.

He was thirty when he arrived in Minneapolis from New York State in 1858. Within a year, he founded a newspaper called the State Atlas for which he penned fiery editorials denouncing Democrats and slavery. Later, he established the Minneapolis Tribune and invested in the city's first street railway. A man of high civic ideals, he was a staunch supporter of the park system, served in Congress, and helped found Lakewood Cemetery. As a member of the Minnesota Agricultural Society, he staged a series of fairs in Minneapolis in the late 1870s and early 1880s. Somewhere along the line, he also became known as Colonel King, even though he was never in the military.[10]

The farm, originally in Richfield Township, was annexed into Minneapolis in 1867. It reached its apogee around 1870, when King's acreage extended from Lyndale Avenue on the east to Lake Street on the north to Lakes Calhoun and Harriet on the west and south. The property soon dwindled away. King sold off 130 acres in 1872 to Lakewood Cemetery. Other large parcels were platted for residential use or donated to the Minneapolis Park Board.[11] The house itself was initially built for farmworkers

William King farm, house, and barns, 3900 Bryant Avenue South, 1875. Reaching 1,400 acres at its maximum, this farm was the largest individually owned property in the history of Minneapolis.

William King House in 1917, three years before its demolition. The woman in the yard is probably Helen Shuart, King's sister-in-law, the house's final occupant.

who tended to King's horses and a herd of prized English cattle that were said to be among the finest in the world. King, who maintained a home on Nicollet Island for many years, did not move out to the farm until the late 1880s, after he had lost the property and then won it back in a celebrated court case.[12]

King's difficulties began in 1877, when he built a resort pavilion on Lake Calhoun. He became overextended and made a deal to borrow $120,000 from a New York financier named Philo Remington. The deal went sour, after which Remington and his lawyers seized Lyndale Farm. Later, Remington sold much of the property to developer Louis Menage, a rather shady character best remembered as the man behind the legendary Metropolitan Building (1890–1962) in downtown Minneapolis. Claiming he had been cheated, King fought back through the courts. The legal warfare did not end until 1885, when the Minnesota Supreme Court upheld a lower court ruling that returned the farm property to King and awarded him $2 million in damages.

Once King got the farm back, he remodeled the house into a summer residence for himself, his wife, and his daughter and her two young children. The Kings also had a son, Preston, who later lent the family name to the Northrup King Seed Company, where he was an executive for many years. Although the renovated house was spacious and well appointed, it was not quite as lavish as many other mansions of the time. The main rooms featured oak and walnut woodwork, textured wallpaper, Brussels carpets, marble fireplace mantles, Tiffany art-glass windows, and antique furniture.

King died in 1900, and the Minneapolis Park Board eventually bought the house and remaining farm property. The home's last occupant was King's sister-in-law, Helen Shuart. A 1917 photograph shows an old woman, presumably Mrs. Shuart, standing in the front yard. Behind her the house, its clapboard walls bereft of paint, is well on the way to ruin. The house was finally razed in 1920 after its furnishings, right down to the dishes and pillowcases, were sold. Lyndale Park now occupies the site,

and a portion of nearby Dupont Avenue is still known as King's Highway.[13]

Before the house came down, the *Tribune* reporter took one last look at the place where so much Minneapolis history had been made: "The late afternoon sun gleamed around the sagging cupola in a splendid halo. A gust of wind swept around and through the ruined south wing. A shutter rattled wearily. Out across the brown grass, toward the bold little bungalows across the street, the old King farmhouse gazed with a mournful sigh."

Frank B. Forman House, 3450 Irving Avenue South, Edwin P. Overmire, 1902 to 1955 (razed)

The pleasant spot on a low bluff above Lake Calhoun's eastern shore where Frank B. Forman built his mansion in 1902 was by then already historic ground. Missionary brothers Gideon and Samuel Pond built a log cabin there in 1834. In the 1870s William King constructed a pavilion on the site that was later enlarged into the fashionable Lyndale Hotel, an all-wood festival of Victoriana that proved to be eminently combustible, burning down in 1888. The site stood vacant until 1901, when Forman—who with his father, Frank W., owned a paint and glass company—acquired it.[14]

Built on the foundations of the old hotel, the mansion evoked the plantation version of Classical Revival architecture. A two-story pedimented portico carried on colossal Ionic columns reigned over the long front facade, which was set well back from Irving Avenue. Behind the portico, white clapboard walls rose to a hipped, balustraded roof. The mansion was divided into two offset volumes, one for the family's living quarters and the other housing a kitchen, laundry, and servants' quarters.

A thirty-by-fifty-foot living room with an oak-beamed ceiling took up much of the main floor. Next to it, past a massive

Frank B. Forman House, 3450 Irving Avenue South, 1903. The house was built on the foundations of the Lyndale Hotel, which burned down in 1888.

brick fireplace, was the dining room, finished in mahogany. Both rooms opened out to a seventy-foot-long veranda overlooking the lake. There were five bedrooms upstairs. The basement included a bowling alley.[15] The grounds, which took in nearly a full square block, offered gardens, fountains, statuary, and a pergola that led to a streetcar station below the bluff. Forman also had a "replica"—it actually was not—of the Ponds' cabin built on his property. One magazine called the mansion a "country residence," and it must have seemed that way before development filled in the blocks around it.

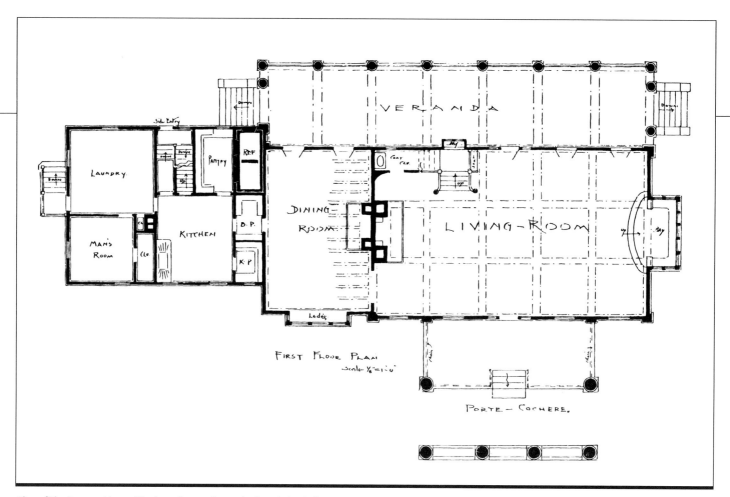

Plan of the Forman House. The broad veranda overlooking Lake Calhoun to the west was seventy feet long.

Forman's tenure in the house was brief and, it appears, unhappy. He died in 1905, at age forty-six, a year or so after suffering what a newspaper, using the common but vague parlance of the time, described as "a nervous breakdown."[16] Oddly, the mansion's architect, Edwin Overmire, died only a few months later, at the even younger age of forty-one.[17]

While the men of the mansion proved to be short-lived, Forman's wife, Marguerite, did not. Although the couple had no children, Marguerite stayed on in the huge house for more than forty years, filling it with antiques from her travels abroad. In time, she became quite the character. One friend called her "eccentric, but the grandest woman I ever knew." She favored "outlandish" attire, staged peculiar dinner parties, and liked to invite neighborhood children into the mansion to play. After she died in 1949, at age eighty-seven, an insurance company bought the property for a new headquarters building. That plan never materialized, however, and the mansion stood until 1955, when it was razed to make way for St. Mary's Greek Orthodox Church.[18]

Living room of the Forman House, 1903. The decorating features included a throne (far left) and a large dead animal.

Charles G. Gates mansion, 2501 Lake of the Isles Parkway East, and sur-roundings, about 1930. This was the largest house ever built in Minneapolis.

Charles G. Gates House, 2501 Lake of the Isles Parkway East, Marshall and Fox (Chicago), 1914 to 1933 (razed)

Among the many mansions that have come and gone in the Twin Cities, none was larger or in the end more spectacularly pointless than the folly on the east shore of Lake of the Isles built for Charles G. Gates. The 38,000-square-foot mansion, modeled on the palaces of the Italian Renaissance and built at a cost of millions, was undeniably magnificent. Yet it turned out to be a marble mirage, quickly consumed by its own excess.

Its builder, Charles G. Gates, was the only son of John W. "Bet You a Million" Gates, a feral, charismatic genius who believed "all life is a gamble." The elder Gates made millions in the barbed-wire business, branched out into steel and coal and oil, played the stock market, and once made $500,000 (not the $1 million of legend) on a bet at a horse race. Charles was spoiled from the start; John once told a reporter, "I want my boy to feel that his daddy is not only his best friend, but his chum."[19]

Marinated in money and alcohol from a young age, Charles—even after marrying in 1899—could not settle down, his life a blur of parties, chorus girls, and cross-country jaunts in his private railroad car (named Bright Eyes). He frequently visited spas, among them the resort at French Lick Springs, Indiana. There, early in 1911, he met a slender young woman named Florence Hopwood. Just twenty-four years old and a recent graduate of Smith College, she was visiting the springs with her father, a buyer for Wyman, Partridge & Company in Minneapolis. Of her first meeting with Gates, Hopwood said years later: "I was facing three people two or three tables away. A young man facing me made me feel different than any time I can recall in my life. I was taken with him at once."[20]

The feeling was mutual, and Gates began visiting Hopwood in Minneapolis, even though he was still married (a divorce from his first wife was pending). In August 1911, John Gates died, leaving behind a $38 million estate to be split between his widow and son. A month later, Charles and Florence were married, after which she convinced him to build a home in Minneapolis, where her parents lived on Lake of the Isles.

By the summer of 1912, Gates had purchased nearly a full block of land (which included two houses that had to be moved) on the lake's east shore between Twenty-Fifth and Twenty-Sixth Streets as well as property to the south he never built on. He had also hired Benjamin Marshall, an old school acquaintance from Chicago, as his architect. Marshall and Charles Fox were partners in a firm, formed in 1905, that specialized in apartment buildings and hotels but also turned out the occasional mansion.

The Gateses watched from a rented home nearby as work began on the mansion in the fall of 1912. Florence recalled that her husband especially enjoyed watching the home's steel frame being erected. Gates also liked hunting, and as the mansion neared completion, he embarked on Bright Eyes to Wyoming, where he, the Prince of Monaco, Buffalo Bill Cody, and a few select friends intended to hunt bear and elk. Gates had recently undergone an appendectomy, and as a precaution he traveled with his personal physician. It did him no good. The hunt produced many dead animals, and Gates soon joined them. While in his railcar at Cody, Wyoming, he suffered a fatal heart attack (or possibly a stroke) on October 28, 1913, at age thirty-seven. After his death, Florence had little choice but to finish the mansion. In the summer of 1914 she moved in.[21]

The four-story mansion, which resembled libraries of the period, was U-shaped, with wings extending from its south side and flanking a courtyard. Its inspiration was the sixteenth-century Palazzo Farnese in Rome, although it was hardly a replica. The exterior walls, rusticated on the lower floor and smooth above, were built of Indiana limestone. Openings on the main floor were arcaded, while the windows above were squared off, with arched or pedimented hoods. A metal cornice and hipped roof completed the design, which was accomplished, if not exactly glowing with warmth.[22]

The Gates mansion, south from Twenty-Fifth Street West, 1916. The design of the home was based on Renaissance palaces, which was appropriate, since Gates inherited a princely fortune.

Gardens on the south side of the Gates mansion, 1916. Charles Gates died of a heart attack in 1913 at age thirty-seven and did not live to see the completed mansion.

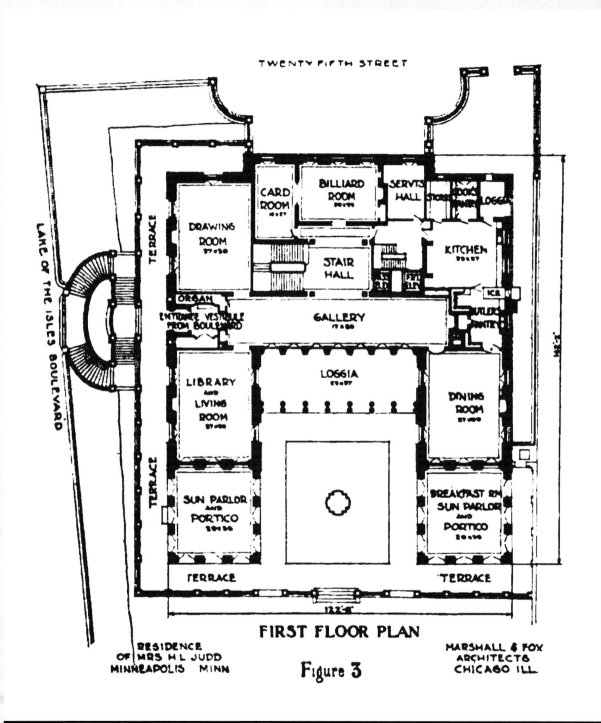

TWENTY FIFTH STREET

CARD ROOM

BILLIARD ROOM

SERVTS HALL

LANE OF THE ISLES BOULEVARD

TERRACE

DRAWING ROOM

STORE PANTRY LOGGIA

KITCHEN

ORGAN

STAIR HALL

ENTRANCE VESTIBULE FROM BOULEVARD

GALLERY

BUTLER PANTRY

ICE

TERRACE

LIBRARY AND LIVING ROOM

LOGGIA

DINING ROOM

SUN PARLOR AND PORTICO

BREAKFAST RM SUN PARLOR AND PORTICO

TERRACE

TERRACE

122'5"

FIRST FLOOR PLAN

RESIDENCE OF MRS H L JUDD MINNEAPOLIS MINN

Figure 3

MARSHALL & FOX ARCHITECTS CHICAGO ILL

Plan of main floor of the Gates mansion—oddly enough, the one floor that did not include a bathroom.

Main-floor gallery of the Gates mansion, looking west, with the stair hall at right, 1916. The gallery was eighty feet long and extended almost the full width of the mansion.

Gates mansion, second-floor corridor and stair hall, 1916. The hallway led to eight bedrooms, two large sitting rooms, dressing rooms, and five bathrooms.

Gates mansion, third-floor loggia off the ballroom, looking northwest across Lake of the Isles, 1916. Gates's widow, Florence, remarried after his death, and she and her new husband put the mansion up for sale in 1920.

Ballroom in the Gates mansion, 1916. Measuring seventy-six by thirty-seven feet, the room was large enough for a marching band.

Although the house had a "front" entry reached from Lake of the Isles Parkway by means of an elaborate double staircase, the working entrance was at ground level off Twenty-Fifth Street, where a short driveway led to doors sheltered by a marquee. Once inside, visitors ascended a staircase made of Botticini marble to the main floor. There, a hall lit by three chandeliers carved from alabaster opened out into an eighty-foot-long gallery that connected to the west entrance off the parkway. The gallery opened through a series of doors to a porch facing the courtyard. It also provided access to the mansion's three most sumptuous rooms: a drawing room outfitted with an Aeolian pipe organ, a walnut-paneled library, both overlooking the lake, and a dining room on the other side of the house. Sunrooms, a billiard room, a card room, and a kitchen were also on the main floor, which oddly enough lacked a bathroom.

Finish materials were of the highest quality. Floors were mostly marble, as were fireplace mantles (the largest, nine feet high, was at the east end of the gallery). The billiard and card rooms were paneled in white oak and had shiplike plank floors. Doorknobs and escutcheons were bronze, all custom made. Artwork (the elder Gates had been quite a collector) and tapestries adorned the walls.

Upstairs there were two master bedroom suites, along with half a dozen guest rooms. All the bedrooms had teak floors and marble baths. The third floor was devoted largely to a vaulted ballroom, seventy-six by thirty-seven feet, from which guests could wander off to a high porch overlooking the lake.[23]

The mechanical provisions were equally impressive. There were two elevators, four boilers, and a twenty-foot-long air-conditioning unit, built by Willis Carrier's firm and reputed to be the first ever installed in a private home. Attending to the mansion and its staff of thirteen, Florence discovered, was a full-time job. "It seemed like I did nothing but shop for food to feed them. My whole life seemed to be running that big house." It was also very costly; the mansion's annual operating expenses ran to $60,000.

Florence was not alone for long. Late in 1914 she met Harold L. Judd, a stock broker from Connecticut. Once again, it was love at first sight, and they were married in January 1915. They lived in the mansion, where their first child was born, for a few years, although they wintered in Florida and also spent time at Judd's Connecticut home. Around 1920, after removing much of the mansion's furniture, the couple put it up for sale. Florence tried to persuade the city to buy it for use as art museum, to no avail.

In 1923 the Judds finally sold their palatial millstone for a mere $150,000 to Dr. Dwight F. Brooks, a St. Paul lumberman. Brooks never lived in the house, which he seems to have viewed as an expensive toy. He allowed charitable groups to hold special events in the mansion and sometimes dropped by with a friend to soak up the deluxe atmosphere and, as one newspaper put it, "smoke and chat in the room that suited their fancy."[24]

After Brook's death in 1930, his estate tried to sell the mansion, but there were no takers as the economy plunged steadily down what looked to be a bottomless hole. Demolition became the last option. Just before New Year's Day, 1933, the *Minneapolis Journal* delivered the verdict: "Gates Mansion, Showplace of Lake District, to Be Wrecked."[25] A month later, the Junior League of Minneapolis staged a fund-raiser by giving tours of the doomed mansion. Over three days, eleven thousand people tramped along the marble corridors, no doubt gazing in wonder at the spectacle of so much money spent for so little ultimate purpose. Wreckers set to work that spring, carefully salvaging all of the valuable fixtures and furnishings. Parts of the mansion are now spread all around the Twin Cities, from homes on Summit Avenue in St. Paul to a North Minneapolis church that bought the three-thousand-pipe organ.[26] Eventually, several large houses, the last not built until 1958, filled in the site of the mansion.

The young widow who oversaw its completion lived on for many years. She and Judd, who had two children, divorced in

The arches of the Gates mansion appear like Roman ruins during its demolition in 1933. Eleven thousand people toured the mansion before it came down.

1935 (seven days later he married one of her cousins). Florence, however, never remarried, and died—still a wealthy woman—in 1970 at age eighty-three. In her memoirs, recorded in the 1950s, she talked about the mansion and its destruction. "I've always regretted that the city didn't buy it because then it would never have been torn down. It was a crime. It was built to last forever."[27] ◆

CHAPTER 12

NICOLLET ISLAND, NORTHEAST, and UNIVERSITY

In 1859 Ebenezer B. West, who ran a factory on Hennepin Island, built a mansion-sized home and boardinghouse on Second Street Southeast in the city of St. Anthony, across the river from Minneapolis. Named after the waterfall that powered its economy, St. Anthony was both older and more populous than its west-bank rival. West's house, which was probably larger than any residence of the time in Minneapolis, reflected St. Anthony's position as the dominant city at the falls—a status that would prove short-lived.

St. Anthony had been established in 1838, after a treaty with the Dakota and Ojibwa opened up the east bank of the Mississippi for settlement. A land rush followed. Franklin Steele, a politically well-connected storekeeper at nearby Fort Snelling who was good at making deals but less adept at making money, won the race, claiming 338 acres at the falls. The city that grew out of Steele's claim developed slowly until the late 1840s, then boomed for much of the next decade as mills and factories sprang up around the falls. Before long, however, St.

Anthony fell behind Minneapolis, whose visionary industrialists had developed superior milling and water power technologies. By 1872, St. Anthony, with about forty-six hundred residents, was barely growing, and it was merged that year into Minneapolis, which had already reached a population of more than thirteen thousand.[1]

The merger came at a time when St. Anthony's pioneering entrepreneurs—millers, manufacturers, and lumbermen being especially prominent—had just begun to build their first mansions. Some of the earliest appeared on the north side of Nicollet Island, located just above the industrial complex at the falls. Originally owned by Steele, the island was acquired in 1865 by William Eastman and John Merriam. Two years later Eastman built a large house on the south side of Grove Street that served in part as a come-on to other wealthy men seeking a place to settle with their families.[2] At about the same time Charles Loring, a successful miller who would go on to lead the Minneapolis park system, built a mansion nearby that he later

Ebenezer West House, 200 Second Street Southeast, about 1868. Shops occupied the lower floor of the house, one of the largest in St. Anthony when it was built in 1859.

sold to William S. King. By the 1880s, a row of six mansions, two owned by members of the Eastman family and another by lumberman John DeLaittre, lined the north side of Grove.[3]

Another precinct with many fine homes developed in the 1860s and later along and near Fifth Street Southeast, not far from the University of Minnesota's main campus. This area was at the edge of St. Anthony's original plat, leaving plenty of space for the large lots favored by mansion builders. There was never a Park Avenue–style mansion row here; instead, the big houses were scattered across an area of more than twenty square blocks.[4]

Quite a few early mansions have survived in this neighborhood, but several of the largest are gone, including the brick Italianate mansion on Tenth Avenue Southeast built in 1877 for

John DeLaittre House (left), 24 Grove Street, and Joel B. Bassett House, 30 Grove Street, shortly before demolition, 1929. Nicollet Island was once home to nearly a dozen mansions.

William Lochren, a lawyer and judge who served in the First Minnesota Regiment in the Civil War. Another of the neighborhood's great houses, at 1125 Fifth, belonged to Benjamin F. Nelson, owner of a paper mill in northeast Minneapolis. Built in 1883, it was the archetypical Queen Anne pile, a merry gathering of towers, gables, and porches that sprawled across a block-long lot. The Samuel Chute House, at 1024 University Avenue Southeast, was of similar vintage and also occupied ample grounds.

By far the most prominent house in this part of Minneapolis was John S. Pillsbury's mansion, built in 1879 for the man who, with his nephew Charles, established the family flour-milling dynasty. The mansion and its grounds took up almost an entire square block at Fifth Street and Tenth Avenue Southeast. Pillsbury was a long-time benefactor of the University of Minnesota and among its first regents. His mansion later became the official home of university presidents.

Northeast Minneapolis, the lower portion of which was

Benjamin F. Nelson House, 1125 Fifth Street Southeast, about 1885. Built for the owner of a northeast Minneapolis paper mill, the house was demolished around 1930.

included in the original plat of St. Anthony, was from the start a largely working-class neighborhood and never developed a mansion district. Even so, it claimed a few wealthy residents, among them members of the Gluek family, who established a brewery at Twentieth Avenue and Marshall Street Northeast in 1857. Brewers liked to live close to their place of work, and in 1888 Louis Gluek, son of company founder Gottlieb Gluek, built a brick mansion at 2004 Marshall. Like the mansion built at about the same time for brewer Theodore Hamm in St. Paul, Gluek's house had a distinctly Germanic cast, and it was long one of the neighborhood's showpieces.[5]

Mansions were still being built in the Fifth Street Southeast neighborhood as late as the early 1900s, but by then other parts of old St. Anthony were already in decline. On Nicollet Island, institutional invasion in the form of DeLaSalle High School ultimately claimed both the Eastman and Loring mansions, as well as a pair of huge row houses built by Eastman in the late 1870s. The island as a whole lost its appeal as an upper-class residential district after 1900, when wealthy families like the DeLaittres began moving to tonier locales. By the 1930s many of the island's mansions were already gone or had been converted into apartments.

The Fifth Street mansion district fared better, but sprawl from the university campus inevitably ate away at some of the old residential blocks, while in other cases mansions were taken over by fraternities or converted to rental properties. The Nelson House came down in the 1930s, as did Ebenezer West's home and boardinghouse. The Pillsbury mansion, which was eminently worthy of preservation on historic and architectural grounds, lasted until the 1960s, when the university demolished it to make way for new faculty apartments.

ISLAND ESTATES

William W. Eastman House, 23–25 Grove Street, ca. 1867; remodeled, Leroy Buffington, 1881 to ca. 1927 (burned)

Charles M. Loring (later William S. King) House, 41 Island Avenue, 1869 to 1920 (razed)

In 1865 William W. Eastman, a young industrialist who had settled eleven years earlier in St. Anthony, joined up with St. Paulite John Merriam to buy Nicollet Island. The forty-eight-acre island, made accessible in 1855 by the opening of the first Hennepin Avenue Suspension Bridge, was largely undeveloped, but the two men hoped to attract industry to the southern end, just above St. Anthony Falls. They were less sure what to do with the rest of the island, at first offering to sell it to the city of Minneapolis, for $47,500, as a park. A referendum to approve that deal failed, however, and so in 1866 the partners platted all of the island north of Hennepin into residential lots.[6]

No doubt in hope of stimulating others to make the island their home, Eastman in about 1867 built a brick house on Grove Street, overlooking the east channel of the Mississippi. The house—square, two stories high, and crowned with a cupola—was hardly exceptional, but it was pleasantly situated on large grounds. Eastman and his wife, Susan, had two young children, and the island—still a little wild—must have been an adventurous place to grow up. In 1881 Eastman hired architect Leroy Buffington to upgrade his mansion. Buffington added a rear wing, remodeled the interior, and attached a dramatic tower to one corner. Four stories high with an arcaded lookout beneath a Gothic-style roof, the tower transformed what had been a rather meat-and-potatoes house into quite a curiosity.[7]

Eastman had by this time made many other improvements to the island. In the 1870s, he constructed three stone row houses; one of them, four stories high and 550 feet long, was the largest ever built in the Twin Cities. He and his partners also succeeded in bringing industry to the south end of the island,

William W. Eastman House, 23–25 Grove Street, after it was enlarged and remodeled, 1891. Eastman built the house in 1867, two years after he and a partner purchased Nicollet Island.

Eastman Flats, 13–59 Eastman Avenue, 1936. This row house extended all the way across Nicollet Island. It was demolished around 1959 but was similar in style to the nearby Grove Streets Flats, which still stand.

but only after an attempt to build a tunnel under the river in 1869 nearly destroyed the falls.

Other members of the Eastman clan, including four of William's siblings, later occupied mansions along Grove. As with any family, there were problems. Eastman's son, Fred, was a notorious alcoholic whose exploits were frequent fodder for the press. William lived in the mansion until his death in 1902. Susan died ten years later, but other family members remained in the house until about 1919. It burned down about eight years later, and the site is now part of DeLaSalle High School's athletic field.

West of Eastman's mansion, where the older portion of DeLaSalle High School now stands, Charles M. Loring built the island's other most notable estate. Loring was one of those Victorians who seem to have packed many lives into one. The son of a Maine sea captain, he sailed to the West Indies as a young man. In 1856, at age twenty-three, he became a successful grain trader in Chicago, then moved to Minneapolis, where he worked as a merchant and also owned several flour mills. A nature lover—he organized the first flower show in Minneapolis—Loring was named president of the Minneapolis Park Board after its creation in 1883.

Charles M. Loring (later William S. King) House, 41 Island Avenue, about 1893. "Nicollet Island was a dreamland in those days," Loring later recalled.

It is easy to see why Nicollet Island, with its oaks and maples and river rushing by on its way to the falls, would have appealed to Loring. The house he, his wife, Emily, and their two children moved into in 1869 was a charming Gothic-Italianate "cottage" on a one-acre lot just south of Grove Street. The home offered plenty of architectural romance: a balconied tower, bay windows, gables with stick work, and porches spilling off in all directions.[8] "Nicollet Island was a dreamland in those days," Loring recalled. "We had a delightful little community there. W.-W. Eastman, the DeLaittre family, our house, and a few others. The island was really a park as it stood. It was thickly grown up to a grove of as beautiful native maples as one would care to see."[9]

Despite these sylvan pleasures, Loring moved away after eight years, selling the property to flamboyant newspaperman and entrepreneur William S. King, who also loved nature and who would also go on to make many contributions to the Minneapolis park system. King's death in 1900 coincided with the arrival of DeLaSalle Institute (now High School) on the island. The institute constructed its original building directly north of the Loring-King House before acquiring the estate in 1914. A few years later the house came down to make way for a second school building, completed in 1922.[10]

William Lochren, about 1900. He fought with the famed First Minnesota Regiment during the Civil War and later became a federal judge.

William Lochren House, 422 Tenth Avenue Southeast, Charles Ferrin, ca. 1877 to 1951 (razed)

On July 8, 1863, just days after the First Minnesota Regiment had sustained horrific casualties at the Battle of Gettysburg, a newspaper reported that William Lochren, a thirty-one-year-old lawyer from the city of St. Anthony, was among the dead. The report turned out to be false. Lochren, a second lieutenant, had not only survived the fight but had come through it unscathed—one of only about fifty of the regiment's three hundred or so members who were not killed or wounded in two days of furious, close-quarters combat. If life is in some measure a matter of luck, then Lochren perhaps enjoyed more than his share.[11]

Born in Ireland but raised in Vermont, Lochren found his way to Minnesota in the early 1850s, "read law," and then began practicing his profession in St. Anthony. Gregarious and articulate, he did well. After returning from the war, he teamed up with William McNair to form a successful law firm. He dabbled

Lochren House, 422 Tenth Avenue Southeast, 1936. The carriage house at left was as impressive as the mansion.

in politics, serving one term in the Minnesota Senate, before being named to the district court bench in 1881.[12]

The mansion he built in about 1877 at the corner of Fifth Street and Tenth Avenue Southeast was in a neighborhood that attracted many of old St. Anthony's elite. Two years after Lochren moved in, John S. Pillsbury built his estate just across Fifth, and Benjamin Nelson would also become a neighbor. The Pillsbury and Nelson mansions were in newly fashionable styles, but Lochren's brick house was a bit old hat. Designed by Charles Ferrin, who later became the Twin City Rapid Transit Company's chief architect, the house offered a familiar Italianate package that included a tower and bracketed eaves. The carriage house, however, was a delight, with a broad arched doorway and a tower balanced on one corner of the second story like a tiny lighthouse.

Lochren remained a district court judge until 1893. Three years later, President Grover Cleveland nominated Lochren for a seat on the federal bench, and the U.S. Senate quickly confirmed the appointment. By this time, Lochren had already written a brief history of the First Minnesota. His account of the regiment's reaction when ordered to charge a Confederate force five times its size still stirs the blood: "Every man realized in an instant what that order meant—death or wounds to us all; the sacrifice of the regiment to gain a few minutes time and save the position, and probably the battlefield—and every man saw and accepted the necessity for the sacrifice."[13]

Lochren seems to have been fortunate in love as well as war, although he certainly bided his time. In 1882, at age fifty, he married twenty-one-year-old Mary Abbott of Farmington, Minnesota. They later had a son, also named William. Lochren retired from the federal bench in 1908 and died four years later. Mary Lochren lived on in the house, with her son, until 1944, when she died. In 1947 the mansion was sold to Alpha Delta Pi Sorority, but it was torn down four years later to make way for a new building, which is now used by a church group.[14]

John S. Pillsbury House, 1005 *Fifth Street Southeast, Leroy Buffington, 1879 to 1964 (razed)*

Among nineteenth-century business and civic leaders in the Twin Cities, few could boast of a more impressive list of achievements than John S. Pillsbury. He started out in the hardware business in St. Anthony in the 1850s on the site where the milling company he later cofounded with his nephew Charles would one day build the world's largest flour mill, the Pillsbury A. He also had a stellar political career that included six years as governor of Minnesota in the 1870s. Perhaps more impor-

John S. Pillsbury House, 1005 Fifth Street Southeast, about 1880. This house was almost identical to one built for Pillsbury's brother, George, in downtown Minneapolis.

tantly, Pillsbury was a University of Minnesota regent for nearly forty years. First appointed in 1864, he helped free the struggling young institution from debt and became one of its chief benefactors, donating $150,000 to build Pillsbury Hall in 1889 and also providing land for the university's experimental farm near its St. Paul campus.[15]

It would be nice to think that Pillsbury's love for the university inspired him to live close to the campus, but in fact he built his first house on the site of his mansion in the 1850s, well before he became a regent.[16] In 1877 he hired Minneapolis architect Leroy Buffington to design a new, much larger home on the property, which took in about two-thirds of a square block at Fifth Street and Tenth Avenue Southeast. Pillsbury had just turned fifty when he began building the mansion for himself, his wife, Mahala, (a sister of his first business partner, Woodbury Fisk) and their four children, then ranging in age from nine to eighteen.

Buffington by this time was becoming the architect of choice for much of the Pillsbury family. John's brother, George, hired Buffington to design a mansion in downtown Minneapolis, and the two houses, both completed in 1879, were strikingly similar. In 1881 Buffington also won the commission for the A Mill. He would go on to design Pillsbury Hall and a downtown mansion for George's son, Frederick.

The John Pillsbury House, built of cream-colored Milwaukee brick, was not one of Buffington's greatest moments, but it did show how architectural tastes were beginning to change at the end of the 1870s. Across Fifth Street, the Lochren House of 1877 had adhered to a familiar Italianate template, but Pillsbury's mansion looked ahead to the stylistic gumbo of the 1880s. It still clung to a few old-time Italianate devices, such as well-defined window hoods, but with its picturesque trio of front gables infilled with stick work, its undulating bays, and its busy roofline, the mansion evoked the Gothic-tinged Eastlake style that would enjoy a brief flowering in the Twin Cities before the Queen Anne craze of the mid-1880s.

Inside, Pillsbury's house offered a varied arsenal of woodwork: oak in the main hall, bird's-eye maple in the front parlor, cherry in the library, and black walnut in the dining room, which was said to include a superb sideboard. The main staircase, paneled in oak and lit by a stained-glass window, featured two landings on its way to the second floor. A ballroom finished in Georgia pine took up much of the attic.[17]

Although the house was large (at least six thousand square feet) and handsomely detailed, it was modest compared to some of the mastodons that stomped into the city's mansion districts in the 1880s and later. William Washburn's mansion was probably three times as large as Pillsbury's, as was the George Partridge House on Lowry Hill. It does not appear that Pillsbury felt overawed by these later displays of wealth, and he never moved to a bigger house. When he died in 1901 at age seventy-three, he seems to have been genuinely mourned, not always the case with multimillionaires. The *Minneapolis Journal* wrote after his death that his life was "a model for all rich men. His possession of wealth never led him to esteem it as the best thing in the world. . . . He lived simply, abhorred display, used his wealth wisely and largely for the public good."[18]

Mahala remained in the home until her death in 1910, after which it was turned over to the University of Minnesota for use as a president's mansion. It is likely the mansion was extensively remodeled at about the same time by giving its dark Victorian interiors a Classical Revival makeover that included white enameled woodwork and wall paintings of classical scenes. At some point, the exterior was also stripped of its original front porch and porte cochere and painted white. The mansion served as the president's residence for more than fifty years. In the early 1960s the university, not always a friend to its own history, tore the mansion down and replaced it with the Pillsbury Court townhomes.

Gluek Brewery and Louis Gluek House, 2004 Marshall Street Northeast, look-ing east across Mississippi River, 1963. The brewery was founded in 1857 by Gottlieb Gluek, Louis's father.

Louis Gluek House, 2004 Marshall Street Northeast, 1888 to 1966 (razed)

Gottlieb Gluek was one of two thousand or so German-born immigrants who settled in the Twin Cities in the 1850s. Most went to St. Paul, but Gluek made his home in St. Anthony, where he went to work for pioneer brewer John Orth. In 1857 Gluek struck out on his own, establishing the Mississippi Brewery along Marshall Street Northeast.[19]

Gluek was producing four thousand barrels annually by 1880, when a fire heavily damaged the brewery. He quickly rebuilt, only to die at age fifty-two before the year was out. His three sons—Louis, who was the oldest, along with Charles and John—took over the company, which became one of Minneapolis's two major breweries (the other, Grain Belt, was located less than a mile away on Marshall). Charles and John later lived in mansions on or near Lowry Hill, but Louis stayed closer to the family business. In 1888 he built a red brick and brownstone home directly south of the brewery complex for himself, his mother, and his seven sisters, the youngest of whom was only twelve.[20]

The house, which like the brewery itself overlooked the Mississippi River, was among the most intriguing and exotic of all the Victorian-era brewers' mansions in the Twin Cities. Its three sculpted and scrolled gables, derived from Dutch and North Germanic architecture, were especially prominent, evoking the Old World the Gluek family had left behind. A porch supported by paired columns and adorned with a richly carved pediment wrapped around the front of the house. Above it, a small semicircular porch with a half-domed roof extended out from one of the bedrooms. Along the roofline, an array of chimneys and dormers added to the mansion's romantic profile.

It is not known who designed the mansion, which was quite different from any other house of its time in the Twin Cities. Most midwestern breweries were designed by specialists based in Chicago or Milwaukee, and it is possible the Glueks found their architect there.

Louis Gluek was single when he built the house, but in 1893, at age thirty-five, he married. He and his wife, Laura, eventually had seven children, and with three generations of Glueks living in the mansion it must have been a very busy household. City directories indicate that Louis and Laura were still living in the mansion as late as 1930, although they were probably wintering in California, where Louis died in 1937. After Louis's death, the mansion was used for a time as the brewery's offices.[21]

Like many other regional brewers, Gluek's ultimately succumbed to competition from national brands. Two years after the company was purchased by G. Heileman Brewing Company of La Crosse, Wisconsin, the old brewery on Marshall was demolished, as was the mansion.[22] The Cold Spring Brewery Company then acquired the Gluek label and continued producing beer under that name until the label was dropped in 2010, ending Gluek's 153-year history in Minnesota. A park now occupies the site of the old mansion. ◆

Louis Gluek House, about 1915. The sculpted and scrolled gables were among its most distinctive features.

CHAPTER 13

SUBURBAN MINNEAPOLIS

Although several small communities, including Richfield and what later became Minnetonka, developed near Minneapolis as early as the 1850s, suburbs as they are commonly thought of today did not really appear until about 1880 as railroad lines began to extend out from the city in all directions. Some of these early suburbs grew around large-scale industrial operations. Hopkins, originally known as West Minneapolis, developed rapidly in the 1880s after the Minneapolis Threshing Machine Company (later Minneapolis-Moline) built a plant there. Industrial development also fueled the growth of St. Louis Park and Robbinsdale in the late nineteenth century.[1]

Mansions were never common in these industrial suburbs, where most of the early housing was of the working-class variety. In Hopkins, the grandest nineteenth-century home was built in 1894 by pioneer settler Daniel Dow. The fifteen-room house, on Second Street South, stood until 1965. Robbinsdale also had at least one notable Victorian mansion, built by the city's founder, Andrew Robbins, on twenty acres overlooking Twin Lake.

Two far larger mansions, true country estates, were once located along the Minnesota River bluffs in Bloomington. The earlier of the two was built just after 1900 by Marion Savage, owner of the renowned pacer Dan Patch. Savage's estate in a sense extended all the way across the Minnesota's wide valley, since from his mansion he could see the stock farm on the south side of the river where Dan Patch and other prized horses lived in equine luxury. East of Savage's estate was Waleswood, the summer home of Minneapolis coal magnate Charles Wales. Large estates run by so-called gentleman farmers were also scattered around Minneapolis. One of the best known, in Brooklyn Center, belonged to flour miller John Martin, who later bequeathed the 750-acre spread to his grandson Earle Brown. It survives today as a meeting and convention center.

By far the greatest gathering of nineteenth- and early-twentieth-century mansions anywhere in the Twin Cities suburbs was at Lake Minnetonka, which began to be widely publicized not long after its "discovery" in the 1850s. Its appeal was immediate and lasting. With its intricate tangle of bays, the lake must

Daniel E. Dow House and grounds, Second Street South between Ninth and Tenth Avenues, Hopkins, about 1900. Built for one of the town's pioneers in 1894, it was razed in 1965.

have seemed to the Victorians like a picturesque Queen Anne house, its irregularities offering a welcome counterpoint to the corseted rigors of everyday life. The first rail line reached the north shore of the lake, at Wayzata, in 1867, and by the 1870s

cottages began springing up around Wayzata Bay and to the south toward what is now Deephaven.[2]

The first large estate on the lake was built in the 1870s by Charles Gibson, a lawyer from St. Louis who escaped that city's notorious heat and humidity by spending summers in Minnesota. One year he found his way out to the lake. He was so enchanted that in 1870 he bought 160 acres along and to the

Frederick C. Pillsbury summerhouse, near Ferndale Road and Pillsbury Drive, Wayzata, about 1890. The house burned down in 1897, eleven years after it was built.

north of what is now St. Louis Bay and built a five-thousand-square-foot summerhouse, which he called Northome. Like many of the all-wood hotels later built on the lake (including the St. Louis, which Gibson owned), Northome was kindling in search of a spark, and it finally burned down in 1894.[3]

By the 1880s, many of Minneapolis's—and a few of St. Paul's—leading families had summer homes at the lake. Some of

them, like Frederick Pillsbury's towered Queen Anne confection in Wayzata, were quite large; others were of more modest size. Most of Minnetonka's greatest estates date to the 1890s and early 1900s. Among them was Cedarhurst, built in 1901 by

Russell M. Bennett on the site of the old Gibson estate. An equally grand exercise in columned classicism, the Lucian Swift mansion (Katahdin), was not far away. In Tonka Bay the eighty-six-acre John Wilcox estate, known as Old Orchard, included a Dutch Colonial–style house built in about 1890 and a separate lookout tower. Minnetonka's most magnificent lost estate was undoubtedly Highcroft, built by grain merchant Frank Peavey

and later owned by his daughter and son-in-law. Until well into the twentieth century, even lake homes as large as Highcroft were seasonal, their occupants returning to the city once cold weather set in.[4]

Like many of Minnetonka's estates of this period, Highcroft—which encompassed well over one hundred acres—was also a working farm. Even larger farm-estates appeared on the lower

John F. Wilcox House and tower, near Birch Bluff Road, Tonka Bay, about 1908. Known as Old Orchard, the eighty-six-acre estate became a resort in the 1930s but was later subdivided.

(western) part of the lake. Albert C. Loring's estate, Woodend, on Halsted's Bay, took in about one thousand acres at its peak during the early 1900s.

Minnetonka also had more than a few island homes of note. Harlow Gale, who with his brother Samuel was among the lake's first summer residents, built an octagonal summer cottage on a tiny island in 1872. The cottage is long gone, but the spit of land on which it stood is still known as Gale Island. Nearby, on Big Island, Norwegian immigrant turned entrepreneur Olaf Searle occupied an estate of more than one hundred acres, only to see his dream dissolve in alcohol and betrayal.

Among Lake Minnetonka's lost mansions are two early-twentieth-century houses of exceptional architectural significance. The Edward Decker House (1913) in Wayzata, designed

Gale Island, Lake Minnetonka, south of Big Island, 1890s. Harlow Gale bought the tiny island (reputedly for $2.85) in 1872 and the next year built an octagonal summer cottage, now gone.

by Purcell and Elmslie of Minneapolis, and Frank Lloyd Wright's Francis Little House (1914) in Deephaven, were the largest Prairie School houses ever built in Minnesota, and had they survived, both would be regarded today as among the state's architectural treasures. Also lost is a much later Modernist work from the 1960s, the Philip and Eleanor Pillsbury House, designed by Ralph Rapson.

Mansions of course still stand in showy abundance all around Lake Minnetonka, but the age of the great estates is all but over, and there will be no new Katahdins or Highcrofts on the lovely wooded shores where Charles Gibson came long ago in search of a cooling summer breeze.

Andrew B. Robbins House, west side of Twin Lake, south of Highway 100, Robbinsdale, 1890 to ca. 1942 (razed)

The suburbs that ring Minneapolis have, for the most part, rather generic names, such as Richfield and Bloomington, or names—Minnetonka, for example—derived from Indian words.

Robbinsdale, on the other hand, is named after its founder, Andrew Bonney Robbins, who was a prominent figure in nineteenth-century Minnesota.

Born in Maine, Robbins moved to Minnesota Territory with his parents in 1855, when he was ten years old. At age seventeen he signed on with the Eighth Minnesota Regiment, which saw service during the Dakota War of 1862 and later fought on Civil War battlefields in Tennessee. After the war, Robbins moved to Willmar, Minnesota, where he worked as railroad station manager before turning to banking and other enterprises. He later relocated to the Twin Cites, where he founded a grain elevator company and invested in real estate. He also married well. His wife, Adelaide, was a sister of millionaire Minneapolis lumberman and art collector Thomas B. Walker.[5]

Robbins first visited the area that would one day bear his name in 1887. Supposedly, he was so impressed by its "many natural advantages, scenic and otherwise," that he promptly

Robbins House and grounds, early 1900s. The sixteen-room house was part of a twenty-acre estate.

Andrew B. Robbins House, west side of Twin Lake, south of Highway 100, Robbinsdale, shortly before demolition, 1942. The owner of the house founded Robbinsdale in the 1880s.

bought ninety acres in what was then part of Crystal Township. He went to work at once to develop his property. He platted streets, established two factories, and built a streetcar line that connected to the Twin City Rapid Transit Company's system in Minneapolis.[6] Even so, the village of Robbinsdale, which was organized in 1893 just as the nation plunged into a depression, was not an immediate success, counting only 520 residents by 1900.

The sixteen-room, Queen Anne–style mansion Robbins built for himself and his family (he and Adelaide had five daughters) was for many years the showpiece of the small community. It was located on the west side of Twin Lake, about a block south of today's Highway 100. The clapboard and shingle-clad house included a round corner tower crowned by a conical roof, a two-story arcaded front porch, and a balustraded porte cochere. A photograph of the home's library suggests that the interior was finished rather simply by the usual overstuffed Victorian standards.

Perhaps more impressive than the house itself were the grounds, which originally took in twenty acres. Robbins loved trees (he planted them all over the village), and he lined the long driveway to his mansion with a row of elms reputed to be "one of the finest in the state." The grounds also included a small pond.

Robbins lived in the mansion until his death, from stomach cancer, in 1910. Adelaide stayed on for at least another ten years. The couple's oldest daughter, Edith—a businesswoman, teacher, and in her day a well-known writer of children's poetry—later occupied the mansion, which was torn down in the 1940s. Houses have now filled in the old grounds of the estate.[7]

BLUFFTOP ESTATES

Marion W. Savage House ("Valley View"), Normandale Boulevard near Masonic Home Drive, Bloomington, Harry Jones, ca. 1903 to 1950 (razed)

Charles E. Wales House ("Waleswood"), near 108th Street West and Overlook Drive, Bloomington, ca. 1914 to 1933 (razed)

Marion W. Savage, remembered today as the owner of the pacer Dan Patch, led a life that was at once extraordinary and improbable. A promotional genius, he turned Dan Patch into an advertising icon, all the while peddling a product that was essentially patent medicine for animals. Today, Dan Patch remains an icon of American horse racing, but only faint traces survive of the world he and his master once inhabited on the Minnesota River.

The son of a country doctor, Savage was raised in Iowa, where as a young man he worked in a drugstore in President Herbert Hoover's hometown of West Branch. Perhaps drawing on that experience, Savage went into the patent medicine

M. W. SAVAGE AND HIS GREAT DAN PATCH 1:55

Marion W. Savage and Dan Patch, about 1905. Savage paid $60,000 for the famed pacer in 1902.

business in Iowa City in the 1880s, selling such nostrums as Dr. Savage's Stomach and Bowel Regulator and "blood purifying syrup." Although patent medicines were big business at the time, their appeal frequently enhanced by a high alcohol content, Savage's cure-alls did not sell well, and his company soon failed.

In 1888 he, his wife, Marietta, and their young son, Erle, moved to Minneapolis, where Savage struck gold with a new concept. He mixed "herbs, roots, barks, and seeds" into a supplement that, when added to feed, would supposedly make livestock fatten more quickly. The concoction's actual ingredients included chalk, charcoal, and a dollop of strychnine, and agricultural experts dismissed Savage's claims as nonsense. It did not matter. Savage was a brilliant salesman, and his International Stock Food Company, which eventually sold a variety of animal and human food products, became an enormous success. By late 1902, when Savage bought Dan Patch for $60,000, the company had three hundred employees and published a catalog mailed all across the country.[8]

At the time of the purchase, Dan Patch was already an equine superstar, the fastest pacer in the world, and three thousand people showed up to see him when he arrived at the Union Depot in Minneapolis on a zero-degree January day in 1903. Savage and the brown stallion immediately became intertwined in all of the stock food company's advertising. Dan Patch by all accounts was gentle and unassuming; his owner was not. Savage's specialized in shamelessly over-the-top self-promotion. One company blurb, summoning up a strange trifecta of virtues, described Savage this way: "He has the energy of a Roosevelt, the heart of a woman and the tenacity of a barnacle."[9]

Savage also had a lot of money. In 1892, with his business booming, he built a mansion at 2600 Portland Avenue in Minneapolis. After weathering the depression of the mid-1890s, Savage's business continued to grow, and once he acquired Dan Patch, he was ready to build on a monumental scale. In 1902, in what would later become the city of Savage, he bought seven hundred acres on the south side of the Minnesota River and built the stock farm of his dreams. Its centerpiece was a Taj Mahal of a barn with five 260-foot-long stables radiating from an octagonal hub crowned by an oriental dome (which enclosed a water tank fed from nearby springs). Later, Savage added the country's first indoor racetrack—a half-mile-long oval lit by 1,600 windows.[10]

As the farm buildings went up, so did Savage's summer home across the river in Bloomington. Designed by Harry Jones, the house was a white Georgian Revival fantasy with a curving, two-story-high Ionic portico flanked by open porches. After Dan Patch paced the mile in a record one minute and fifty-five seconds at the 1906 Minnesota State Fair, the horseshoes he wore that day were embedded in the porches' concrete floors. Inside, the living room was two stories high at the center. An adjoining dining room opened into an angled wing containing the kitchen and servants' quarters. The second floor, reached by a marble staircase, included hallways with vaulted plaster ceilings that led to the bedrooms. There was also a penthouse office where Savage often worked.[11]

Savage was at the height of his success when he built his house in the country, but he soon suffered a series of reverses. A flood in 1907 damaged his farm, and in 1908 he lost a bid to run as the Republican nominee for governor of Minnesota. Even so, Dan Patch continued to be a lucrative endorsement machine, his image appearing on all manner of products and in countless advertisements. The horse was getting old, however, and ran his last race in 1910. Savage, meanwhile, had decided, unwisely, to build a railroad run by gasoline-electric locomotives from Minneapolis to Chicago. The Dan Patch Line, as it inevitably became known, got only as far as Northfield, Minnesota, and by 1916 the project was deeply mired in debt.

As he tried to stave off creditors that summer, Savage fell ill and was admitted to a Minneapolis hospital, where on July 11 he learned that Dan Patch, then twenty years old, had collapsed

Covered racetrack and barn at Savage's stock farm, in what is now the city of Savage, about 1915. The half-mile track was lit by 1,600 windows.

Horse barn at Savage's stock farm, about 1910. The barn's onion-shaped dome held a water tank and was adorned with a sign: "The 4 Fastest Stallions Ever Owned by One Farm."

in his stall and died. The next day, a heart attack killed Savage at age fifty-seven. Afterward, his world along the Minnesota faded away. The farm was sold in 1919, and within three years both the indoor track (destroyed by a windstorm) and the great barn (leveled by fire) were gone. Later, the magnificent white mansion across the river was converted into a Masonic home for the aged. It was finally razed in 1950. All is not lost, however. The outlines of the racetrack are still visible in aerial views of the old farm site, serving as a ghostly reminder of that brief glorious time when Dan Patch and his proud owner lived like kings in the valley of the Minnesota.[12]

About two miles east of Savage's estate was an even more remarkable place, built by Minneapolis coal tycoon Charles E. Wales. Unlike Savage, Wales was not a high-profile figure, and his estate, known as Waleswood, never garnered a great deal of publicity. It should have. The estate offered an intriguing pair of buildings linked by an unusual twin tunnel, as well as a tall white tower that looked very much like a lighthouse guarding the river valley.

Perched above the deep ravine of Nine Mile Creek on almost five hundred acres of land, the estate occupied property that had been owned by the Wales family since at least the 1890s. Born in 1852 in St. Anthony, where his parents had settled just a year earlier, Wales went to work in the coal business at an early age. While still in his twenties, he organized a fuel company that later was merged into a national conglomerate. He also had extensive real estate holdings in the Twin Cities and Duluth.[13]

Wales's first wife died in the early 1900s, and it is possible that his second marriage, in 1911, enabled him to build such a lavish estate, since his new wife, Sarah Smythe, came from a very wealthy Chicago family.[14] According to one account, which may be apocryphal, the couple actually built two mansions on the property. The first was constructed while they were on a prolonged European honeymoon. Wales, so the story goes, hated the mansion when he finally saw it, ordered its demolition, and then immediately built another home more to his liking.[15]

If so, his tastes were certainly unusual. The mansion, which had twenty-one rooms and six baths, was an ungainly collection of Colonial Revival elements dominated by a five-story corner tower with inward sloping walls. The tower, which may well have had an elevator, culminated in a lookout ringed by a projecting balcony. A large telescope was said to be mounted somewhere inside. Below the tower, first- and second-floor porches and sunrooms ran along the entire east side of the mansion, looking out over the creek and river valley. There was also a rooftop deck. No interior photographs of the house have been located, but the rooms must have been sunny given the sheer amount of wall space devoted to windows.

Savage House, portico with Ionic columns, about 1905. A boldly scaled split pediment presided over double entry doors.

Savage and his younger son, Harold, gaze across the Minnesota River toward the stock farm, about 1905. Savage's mini-empire on the river did not survive long after his death in 1916.

Living room in the Savage House, about 1905. Vaulted ceilings decorated with stencils rose above the balcony.

Charles E. Wales estate, near present-day 108th Street West and Overlook Drive, Bloomington, looking south, about 1915. Wales made his money in coal and real estate.

Wales House and lookout tower, 1914. A sheltered walkway and a tunnel connected the main house to a clubhouse at right.

Clubhouse of Wales estate, 1918. This building included a ballroom, a bowling alley, and a heated swimming pool.

The estate's other major building was a clubhouse that connected to the mansion via a 125-foot-long pergola and, below, a twin tunnel—one side for family and guests, the other for servants. The clubhouse offered quite a suite of amenities, including a ballroom, a heated swimming pool, and a bowling alley. A central boiler heated the complex (it is a good guess the fuel was coal), and the plumbing system included tanks to collect rainwater, which was then heated and piped into some of the bathrooms. Other buildings on the property included barns, a poultry house, and a sixteen-stall garage.[16]

The estate as completed in 1914 was not around for long. In 1921, Wales subdivided much of his property into one-acre or larger residential lots, but sales do not seem to have been especially robust. By then, he was also touting the mansion and clubhouse as ideal for institutional use, but he found no takers. Once the Great Depression hit, the real estate market collapsed, and Wales lost any chance of selling the mansion or clubhouse. In 1933, a year after his death at age eighty, both buildings were torn down. Today, hundreds of houses—many dating to the 1950s—fill in what is still called the Waleswood Addition.

Emile Amblard Estate ("Eden"), Coney Island, Lake Waconia, 1893 and later to ca. 1970s (ruins)

In 1890 Emile Amblard, a French wine merchant who traveled throughout the United States and Canada, visited an old friend in Minneapolis. One morning they took a train out to the village of Waconia, on the shores of what was then called Clearwater Lake, for a day of fishing. The lake was at that time a popular resort destination, although on nowhere near the scale of Lake Minnetonka a few miles to the northeast. While at the lake, Amblard took a boat out to its most distinctive natural feature: Coney Island of the West. The island's thirty-two wooded acres were home to a resort hotel, established in 1884, as well as several cottages. Amblard was smitten, and he soon returned to build an unusual estate on the island, where he would spend summers for the rest of his life.

Born in Paris in 1840 to a well-to-do family, Amblard was not immune to the call of adventure, and in 1870 he fought in the Franco-Prussian War. The war was a disaster for France, but Amblard came out of it with nothing worse than a saber wound, leaving a scar of which he was said to be very proud. After the war, he became a traveling sales representative for a firm that distributed French wines in the United States, Canada, and Mexico. His work appears to have been lucrative but not onerous, since he was able to spend a good part of every year at his Coney Island estate.

Amblard bought his first parcel on the western side of the island in 1893 and expanded his holdings over the next decade. In 1894, he also married, apparently for the second time. His new bride, Mary Wood, the daughter of a prominent Canadian jurist, was just twenty-two years old. By 1899, when he built Villa Emile, the largest cottage on the estate, Amblard was a well-known figure in Waconia. Suave and charming, he favored white summer linens, always wore a sailor's cap for photographs, and sported a handsome, well-maintained mustache. Given his aristocratic bearing, it was perhaps inevitable that a local newspaper dubbed him "the Duke of Clearwater Lake."

Eden, as Amblard called his estate, never included a mansion per se. Instead, it was more like a small private resort offering an array of cottages, pavilions, and outbuildings scattered around parklike grounds. At its center was Villa Emile, a wooden cottage designed, suitably enough, in the French Second Empire style. Looking like a gaudy little riverboat, it featured porches on three sides as well as a tower. There was also a five-room guest cottage (Villa Topsy, named after Amblard's dog) and a private retreat for Mary and her mother, who often summered at the estate. Rounding out the estate's collection of structures were a boathouse (Amblard's fleet consisted of a sailboat, several rowboats, and, by 1905, a gasoline-powered

Advertisement for Coney Isle, Lake Waconia, about 1899. The thirty-two-acre island was once the site of a resort hotel and private cottages.

launch), several pavilions and gazebos, a billiard room, and a chess room.

Amblard also devoted considerable attention to the grounds. He laid out broad walkways bordered by brick retaining walls, built stairways and fences, and planted trees, shrubs,

and perennials, including tiger lilies that still bloom on the island. Beginning in 1913, he opened up part of his property as a public park, which became a favorite destination for picnickers.

During the winter months, Amblard spent much of his time on the road, but as he grew older he settled down in Minneapolis, where he owned a house on Blaisdell Avenue. He also built a garage and clubhouse in Waconia that he hoped would one day serve as the headquarters of an automobile club. That

Emile Amblard, looking jaunty outside Villa Emile, Coney Island, about 1900. He was known as the Duke of Clearwater Lake, and his funeral in 1914 was one of the largest ever held in Waconia.

idea did not pan out, but Amblard did run a dining room for a time in the club building.[17]

With his health declining, Amblard visited France late in 1913, then returned to Waconia for another summer at the lake. In July 1914 he underwent surgery for an unknown ailment at Swedish Hospital in Minneapolis but died a week later, at age seventy-four. His funeral, at Waconia City Hall, was the largest in the city's history up to that point. The Frenchman who fell in love with summer in Minnesota was buried on a high spot overlooking Lake Waconia so that, as a newspaper writer put it, "when the trumpet of the resurrection summons him, his vision may first fall upon his beloved island."[18]

Mary Amblard seems to have been far less sentimental about Eden than her husband. A month after his death, she sold the estate to a Minneapolis businessman. Later, she remarried and moved to California. Over the next half century, there were several other owners of the property. By the 1970s, however, Eden had fallen into a state of ruin, and little remains today of Coney Island's unique French estate.

Classics by the Lake

Lucian Swift (later Albert W. Strong) House ("Katahdin"), north of Lakeview Avenue near North Lane, Deephaven, 1898 to ca. 1920s (burned)

Frank H. Peavey (later Frank. T. Heffelfinger) House ("Highcroft"), Highcroft Road near Highcroft Lane, Wayzata, William Channing Whitney, 1895 and later to 1953 (razed)

By 1890, Lake Minnetonka had firmly established itself as *the* summer resort for wealthy Minneapolitans. The first generation of summer homes, mainly built in the 1880s, often had the look of cabins on steroids; they were large but not especially refined. As the new century approached, the lake's woodsy shores began to harbor a new kind of summerhouse—elegant, classical in spirit, and set amid professionally landscaped grounds. Many of the finest estates were along the Upper Lake in Deephaven, Woodland, and the Ferndale section of Wayzata.

Among the most prominent of these estates was Katahdin, on Swift's Point near the entrance to Carson's Bay. The point takes its name from the estate's builder, Lucian Swift, who was manager and co-owner of the *Minneapolis Journal*.[19] The estate, named after Maine's highest mountain, was part of the Cottagewood development platted in 1876 by Minneapolis real estate mogul Samuel Gale. Swift's clapboarded mansion was hardly a cottage. Classical Revival in style, it featured an unusual central rotunda from which a two-story porch thrust out toward the lake. The rotunda, thirty feet in diameter and decorated in green and gold, led to a grand staircase as well as to the living and dining rooms. Parked at the center of the rotunda was a billiard table, suggesting that Swift, if nothing else, had his recreational priorities in order.[20]

Swift and his wife, Minnie, entertained often at the mansion, which like others of its time at the lake was mainly a summer retreat. There was, however, a furnace, and the Swifts sometimes hosted events during the Christmas season. Swift retired

Lucian Swift (later Albert W. Strong) House, north of Lakewood Avenue near North Lane, Deephaven, about 1905. This site on Lake Minnetonka is still known as Swift's Point.

Swift House and its many porches, about 1905. Lucian Swift was manager and co-owner of the Minneapolis Journal, once one of the city's leading newspapers.

from the *Journal* in 1908 but pursued other business interests until his death in 1926. By that time, his daughter, Grace, and her husband, Albert W. Strong, had become Katahdin's owners. They remained so until fire swept the mansion away in the 1920s.[21]

The most celebrated of Minnetonka's lost estates is Highcroft, built by Frank H. Peavey, whose "untiring energy, industry and pluck"—in the words of one newspaper—propelled an extraordinary career. It was said of J. P. Morgan that looking into his eyes was like staring into the headlamps of an oncoming locomotive. So it must have been with Peavey, who in an 1899 photograph looks out at the world with his arms folded in a gesture of supreme confidence, conveying a sense of indomitable force and purpose.

Born in Maine, Peavey went west to Chicago at age fifteen, then migrated to Sioux City, Iowa, where he got into the grain business. By the 1880s, when he relocated to Minneapolis, he

Frank H. Peavey, master of grain, about 1899.

was on his way to owning more grain elevators than anyone else in the world. Peavey was also an innovator, hiring engineer Charles Haglin to create the world's first reinforced concrete grain elevator. Haglin's prototype, built in 1899 in St. Louis Park, revolutionized grain storage and is now a National Historic Landmark.[22]

Peavey's 111-acre estate along the north side of Lake Minnetonka west of Wayzata extended from Ferndale Road north to the Great Northern Railway tracks (now the Luce Line Trail) and west to the small body of water called Peavey Lake. His neighbors at one time included flour miller Charles Pillsbury, lumberman Charles Bovey, and real estate developer Edmund J. Phelps. Peavey's property, a working farm where he bred Guernsey cattle and other livestock, was the largest of them all.

In 1895 Peavey set about crowning his property with a mansion, which its decorator, John Bradstreet, named Highcroft, a Scottish term with a nice ring to it. Peavey and his wife, Mary (the daughter of a former U.S. senator from Iowa), selected William Channing Whitney, who was the all-but-official architect of Minnetonka's moneyed class, as their designer. The result was

Peavey House ("Highcroft"), Highcroft Road near Highcroft Lane, Wayzata, about 1900. The Georgian Revival–style mansion was among the grandest homes ever built on Lake Minnetonka.

*Peavey House and formal gardens, about 1900. Peavey bred Jersey cattle
and other livestock on the 111-acre estate.*

Great hall in the Peavey House, about 1900. The room measured sixty by forty feet and featured a beamed ceiling studded with incandescent lights.

one of Whitney's better efforts, a Georgian Revival mansion that rose in red-brick splendor above Wayzata Bay.

The mansion featured a tall central block flanked by wings terminating in rounded porches and sunrooms that added a dynamic note to the design. The main entry, reached via a two-thousand-foot-long drive off Ferndale Road, was on the northwest side of the house in a courtyard set between two low service wings. The lake front, dominated by a two-story portico, was more monumental. Frederick Law Olmsted's firm in Boston planned the grounds and gardens surrounding the mansion, which unlike many of Minnetonka's great houses was not hidden away in thick woods.[23]

The heart of the twenty-three-room mansion was a great hall, sixty by forty feet and lit by incandescent lights. It featured fireplaces at either end, a grand staircase, beamed ceilings, and costly furnishings that included European antiques and oriental carpets. The adjacent dining room had a table that could seat up to forty guests in a pinch. Among the mansion's many amenities was an indoor swimming pool. A six-hundred-foot tunnel carrying steam pipes and electrical conduits connected the mansion to a power plant by Peavey Lake. Water was also pumped up to serve the mansion and grounds.[24]

Peavey's tenure at Highcroft was brief. On December 29, 1901, during a business trip to Chicago, he died of pneumonia at age fifty-one. "Frank H. Peavey Is Called from Earth," headlined the *Minneapolis Journal* the next day, calling him "one of the foremost men of the northwest." The story said Peavey "enjoyed nothing so much as to spend a day at 'Highcroft' . . . surrounded by his family and their friends. Of recent years 'Highcroft' has been his hobby, and the hours he spent there were the happiest of his life."[25]

After Peavey died, his daughter, Lucia, and her husband, Frank T. Heffelfinger, took over the estate and made it their primary residence. A decade or so after Lucia's death in 1941, the estate was subdivided. The mansion came down in 1953. Houses, a school, and a golf course now occupy the site.

Olaf O. Searle House, Big Island, Lake Minnetonka, ca. 1891 to ca. 1930s (burned)

Long known to the Dakota people, who tapped its maples for syrup, Big Island was claimed in the 1850s by brothers William and John Morse. The Morses had a niece who would become famous—Lizzie Borden—but confined their own ax work to the island's forests, carving out a homesite for William and his family. In the 1880s William sold or subdivided much of the island, and thirty or so cabins soon dotted its wooded shores.[26] The island's days as a place for rustic living changed in 1891, when Olaf O. Searle arrived with a vision in his head and money in his pocket. After buying 125 acres in the center of the island, Searle created a dreamland where he, his wife, Dagmar, and their young son, Ralph, could savor the pleasures of summer at the lake.

Searle was hardly the typical Minnetonka grandee. Unlike the transplanted New Englanders who owned many of the lake's estates, Searle was a Norwegian immigrant who had arrived in Minnesota in 1881 without so much as the proverbial penny in his pocket. His fortunes quickly changed. After a stint with the St. Paul, Minneapolis and Manitoba Railway, Searle and a partner, Aleck Johnson, formed a company to sell steamship tickets and farmland to mostly Scandinavian emigrants. The company was a tremendous success. Searle also went into banking and real estate, and he became so rich that he was able to pour an estimated $250,000 into his island estate.[27]

He began by building a Colonial Revival–style mansion. The twenty-one-room home was not quite Highcroft, but it was impressive enough, offering porches galore, steam heat, and gaslights. The interior, adorned with hand-carved woodwork and murals, included a library stocked with $25,000 worth of books. The cellar was said to be equally well stocked with fine wines and liquors.

The grounds were extraordinary. Searle laid out a Japanese garden, planted Russian olive and other fruit trees, built

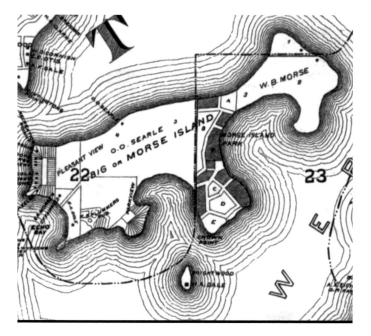

Olaf Searle's estate at the center of Big Island, Lake Minnetonka, from an 1898 plat map. Searle co-owned a company that sold steamship tickets and land to Scandinavian immigrants like himself.

Olaf Searle's house and estate, 1906, from a Lake Minnetonka souvenir book. Searle put about $250,000—then an enormous amount—into his lakeside dream.

a towered boathouse, and installed a dock large enough to accommodate the lake's big steamers. His most audacious "improvement" was a channel and lagoon that cut Big Island in two and, perhaps more to the point, separated Searle from his neighbors. It is hard to imagine how many studies, hearings, reviews, and permits would be required to undertake such a project today, but Searle seems to have been unencumbered by any pesky regulations. One account says that he simply hired a crew of laborers and told them to dig; realists suspect he may have brought in a steam-powered dredge. At the north end of the channel, which still divides the island, the excavators left a spit of land (now called Mahpiyata Island), which Searle connected to his estate with a footbridge.[28]

The Searles entertained frequently, took Ralph for pony rides, and lived what looked to be an enchanted existence. Perhaps it was for a time, but trouble, as always, slunk into para-

RALPH AND HIS PONY. · SIDE VIEW ·

O. O. SEARLE BIG ISLAND

BOAT HOUSE AND GROUNDS · THE LAGOON ·

Olaf O. Searle's Beautiful Home on Big Island, Minnetonka.

dise. Dagmar, or so it is alleged, was all too fond of the wine cellar, and Searle may have had his own battles with alcohol. He was also struck hard by the depression of 1893. One or more of his banks failed, and in 1897 he was indicted in Minneapolis for declaring a dividend without the money to pay for it—hardly the Mount Everest of crimes but suggestive of his financial difficulties. He or his company also defaulted on some North Dakota farmland, and it is possible the Big Island estate fell into foreclosure, at least for a time.[29]

Searle survived these financial setbacks, and he was still summering on Big Island in 1905, when Dagmar died at age thirty-eight. A year later, Searle's estate, along with advertisements for his company, appeared in a souvenir booklet called *Picturesque Minnetonka*, which included photographs of his new neighbor to the east, the Big Island Amusement Park. With its noisy crowds, the park must have been an unwelcome intrusion, especially since Searle had no moat on the east side of his property.[30]

It is unclear how long Searle occupied his estate, but he still owned the property as late as 1916, when he sought approval to build a bridge from the mainland to the island. The plan failed and so, before long, did Searle. Three years earlier, he had married a twenty-year-old woman who, with her mother, may have been fortune hunters (one history refers to them as "a pair of harpies").[31] Searle later obtained a divorce, but not before he had apparently been picked clean, and the 1920 census lists him as a "lodger" in a Minneapolis boardinghouse. By then, he had left Big Island for good. Searle died, in St. Paul, in 1926. The abandoned mansion went up in flames a few years later, although its foundations remain, the last traces of Olaf Searle's strange and marvelous island dream.

Prairie School Masterpieces

Edward W. Decker House, 250 Bushaway Road, Wayzata, Purcell and Elmslie, 1913 to ca. 1948 (razed except for garage and breezeway)

Francis W. Little House, 3350 Northome Road, Deephaven, Frank Lloyd Wright, 1915 to 1972 (dismantled)

In the late 1890s in Chicago, Frank Lloyd Wright created a new kind of house: long and flowing, with banded windows, broad eaves, and dynamic pinwheeling floor plans. Wright and his followers, including the Minneapolis firm of Purcell and Elmslie, later became known as the Prairie School. Although many Prairie School buildings remain in Minnesota, two exceptional houses, both at Lake Minnetonka, are gone.

The first, located just north of the lake in Wayzata, was built in 1913 for Minneapolis banker Edward W. Decker. Its designers, William Purcell and George Elmslie, had impeccable Prairie School credentials. Purcell grew up in Oak Park, Illinois, a Chicago suburb where Wright maintained his home and studio. After graduating from Cornell University, Purcell returned to Chicago, where he met George Elmslie. Born in Scotland, Elmslie was then working as chief draftsman for Louis Sullivan, Wright's old mentor. In 1909 Purcell and Elmslie formed their own firm in Minneapolis and began designing "progressive" houses in the manner pioneered by Wright.[32]

How a conservative businessman like Decker came to hire architectural radicals like Purcell and Elmslie remains something of a mystery. Years later, Purcell could only speculate that "it is possible Decker liked bright young businessmen."[33] Purcell and Elmslie's first scheme for the house, which ultimately cost $60,000, included a six-story tower that Decker rejected as too costly.

As built, the two-story house was cruciform in plan, its semicircular living room thrust forward like the nose of an airplane. A pair of screen porches flanked the living room, while above a line of twelve leaded-glass casement windows snuggled under the eaves. The rear of the house included a stair hall and dining room, a kitchen with attached servants' quarters, and a three-stall garage reached by a breezeway. Upstairs, there were seven bedrooms. The house's design was not entirely original; a year or so earlier Purcell and Elmslie had created a very similar home in Wood's Hole, Massachusetts.[34]

The interior offered a crisp and unified look: brick or wood-paneled walls, built-in benches and bookcases, integrated light fixtures, and tiled floors. Elmslie added marvelous ornament in the form of leaded-glass windows, stencil work, and fretsawn wood. He designed much of the furniture as well. Situated on a hill amid nine wooded acres, the house must have offered many summer delights for Decker, his wife, Susie, and their five children. The Deckers also used the house in winter, but its spread-out form and large amount of glass made it difficult to heat, even with three furnaces.[35]

Decker's fortunes turned sour in the 1930s. As president of Northwestern National Bank in Minneapolis, he had led the way in creating Northwest Bancorporation, a holding company that swallowed many smaller banks. Decker was among twenty bankers accused in federal court of fraud, but the charges were dropped after he resigned from the bank.[36] Even so, his personal finances suffered, and he lost the house on Busha-way Road. In 1948 the new owner tore it down—except for the garage and breezeway, which still stand—and replaced it with a French Provincial–style mansion.[37] It was a cruel ending for one of Lake Minnetonka's most extraordinary houses.

Frank Lloyd Wright designed the lake's other Prairie master-piece. It was built in 1914 for Francis Little, a lawyer and utility company owner from Illinois, his wife, Mary, and their daughter, Eleanor. The Littles knew Wright well—he had designed an earlier house for them in Peoria, Illinois—and in 1908 they hired him to create a summer home along the south shore of Robinson's Bay in Deephaven. It did not happen quickly, mainly because Wright was entangled in personal affairs. In 1909 he

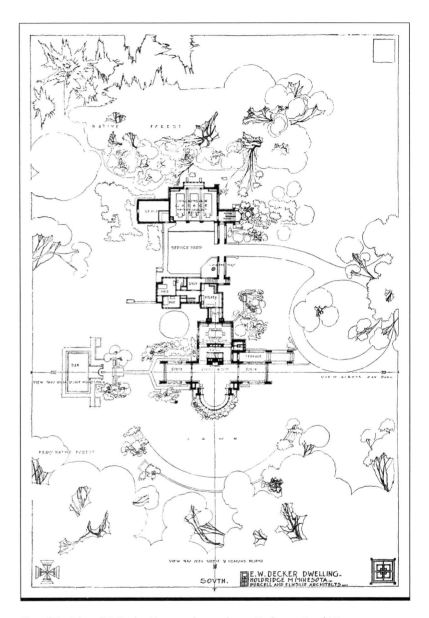

Plan of the Edward W. Decker House and grounds, 250 Bushaway Road, Wayzata, about 1912. The architects, William Purcell and George Elmslie, were leading practitioners of the Prairie School style in Minnesota.

Decker House, 1913. Screened porches extended on either side of the project-
ing semicircular living room.

Living room of the Decker House, 1913. Free-flowing plans and numerous built-ins were among the hallmarks of Prairie School homes.

Dining room of the Decker House, 1913. George Elmslie designed the furniture, which included elegant, though not especially comfortable, high-back chairs.

abandoned his wife and children and went to Europe with his new love, Mamah Borthwick Cheney. Before doing so, Wright had borrowed $10,000 from Little, who wisely insisted on collateral given the great architect's reputation as a deadbeat, and ultimately got his money back. While waiting for Wright, Little built a cottage on the property and summered there until the new house was finally finished.[38] Little was patient because he understood that Wright was capable of creating houses of such incandescent beauty that to live in one was akin to a religious experience, even if many devils—leaky roofs, poor heating, sagging cantilevers—lurked amid the details.

The Little House, Wright's first in Minnesota, proved to be worth the wait. Consisting of two offset brick volumes arranged like trains on adjacent tracks, the house with its all of its ter-

races, pavilions, and walls stretched an astounding 250 feet, its rows of windows marching along in rhythmic majesty beneath low-slung roofs. The home straddled two hills, with its lower level tucked into the valley between them.[39]

Within, a fifty-five-foot-long living room lined by leaded-glass windows was one of those Zen-like spaces, calm and clean, that Wright was somehow able to create out of the tumult of his life. The ceiling was high by Wright's standards, an accommodation made to improve the acoustics (Mary Little was a pianist and gave concerts in the house). Past the living room, the house jogged to the south to the bedroom wing. The dining room and kitchen were in the lower level. Washing the windows must have been a chore; there were at least 120 on the main floor alone.[40]

At about the time the Little House was completed, Wright's life came apart in fire and blood. In August 1914, while Wright was in Chicago, a deranged servant torched his Wisconsin estate and killed Mamah Cheney, her two children, and four

Decker House, breezeway and garage (at right), 1913. These are the only parts of the house that remain standing.

Plan of the Francis W. Little House, 3350 Northome Road, Deephaven. This was among the last great Prairie houses designed by Frank Lloyd Wright, who invented the style.

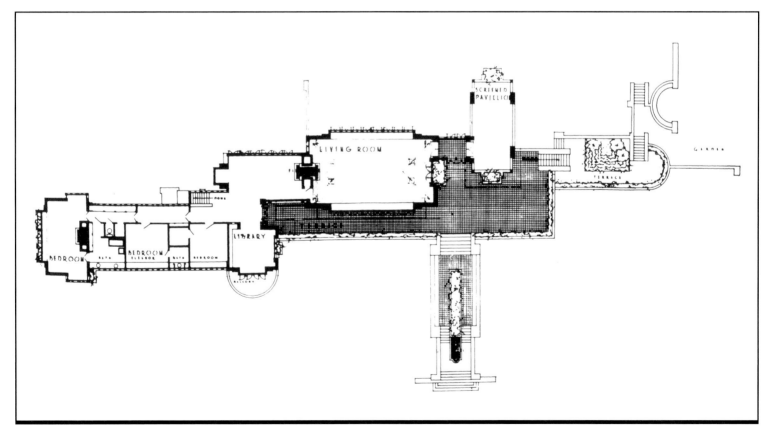

Little House, about 1915. The home was gorgeous down to the last detail but proved all but impossible to heat.

other people. Wright eventually rebuilt his life, but his Prairie School period was over.

In 1926 he returned to Lake Minnetonka for an adventure more comic than tragic. Traveling with twenty-eight-year-old Olga Ivanovna Lazovich (known as Oglivanna) and their infant daughter, the couple stopped to spend the night at a cottage

in Tonka Bay. As Wright, who was nearly sixty at the time, later wrote in his intermittently truthful *Autobiography*, "About half-past nine came a rude knock on the door of the living room. . . . I went to the door and opened it. A dozen or more rough-looking characters . . . shouldered their way into the room and sur-rounded us." The "characters" turned out to be deputy sheriffs. Wright and Oglivanna were arrested—on phony white slavery charges brought by Wright's estranged and soon-to-be divorced

Living room of the Little House as it would have appeared about 1915. All of the windows featured leaded-glass patterns designed by Wright.

Frank Lloyd Wright under arrest at his Lake Minnetonka "love nest," Tonka Bay, 1926. The famed architect and his lover spent two nights in the Hennepin County jail on phony white slavery charges.

wife, Miriam Noel—and hauled off to the Hennepin County jail amid the bursting flashbulbs of press photographers. The couple, who would marry in 1928, spent two nights behind bars (the jail, Wright told reporters with his usual aplomb, was badly designed) before the charges were dismissed.[41]

Francis Little was not able help his old friend. He had died in 1923, at age sixty-four. After his death, Mary moved into the cottage on the property and gave the house to Eleanor and her husband, Raymond Stevenson. Heating and maintaining the

Dismantling the living room of the Little House, about 1972. The room was later installed in the Metropolitan Museum of Art in New York City.

house were constant challenges, and by the 1960s the Stevensons wanted a smaller place. No local buyers could be found who were willing to preserve the house (rather than it tear it down for the lot). The Stevensons finally sold their gorgeously impractical jewel to the Metropolitan Museum of Art in New York in 1972. The house was then carefully dismantled. The living room was later installed in one of the Metropolitan's galleries, while a hallway now resides in the Minneapolis Institute of Arts.[42]

Philip W. and Eleanor Pillsbury House, 300 Ferndale Road West, Wayzata, Ralph Rapson, 1963 to 1997 (razed)

After World War II a style of architecture called Midcentury Modernism rose to prominence across the United States. Its practitioners touted efficiency, rationality and simplicity, all evident in popular housing types of the period like the ranch house and the rambler. High-style houses were a different story, however. Midcentury Modern architects in Minnesota and elsewhere produced a dizzying variety of houses that, despite their differences, shared a common urge to break away from traditional residential models. One of the masterpieces of this era in

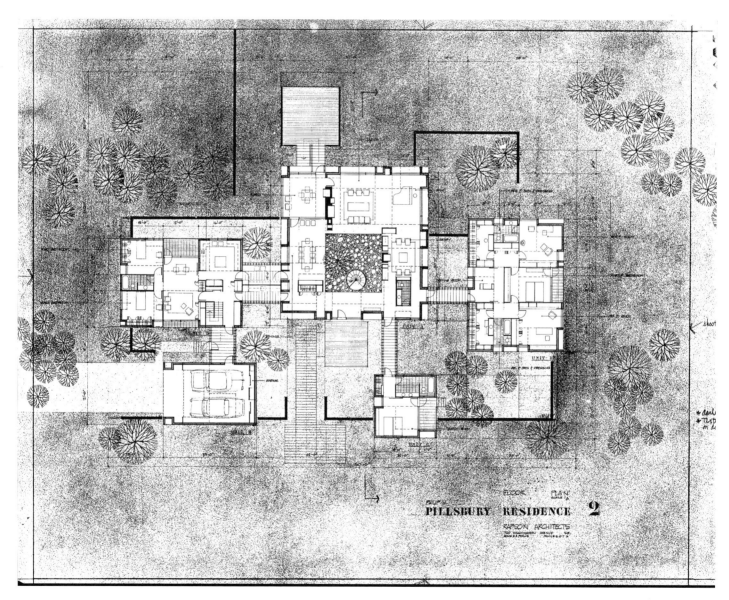

Plan of the Philip W. and Eleanor Pillsbury House, 300 Ferndale Road West, Wayzata. The house consisted of a series of pavilions linked by "bridges."

Pillsbury House, about 1964. The home was designed by architect Ralph Rapson at the same time he was working on the first Guthrie Theater in Minneapolis; both buildings are now gone.

*Living room in the Pillsbury House, about 1964. The ceiling provided much of
the architectural drama with its numerous steps and projections.*

Minnesota was the Philip and Eleanor Pillsbury House on Lake Minnetonka in Wayzata.

The house was built for Philip W. Pillsbury, president of the family's food company and a grandson of one its founders, and his wife, Eleanor. The property, site of three previous houses, had been owned by members of the family since the 1880s. Philip inherited it in 1959 after his mother's death. Eleanor had always wanted to build a house of her own, and in 1961 she got her chance. The daughter of a University of Minnesota classics professor, she had definite tastes and wanted a modern house. She and her husband chose Ralph Rapson, who had headed the University of Minnesota's School of Architecture since 1954, as their architect. While Philip tended to the project budget—a firm $260,000—Eleanor worked with Rapson to develop and refine what proved to be one of his outstanding designs.

Rapson was at the time perhaps Minnesota's most visible architect. He was already at work on what would become his most famous building, the Guthrie Theater in Minneapolis, also completed in 1963. Before that, he had built a reputation as designer of houses, churches, and several American embassy buildings in Europe. His style was jazzy and jumpy in an appealing way, yet always maintained its formal rigor.

The Pillsbury House consisted of five pavilions organized asymmetrically around a series of courtyards and linked by narrow, glassed-walled "bridges," as Rapson called them. This complex arrangement made the nine-thousand-square foot brick and concrete house seem much larger than it actually was. It also created unusually dynamic views, not only of the lake but also in and through the house's twenty or so rooms.

The largest pavilion was the "public" part of the house and consisted of a skylit foyer (where spiral steps led down to the lower level), living, dining, and music rooms, a library, and a half bath. The scale of these rooms—the largest, the living room,

measured about sixteen by thirty-two feet—was modest compared to those of earlier and later eras. Other pavilions contained family bedrooms and bathrooms, a guest bedroom with bath, the kitchen and maids' quarters, and a two-car garage. The lower level, from which doors led out to the lake, included a lap pool. A projecting rear balcony, midway between the main and lower levels, provided an open-air view of the lake.

The home's sculptural interior, designed in part to accommodate the Pillsburys' extensive collection of Asian art, was light-filled and lively, with a mix of brick and plaster walls, windows of varying sizes and shapes, wood floors and numerous built-ins. Much of the architectural action, however, focused on the ceilings, which stepped up, down, and around numerous skylights and monitors. The home's overall design, according to one of the Pillsburys' sons, Henry, also reinforced the "proposition that a family is best a federation. Each pavilion . . . was its own democracy; the whole was a robust little republic."[43]

Eleanor Pillsbury died only eight years after the house was completed. Philip later remarried and lived in the house until his death in 1984. His second wife then moved out, and the house was rented until the family put it up for sale in 1995, hoping it would find a sympathetic new owner. It did not. The house's peculiar layout, high maintenance costs, and numerous built-ins deterred potential buyers, and when the property was finally sold in 1996, the new owner wanted the land, not the house. Despite protests from the local architectural community, Rapson's Modernist monument was razed in 1997 and replaced by a larger and showier, but hardly better, new house.

"It does hurt," Rapson said when asked about the home's destruction. His beloved Guthrie Theater came down nine years later, and by the time Rapson died, at age ninety-three in 2008, he had endured the misfortune of outliving many of his finest buildings.[44] ◆

NOTES

Introduction

1. *Minneapolis Tribune*, 3 September 1922, A2.
2. *Minneapolis and St. Paul Pioneer Press*, 10 September 1882, 6.
3. Ernest R. Sandeen, *St. Paul's Historic Summit Avenue* (St. Paul: Living Historical Museum, 1978; reprint, Minneapolis: University of Minnesota Press, 2004), 1–5.
4. J. Fletcher Williams, *A History of the City of Saint Paul to 1875* (St. Paul: Minnesota Historical Society, 1876; reprint, 1983), 379.
5. *St. Paul Railroad and Real Estate Advertiser*, 22 August 1857.
6. *St. Paul Pioneer Press*, 7 October 1923, section 4, 4.
7. E. Dudley Parsons, *The Story of Minneapolis* (Minneapolis: privately published, 1913), 95–98.
8. *Minneapolis Tribune*, 4 April 1920.

1. Lowertown and Dayton's Bluff

1. *St. Paul Pioneer Press*, 7 October 1923, section 4, 4.
2. Marshall R. Hatfield, "Lafayette Park and the Vanished Homes of St. Paul's Elite," *Ramsey County History* 29, 2 (Summer 1994): 4–21.
3. Henry A. Castle, *A History of Saint Paul and Vicinity*, 3 vols. (Chicago and New York: Lewis Publishing Co., 1912), 1:392.

4. Larry Millett, *Twin Cities Then and Now* (St. Paul: Minnesota Historical Society Press, 1996), 134–37.
5. *St. Paul Pioneer Press*, 31 May 1903.
6. Paul Clifford Larson, "Dayton's Bluff Historic Site Survey," final report to the Department of Planning and the Heritage Preservation Commission of the City of St. Paul, August 1989.
7. *Minneapolis and St. Paul Pioneer Press*, 14 May 1882, 11; *St. Paul Pioneer Press*, 18 March 1883, 5.
8. Maria Rice Dawson, "A Letter to My Grandchildren about My Childhood Home 'Trout Brook,'" typed manuscript, Minnesota Historical Society, 1953.
9. Thomas M. Newson, *Pen Pictures of St. Paul, Minnesota, and Biographical Sketches of Old Settlers, from the Earliest Settlement of the City, up to and including the Year 1857* (St. Paul: The Author, 1886), 154.
10. Hatfield, "Lafayette Park," 6–8.
11. J. Fletcher Williams, *A History of the City of Saint Paul to 1875* (St. Paul: Minnesota Historical Society, 1876; reprint, 1983), 172.
12. Christopher Andrews, ed., *History of St. Paul, Minnesota, with Illustrations and Biographical Sketches of Some of Its Prominent Men and Pioneers* (Syracuse, N.Y.: D. Mason and Co., 1890), 54.
13. *Weekly Minnesotan*, 3 October 1857.

14. *St. Paul Pioneer and Democrat*, 2 September 1860.

15. Larry Millett, *Lost Twin Cities* (St. Paul: Minnesota Historical Society Press, 1992), 80–81.

16. Frank P. Donovan Jr. and Cushing F. Wright, *The First through a Century, 1853-1953: A History of the First National Bank of Saint Paul* (St. Paul: Webb Publishing Co., 1954), 15–25.

17. Merrill E. Jarchow, *Amherst H. Wilder and His Enduring Legacy* (St. Paul: Amherst H. Wilder Foundation, 1989), 20–21.

18. *St. Paul Pioneer and Democrat*, 9 December 1863.

19. Rhoda A. Gilman, *Henry Hastings Sibley, Divided Heart* (St. Paul: Minnesota Historical Society Press, 2004), 73–76.

20. *St. Paul Pioneer Press*, 4 February 1886.

21. Gilman, *Henry Hastings Sibley*, 210–11.

22. Ibid., 231–32.

23. *St. Paul Pioneer Press*, 5 July 1936.

24. Alan K. Lathrop, *Minnesota Architects: A Biographical Dictionary* (Minneapolis: University of Minnesota Press, 2010), 193–94.

25. Jeffrey A. Hess and Paul Clifford Larson, *St. Paul's Architecture: A History* (Minneapolis: University of Minnesota Press, 2006), 28, 32–34, 39.

26. *Saint Paul Daily Press*, 15 July 1866, 4.

27. *St. Paul Pioneer Press*, 24 July 1887.

28. Barry L. and Joan Miller Cotter, "Truman M. Smith: From Banker to Market Gardener," *Ramsey County History* 43, 3 (Fall 2008): 3–11; and 44, 2 (Summer 2009): 3–12.

29. *St. Paul Pioneer Press*, 2 May 1871, 1; and 1 June 1871, 1.

30. *New York Times*, 1 August 1897; *St. Paul Daily Globe*, 17 October 1897, 17.

31. Gareth Hiebert, *St. Paul Is My Beat* (St. Paul: North Central Publishing Co., 1958), 108–10.

32. Donovan and Wright, *First through a Century*, 27.

33. *St. Paul Pioneer and Democrat*, 9 December 1863.

34. *New York Times*, 24 October 1900.

35. *Northwest Magazine*, March 1885, 10.

36. Millett, *Lost Twin Cities*, 196–97.

37. Moira Harris, ed., *Louise's Legacy: Hamm Family Stories* (St. Paul: Pogo Press, 1998), 18–19, 30.

38. Doug Hoverson, *Land of Amber Waters: The History of Brewing in Minnesota* (Minneapolis: University of Minnesota Press, 2007), 292–93.

39. Paul Maccabee, *John Dillinger Slept Here* (St. Paul: Minnesota Historical Society Press, 1995), 148–57.

40. Andrews, *History of St. Paul*, 197–200.

41. *St. Paul Daily Globe*, 1 January 1888, 14.

42. *St. Paul Pioneer Press*, 1 December 1907; and 21 March 1908.

43. Ethel McClure, "The Protestant Home of St. Paul: A Pioneer Venture in Caring for the Aged," *Minnesota History*, June 1962, 85.

2. Capitol Heights, Central Park, and College Avenue

1. *St. Paul Dispatch*, 11 May 1948, 16.

2. Thomas M. Newson, *Pen Pictures of St. Paul, Minnesota, and Biographical Sketches of Old Settlers, from the Earliest Settlement of the City, up to and including the Year 1857* (St. Paul: The Author, 1886), 345–46.

3. Donald Empson, *The Street Where You Live* (Minneapolis: University of Minnesota Press, 2006), 56.

4. Paul D. Nelson, "The Life and Death of Central Park—A Small Part of the Past Illuminated," *Ramsey County History* 39, 3 (Fall 2004): 4–16.

5. *Little Sketches of Big Folks, Minnesota 1907* (St. Paul: R. L. Polk & Co., 1907), 264.

6. *St. Paul Pioneer Press*, 4 July 1907.

7. *St. Paul Pioneer*, 8 December 1869, 1.

8. Newson, *Pen Pictures*, 730.

9. *St. Paul Dispatch*, 1 July 1953.

10. David P. Handlin, *The American Home: Architecture and Society, 1815-1915* (Boston and Toronto: Little, Brown and Company, 1979), 288–90.

11. Newson, *Pen Pictures*, 314.

12. *St. Paul Railroad and Real Estate Advertiser*, 22 August 1857.

13. Empson, *Street Where You Live*, 181.

14. Newson, *Pen Pictures*, 604.

15. Frank P. Donovan Jr. and Cushing F. Wright, *The First through a Century, 1853-1953: A History of the First National Bank of Saint Paul* (St. Paul: Webb Publishing Co., 1954), 57–58.

16. Paul Clifford Larson, *Minnesota Architect: The Life and Work of Clarence H. Johnston* (Afton, Minn.: Afton Historical Society Press, 1996), 24–25.

17. *St. Paul Daily Globe*, 23 April 1882, 1.

18. Theodore Blegen, *Minnesota: A History of the State* (Minneapolis: University of Minnesota Press, 1963), 386–87.

19. *Minneapolis Tribune*, 11 April 1896, 5.

20. *St. Paul and Minneapolis Pioneer Press*, 23 December 1888.

21. Alan K. Lathrop, *Minnesota Architects: A Biographical Dictionary* (Minneapolis: University of Minnesota Press, 2010), 162.

22. *St. Paul Pioneer Press*, 21 August 1887, 10.

23. George E. Warner and Charles M. Foote, comps., *History of Ramsey County and the City of St. Paul, including the Explorers and Pioneers of Minnesota, by Rev. Edward D. Neill, and Outlines*

of the *History of Minnesota*, by J. Fletcher Williams (Minneapolis: North Star Publishing Co., 1881), 569.

24. Lathrop, *Minnesota Architects*, 218.

25. *St. Paul Daily News*, 26 September 1889, 2.

26. *St. Paul Pioneer Press*, 11 May 1948, 16.

27. *St. Paul Dispatch*, 15 January 1964.

28. David A. Walker, *Iron Frontier: The Discovery and Early Development of Minnesota's Three Ranges* (St. Paul: Minnesota Historical Society Press, 1979), 24–38, 51–52.

29. Nelson, "The Life and Death of Central Park," 6–7.

30. Larson, *Minnesota Architect*, 56.

31. *St. Paul Dispatch*, 22 June 1956.

3. Summit Avenue and the Hill District

1. Ernest R. Sandeen, *St. Paul's Historic Summit Avenue* (St. Paul: Living Historical Museum, 1978; reprint, Minneapolis: University of Minnesota Press, 2004), 6–7.

2. Russell L. Olson, *The Electric Railways of Minnesota* (Hopkins, Minn.: Minnesota Transportation Museum, 1976), 32.

3. *St. Paul and Minneapolis Pioneer Press*, 25 March 1883, 10.

4. Larry Millett, *Lost Twin Cities* (St. Paul: Minnesota Historical Society Press, 1992), 286–87.

5. Sandeen, *St. Paul's Historic Summit Avenue*, 16.

6. "Norman Kittson and the Fur Trade," *Ramsey County History* 6, 2 (Fall 1969): 18–22.

7. *Northwestern Architect and Improvement Record* 5, 5 (May 1887): 37.

8. *St. Paul Daily Globe*, 31 December 1887, 14.

9. Millett, *Lost Twin Cities*, 164–65.

10. Merrill E. Jarchow, *Amherst H. Wilder and His Enduring Legacy* (St. Paul: Amherst H. Wilder Foundation, 1989), 143–48.

11. Millett, *Lost Twin Cities*, 192–93.

12. *St. Paul and Minneapolis Pioneer Press*, 28 August 1887, 13.

13. Paul Clifford Larson, *Minnesota Architect: The Life and Work of Clarence H. Johnston* (Afton, Minn.: Afton Historical Society Press, 1996), 50–53.

14. Jarchow, *Amherst H. Wilder*, 192–219.

15. James M. Reardon, *The Catholic Church in the Diocese of St. Paul* (St. Paul: North Central Publishing Co., 1952), 374.

16. *St. Paul Dispatch*, 18 June 1959, 8.

17. *Inland Architect and Builder* 5, 6 (July 1885): 98.

18. Henry A. Castle, *A History of Saint Paul and Vicinity*, 3 vols. (Chicago and New York: Lewis Publishing Co., 1912), 2:765–67.

19. Alan K. Lathrop, *Minnesota Architects: A Biographical Dictionary* (Minneapolis: University of Minnesota Press, 2010), 77–78.

20. *St. Paul and Minneapolis Pioneer Press*, 28 August 1887, 13.

21. Sandeen, *St. Paul's Historic Summit Avenue*, 24–25.

22. *Little Sketches of Big Folks, Minnesota 1907* (St. Paul: R. L. Polk & Co., 1907), 205.

23. Arnold Lewis, *American Country Houses of the Gilded Age (Sheldon's "Artistic Country-Seats")* (New York: Dover Publications, 1982), plate no. 79.

24. Marion D. Shutter and J. S. McLain, eds., *Progressive Men of Minnesota: Biographical Sketches and Portraits of the Leaders in Business, Politics and the Professions; Together with an Historical and Descriptive Sketch of the State* (Minneapolis: Minneapolis Journal, 1897), 178–79.

25. Sandeen, *St. Paul's Historic Summit Avenue*, 25–26.

26. *St. Paul Pioneer Press*, 3 December 1883, 12.

27. Donald Empson, *The Street Where You Live* (Minneapolis: University of Minnesota Press, 2006), 199.

28. Larson, *Minnesota Architect*, 53–55.

29. Rebecca Ganzel, ed., *A Grand History: The Summit Hill Neighborhood's First 200 Years* (St. Paul: Summit Hill Association, 2010), 52.

30. *Northwest Magazine* 6 (February 1888): 33–34.

31. *St. Paul and Minneapolis Pioneer Press*, 21 August 1887, 10.

32. Mary T. Hill diary, Hill Family Collection, Minnesota Historical Society.

33. Thomas M. Newson, *Pen Pictures of St. Paul, Minnesota, and Biographical Sketches of Old Settlers, from the Earliest Settlement of the City, up to and including the Year 1857* (St. Paul: The Author, 1886), 37.

34. J. Fletcher Williams, *A History of the City of Saint Paul to 1875* (St. Paul: Minnesota Historical Society, 1876; reprint, 1983), 133–34.

35. *St. Paul Pioneer and Democrat*, 25 November 1860, 1.

36. *St. Paul Dispatch*, 4 March 1959.

4. Rice Park, West Seventh, and the West Side

1. Larry Millett, *AIA Guide to Downtown St. Paul* (St. Paul: Minnesota Historical Society Press, 2010), 32–33.

2. Larry Millett, *Lost Twin Cities* (St. Paul: Minnesota Historical Society Press, 1992), 133.

3. Tom Schroeder, *Historic Homes of St. Paul's Uppertown and Irvine Park* (St. Paul: Preservation Alliance of Minnesota and Historic Irvine Park Association, 2001), 3–6.

4. *A Brief History of the Irvine Park District: The People and Architecture of an Extraordinary Neighborhood* (St. Paul: Historic Irvine Park Association, 1986), 2–7.

5. *St. Paul Pioneer and Democrat,* 25 November 1860, 1.

6. Eric C. Hanson, *The Cathedral of Saint Paul: An Architectural Biography* (St. Paul: Cathedral of Saint Paul, 1990), 43, 13–14.

7. James Michael Reardon, *The Catholic Church in the Diocese of St. Paul* (St. Paul: North Central Publishing Co., 1952), 137–42, 153, 379–80.

8. Millett, *Lost Twin Cities,* 76–77.

9. Charles E. Flandrau, *Encyclopedia of Biography of Minnesota* (Chicago: Century Publishing and Engraving Co., 1900), 385–86.

10. Thomas M. Newson, *Pen Pictures of St. Paul Minnesota, and Biographical Sketches of Old Settlers, from the Earliest Settlement of the City, up to and including the Year 1857* (St. Paul: The Author, 1886), 588.

11. Supplement to *Northwest Builder and Decorator,* 1890, plates 40, 41, and 42.

12. Alan K. Lathrop, *Minnesota Architects: A Biographical Dictionary* (Minneapolis: University of Minnesota Press, 2010), 201–2.

13. *St. Paul Pioneer Press,* 19 July 1925, second sec., 2.

14. Larry Millett, "Franklin (Auditorium) Street, St. Paul," *Minnesota History* 62, 2 (Summer 2010): 47.

15. Flandrau, *Encyclopedia of Biography of Minnesota,* 431–32.

16. Newson, *Pen Pictures,* 217–18.

17. George S. Hage, *Newspapers on the Minnesota Frontier, 1849–1860* (St. Paul: Minnesota Historical Society, 1967), 41–45.

18. *St. Paul Dispatch,* 1 June 1956.

19. *St. Paul Pioneer Press,* 30 July 1884, 4.

20. *Brief History of the Irvine Park District,* 27.

21. *St. Paul Downtowner,* 13 May 1981, 6.

22. *St. Paul Pioneer Press,* 7 May 1986, 1D.

23. Larry Haeg, *In Gatsby's Shadow: The Story of Charles Macomb Flandrau* (Iowa City: University of Iowa Press, 2004).

24. *St. Paul Pioneer Press,* 7 October 1923, fourth sec., 4.

25. Georgia Ray, "In Search of the Real Grace Flandrau," *Minnesota History* 56, 6 (Summer 1999): 306–21.

26. City of St. Paul building permit, 225 Prescott Street.

27. Nancy Johnston Hall and Mary Bround Smith, *Traditions United: The History of St. Luke's and Charles T. Miller Hospitals and Their Service to St. Paul* (St. Paul: United Hospital Foundation, 1987), 99–105.

28. *St. Paul Pioneer Press,* 13 February 2006, B1.

29. City of St. Paul building permit, 334 Cherokee Avenue.

30. *St. Paul Pioneer Press,* 23 July 1961.

5. Around St. Paul

1. *St. Paul Dispatch,* 23 May 1957.

2. Thomas M. Newson, *Pen Pictures of St. Paul, Minnesota, and Biographical Sketches of Old Settlers, from the Earliest Settlement of the City, up to and including the Year 1857* (St. Paul: The Author, 1886), 797.

3. Larry Millett, *AIA Guide to the Twin Cities* (St. Paul: Minnesota Historical Society Press, 2007), 520.

4. Judith A. Martin and David A. Lanegran, *Where We Live: The Residential Districts of Minneapolis and Saint Paul* (Minneapolis: University of Minnesota Press, 1983), 42–45, 89–93.

5. Newson, *Pen Pictures,* 322–26.

6. James Sazevich, "The Como Park Hotel," unpublished research paper, 2010.

7. *Pioneer Democrat Weekly,* 11 October 1858.

8. *St. Paul Pioneer Press,* 14 June 1866.

9. *St. Paul Pioneer Press,* 11 August 1869, 4; *St. Paul Dispatch,* 11 August 1869, 2.

10. *St. Paul Daily Globe,* 7 June 1880, 3.

11. *St. Paul Daily Globe,* 24 August 1892.

12. David A. Lanegran with Judith Frost Flinn, *St. Anthony Park: Portrait of a Community* (St. Paul: District 12 Community Council and St. Anthony Park Association, 1987), 1–23, 119–20.

13. *Northwest Magazine,* April 1887, 47.

14. *St. Paul and Minneapolis Pioneer Press,* 20 March 1887; 13 August 1887, 10.; 21 August 1887, 10.

15. Newson, *Pen Pictures,* 82–83.

16. A. T. Andreas, *Illustrated Historical Atlas of the State of Minnesota* (Chicago: A. T. Andreas, 1874), 37.

17. *St. Paul Pioneer and Democrat,* 11 December 1863.

18. *St. Paul Pioneer Press,* 10 May 1876.

19. Donald Empson, "History Resided at Nettleton-Wardell Home," *St. Paul Dispatch,* 4 March 1975, 10N.

20. Henry A. Castle, *Minnesota: Its Story and Biography* (Chicago: Lewis Publishing Co., 1915), 756–57.

21. Jay Pfaender, "Stonebridge: The Story of a Lost Estate and Oliver Crosby, the Inventive Genius Who Created It," *Ramsey County History* 40, 3 (Fall 2005): 4–19.

22. Paul Clifford Larson, *Minnesota Architect: The Life and Work of Clarence H. Johnston* (Afton, Minn.: Afton Historical Society Press, 1996), 142–43.

23. *St. Paul Pioneer Press,* 22 February 1953, local sec., 1.

6. Suburban St. Paul

1. Arnold Lewis, *American Country Houses of the Gilded Age (Sheldon's "Artistic Country-Seats")* (New York: Dover Publications, 1982), xii–xvii.

2. Paul Clifford Larson, *A Place at the Lake* (Afton, Minn.: Afton Historical Society Press, 1998), 70–93.

3. Paul Clifford Larson, *A Walk through Dellwood* (Dellwood, Minn.: City of Dellwood, 2007), 25–50.

4. Norene A. Roberts, "North Hill (Original Town) Stillwater Residential Area," report submitted to City of Stillwater Heritage Preservation Commission, 1995, 16–25.

5. Larson, *Walk through Dellwood*, 31–33.

6. Ibid., 76, 115.

7. Geoffrey Blodgett, *Cass Gilbert, the Early Years* (St. Paul: Minnesota Historical Society Press, 2001), 66–67.

8. Paul Clifford Larson, *Minnesota Architect: The Life and Work of Clarence H. Johnston* (Afton, Minn.: Afton Historical Society Press, 1996), 38–39.

9. Larson, *Place at the Lake*, 82–83.

10. Thomas R. Blanck and Charles Locks, "Launching a Career: Residential and Ecclesiastical Work from the St. Paul Office," in *Cass Gilbert, Life and Work*, ed. Barbara S. Christen and Steven Flanders (New York: W. W. Norton Co., 2001), 58.

11. Thelma Jones, *Once upon a Lake* (Minneapolis: Ross and Haines, 1957; rev. ed., 1969), 299–300, 340.

12. Joan C. Brainard and Richard E. Leonard, *Three Bold Ventures: The History of North Oaks, Minnesota* (Edina, Minn.: Beaver's Pond Press, 2007).

13. Albro Martin, *James J. Hill and the Opening of the Northwest* (New York: Oxford University Press, 1976; reprint, St. Paul: Minnesota Historical Society Press, 1991), 310–14.

14. Robert Grau, *The Business Man in the Amusement World: A Volume of Progress in the Field of Theatre* (New York: Broadway Publishing Co., 1910), 200–202.

15. Roger Bergerson, *Winging It at a Country Crossroads: The Ups and Downs of Minnesota's First Real Airport* (St. Paul: Bergerson and Cunningham, 2008), 7–9.

16. *Western Architect*, March 1907.

17. *Symphony*, ca. 1910; information provided by James Sazevich.

18. *St. Paul Dispatch*, 27 July 1922.

19. *St. Paul Dispatch*, 16 May 1923; *St. Paul Pioneer Press*, 13 May 1924.

20. *St. Paul Pioneer Press*, 13 May 1924; 29 October 1929.

21. Larry Millett, *AIA Guide to the Twin Cities* (St. Paul: Minnesota Historical Society Press, 2007), 583.

22. Agnes M. Larson, *The White Pine Industry in Minnesota: A History* (Minneapolis: University of Minnesota Press, 1949; reprint, 2007), 11–28, 53–70; James Taylor Dunn, *The St. Croix: Midwest Border River* (New York: Henry Holt and Co., 1965; reprint, St. Paul: Minnesota Historical Society Press, 1979), 107–9.

23. Eileen M. McMahon and Theodore J. Karamanski, *Time and the River: A History of the Saint Croix* (Omaha: Midwest Regional Office, National Park Service, 2002), n.p.

24. David B. Peterson, "The Isaac Staples Mansion," a research paper prepared for River Town Restoration, Inc., Stillwater, Minn., 1979.

25. Patricia Condon Johnston, *Stillwater: Minnesota's Birthplace in Photographs by John Runk* (Afton, Minn.: Johnston Publishing, 1995), 37–39.

7. Central Downtown

1. Agnes von Scholten, "The Elegant Eighties in Minneapolis Society," *Minneapolis Journal*, 7 March 1937, in Calvin F. Schmid, *Social Saga of Two Cities: An Ecological and Statistical Study of Social Trends in Minneapolis and St. Paul* (Minneapolis: Council of Social Agencies, Bureau of Social Research, 1937), 74.

2. E. V. Smalley, "Progressive Minneapolis," *Northwest Magazine*, February 1895, 21.

3. Schmid, *Social Saga of Two Cities*, 56.

4. *Minneapolis Journal*, 3 July 1921, second sec., 1.

5. Lincoln Steffens, "The Shame of Minneapolis," *McClure's*, January 1903, 229–38; republished in *The Shame of the Cities* (New York: McClure, Philips and Co., 1904).

6. George E. Warner and Charles M. Foote, comps., *History of Hennepin County and the City of Minneapolis, including the Explorers and Pioneers of Minnesota, by Rev. Edward D. Neill and Outlines of the History of Minnesota, by J. Fletcher Williams* (Minneapolis: North Star Publishing Co., 1881), 500–501.

7. Iric Nathanson, *Minneapolis in the Twentieth Century: The Growth of an American City* (St. Paul: Minnesota Historical Society Press, 2010), 41–53.

8. Isaac Atwater, ed., *History of the City of Minneapolis, Minnesota* (New York: Munsell and Co., 1893), 234–36.

9. Donald Torbert, "Minneapolis Architecture and Architects, 1848–1908: A Study of Style Trends in Architecture in a Midwestern City Together with a Catalogue of Representative Buildings" (Ph.D. diss., University of Minnesota, 1951), 92.

10. Annette Atkins, "At Home in the Heart of the City," *Minnesota History* 58 (Spring/Summer 2003): 286–304.

11. Larry Millett, *Lost Twin Cities* (St. Paul: Minnesota Historical Society Press, 1992), 40, 135, 176–77.

12. Marion D. Shutter, ed., *History of Minneapolis: Gateway to the Northwest*, 3 vols. (Chicago and Minneapolis: S. J. Clarke Publishing Co., 1923), 2:196–98; Atwater, *History of Minneapolis*, 99.

13. Torbert, "Minneapolis Architecture and Architects," 99–100.

14. *Minneapolis Tribune*, 13 July 1885, 1.

15. William C. Edgar and Loring M. Staples, *Minneapolis Club: A Review of Its History* (Minneapolis: Minneapolis Club, 1974), 12–14.

16. *Minneapolis Tribune*, 9 September 1923, second sec., 9.

17. Atwater, *History of Minneapolis*, 599–607.

18. *Minneapolis Illustrated*, 1891, 7.

19. *Saturday Evening Spectator*, 1 September 1888, 1.

20. Eileen Manning Michaels, *Reconfiguring Harvey Ellis* (Edina, Minn.: Beaver's Pond Press, 2004), 89–93.

8. Loring Park, Hawthorne Park, and Oak Lake

1. Steve Trimble, *In the Shadow of the City: A History of the Loring Park Neighborhood* (Minneapolis: Minneapolis Community College Foundation, 1989), 12–40.

2. Calvin F. Schmid, *Social Saga of Two Cities: An Ecological and Statistical Study of Social Trends in Minneapolis and St. Paul* (Minneapolis: Council of Social Agencies, Bureau of Social Research, 1937), 75–79.

3. Carole Zellie, "The Harmon Place Historic District," final report prepared for the Minneapolis Heritage Preservation Commission, 2001, 5–15.

4. Donald Torbert, "Minneapolis Architecture and Architects, 1848–1908: A Study of Style Trends in Architecture in a Midwestern City Together with a Catalogue of Representative Buildings" (Ph.D. diss., University of Minnesota, 1951), 212.

5. Trimble, *Shadow of the City*, 47.

6. *Minneapolis Journal*, 6 March 1933, 5.

7. Eileen Manning Michaels, *Reconfiguring Harvey Ellis* (Edina, Minn.: Beaver's Pond Press, 2004), 92–96.

8. *St. Paul Pioneer Press*, 16 September 1888, 13.

9. Larry Millett, *Lost Twin Cities* (St. Paul: Minnesota Historical Society Press, 1992), 202–3; Trimble, *Shadow of the City*, 28–29.

10. Isaac Atwater, ed., *History of the City of Minneapolis, Minnesota* (New York: Munsell and Co., 1893), 1:23.

11. Alan K. Lathrop, *Minnesota Architects: A Biographical Dictionary* (Minneapolis: University of Minnesota Press, 2010), 226.

12. Trimble, *Shadow of the City*, 25, 37.

13. Ibid., 14, 20–21, 30–31.

14. David C. Smith, *City of Parks: The Story of Minneapolis Parks* (Minneapolis: The Foundation for Minneapolis Parks, 2008), 6–7.

15. "The Adventurous Velies," at www.bleedinggreen.com.

16. "Scouting History in the Viking Council, 1910–1976," at www.scoutingbsa.com/Council_Info/Council/History.

17. Millett, *Lost Twin Cities*, 278–79, 282–83.

18. *Minneapolis Star*, 17 June 1947, 1.

19. *Minneapolis Tribune*, 23 May 1968, 28.

20. Atwater, *History of Minneapolis*, 1:456–60.

21. Isaac Atwater, "Honorable Eugene Wilson," *Magazine of Western History* 8 (August 1888): 369–72.

22. Smith, *City of Parks*, 7, 18, 185–86.

23. Jack El-Hai, "Lost Minnesota," *Architecture Minnesota* 17, 4 (July–August 1991): 110.

24. James Michael Reardon, *The Catholic Church in the Diocese of St. Paul* (St. Paul: North Central Publishing Co., 1952), 383–84.

25. *Minneapolis Tribune*, 16 May 1914, 21.

26. *Encyclopedia of Connecticut Biography*, 4 vols. (Boston: The American Historical Society, 1917), 4:8–14.

27. *History of Winona County Together with Biographical Matter, Statistics, Etc.* (Chicago: H. H. Hillard Co., 1883), 814–15.

28. "Hilltopper" (Tourtellotte Memorial High School Alumni Association newsletter), September 2009, 1–5; October-November 2009, 5.

29. *Minneapolis Tribune*, 10 May 1895, 5.

30. *Minneapolis Tribune*, 13 September 1912, 1.

31. *Minneapolis Tribune*, 16 May 1914, 21.

9. Stevens Square, Washburn-Fair Oaks, and Park Avenue

1. *Minneapolis Tribune*, 27 August 1922, E6.

2. Carole Zellie, "Stevens Square Historic District," National Register of Historic Places Nomination Form, 1993; Steve Trimble, *In the Shadow of the City: A History of the Loring Park Neighborhood* (Minneapolis: Minneapolis Community College Foundation, 1989), 14–15.

3. "Washburn-Fair Oaks Mansion District," National Register of Historic Places Nomination Form, 1976.

4. Charles Nelson, "Historical Park Avenue," from "Historical Building Survey for the Minneapolis Model City," 1971.

5. Isaac Atwater, ed., *History of the City of Minneapolis, Minnesota* (New York: Munsell and Co., 1893), 2:973–79; Trimble, *Shadow of the City*, 14–15.

6. *Minneapolis Tribune*, 27 August 1922, E6.

7. Liddy J. Howard, "Stevens Square–Loring Heights: A Community Defined," *Neighborhood Planning for Community Revitalization*, May 1997.

8. Atwater, *History of Minneapolis*, 2:614–18.

9. Kerek Kelsey, *Prairie Lightning: The Rise and Fall of William Drew Washburn* (Lakeville, Minn.: Pogo Press, 2010), 6–90.

10. Larry Millett, *Lost Twin Cities* (St. Paul: Minnesota Historical Society Press, 1992), 168–69.

11. Arnold Lewis, *American Country Houses of the Gilded Age (Sheldon's "Artistic Country-Seats")* (New York: Dover Publications, 1982), plate 72.

12. *Saturday Evening Spectator*, 15 January 1887, 15.

13. *Northwest Magazine*, January 1885, 4–5; *St. Paul Daily Globe*, 27 January 1889, 3; *Daily Globe* (Minneapolis edition), 1 May 1889, 8.

14. Jack El-Hai, *Lost Minnesota: Stories of Vanished Places* (Minneapolis: University of Minnesota Press, 2000), 12–13.

15. Kelsey, *Prairie Lightning*, 142–58.

16. Scott F. Anfinson, "Archaeology of the Central Minneapolis Riverfront, Part 1," *Minnesota Archaeologist* 48, 1 (1989): 41–44.

17. George E. Warner and Charles M. Foote, comps., *History of Hennepin County and the City of Minneapolis, including the Explorers and Pioneers of Minnesota, by Rev. Edward D. Neill and Outlines of the History of Minnesota, by J. Fletcher Williams* (Minneapolis: North Star Publishing Co., 1881), 572.

18. Lewis, *American Country Houses*, plate 66.

19. Jack El-Hai, "Lost Minnesota," *Architecture Minnesota*, May–June 1997, 120.

20. Warner and Foote, *History of Hennepin County*, 427, 506; Horace B. Hudson, ed., *A Half Century of Minneapolis* (Minneapolis: Hudson Publishing Co., 1908), 242, 335–38.

21. James K. Wilson, "Improvement of Architecture in This Country," *Inland Architect and Builder* 4, 6 (January 1885): 75–77.

22. *Little Sketches of Big Folks, Minnesota 1907* (St. Paul: R. L. Polk & Co., 1907), 34.

23. Alan K. Lathrop, *Minnesota Architects: A Biographical Dictionary* (Minneapolis: University of Minnesota Press, 2010), 190–91.

24. *Saturday Evening Spectator*, 15 January 1887, 9.

25. Atwater, *History of Minneapolis*, 2:667–68; Albert Nelson Marquis, ed., *The Book of Minnesotans: A Biographical Dictionary of Leading Living Men in the State of Minnesota* (Chicago: A. N. Marquis & Company, 1907), 168.

26. Lathrop, *Minnesota Architects*, 56–57.

27. "Mr. Justus Miles Forman, Salon Class Passenger, The Lusitania Resource," www.rmslusitania.info.

28. Marion D. Shutter, ed., *History of Minneapolis, Gateway to the Northwest*, 3 vols. (Chicago and Minneapolis: S. J. Clarke Publishing Co., 1923), 2:242–45.

29. Lathrop, *Minnesota Architects*, 226.

10. *Lowry Hill*

1. A. T. Andreas, *Illustrated Historical Atlas of the State of Minnesota* (Chicago: A. T. Andreas, 1874), 228.

2. David A. Lanegran and Ernest R. Sandeen, *The Lake District of Minneapolis: A History of the Calhoun-Isles Community* (St. Paul: Living Historical Museum, 1979), 13–14.

3. Peter Sussman, "William S. Nott House," National Register of Historic Places nomination form, 1984, 5–6.

4. Goodrich Lowry, *Streetcar Man: Tom Lowry and the Twin City Rapid Transit Company* (Minneapolis: Lerner Publications Co., 1978), 9–32.

5. Ibid., 3–32, 49–50.

6. *New York Times*, 5 February 1909; *Minneapolis Tribune*, 5 February 1909, 1.

7. *Minneapolis Tribune*, 28 October 1915, 14; and 3 November 1915, 10.

8. Cathy Madison, *Walker Art Center: Art Spaces* (Minneapolis: Walker Art Center, 2005), 5–13.

9. Jack El-Hai, "Lost Minnesota," *Architecture Minnesota*, January–February 1994, 58.

10. Marion D. Shutter, ed., *History of Minneapolis, Gateway to the Northwest*, 3 vols. (Chicago and Minneapolis: S. J. Clarke Publishing Co., 1923), 2:34–37, 50–53.

11. Lanegran and Sandeen, *Lake District of Minneapolis*, 71.

12. *Improvement Bulletin*, 19 February 1898, 7.

13. *Minneapolis Tribune*, 14 February 1904, 28; *Western Architect* 13 (March 1904): 25.

14. *Lake Area News*, July 1993, 30–31.

15. *Minneapolis Star*, 1 October 1954, 29.

16. Albert Nelson Marquis, ed., *The Book of Minnesotans: A Biographical Dictionary of Leading Living Men in the State of Minnesota* (Chicago: A. N. Marquis & Company, 1907), 114; Shutter, *History of Minneapolis*, 2:162–67.

17. *Minneapolis Journal*, 5 November 1911.

18. *Minneapolis Times*, 1 April 1935.

19. *Minneapolis Star*, 27 January 1959, 8B.

20. Shutter, *History of Minneapolis*, 2:458–61; Marquis, *Book of Minnesotans*, 502.

21. Alan K. Lathrop, *Minnesota Architects: A Biographical Dictionary* (Minneapolis: University of Minnesota Press, 2010), 119.

22. *Minneapolis Tribune*, 10 April 1919, 10.

23. Isaac Atwater, ed., *History of the City of Minneapolis, Minnesota* (New York: Munsell and Co., 1893), 2:610–13.

24. *St. Paul Pioneer Press*, 12 May 1882, 3.

25. *Minneapolis Tribune*, 10 September 1967, 1B; and 24 September 1967; *Minneapolis Star*, 25 October 1967.

26. *Hill and Lake Press*, 6 December 1980.

11. The Lake District

1. David C. Smith, *City of Parks: The Story of Minneapolis Parks* (Minneapolis: The Foundation for Minneapolis Parks, 2008), 104–13.

2. David A. Lanegran and Ernest R. Sandeen, *The Lake District of Minneapolis: A History of the Calhoun-Isles Community* (St. Paul: Living Historical Museum, 1979), 5–42, 51–52.

3. George E. Warner and Charles M. Foote, comps., *History of Hennepin County and the City of Minneapolis, including the Explorers and Pioneers of Minnesota, by Rev. Edward D. Neill and Outlines of the History of Minnesota, by J. Fletcher Williams* (Minneapolis: North Star Publishing Co., 1881), 624–25; information about Roswell Russell's first house based on research by Bob Glancy.

4. Thatcher Imboden and Cedar Imboden Phillips, *Uptown Minneapolis* (Chicago: Arcadia Publishing, 2004), 32–33, 35.

5. *St. Paul Dispatch*, 7 August 1946.

6. John W. Leonard, ed., *Who's Who in America, 1899–1900* (Chicago: A. N. Marquis & Company, 1900), 595.

7. Linden Hills History Study Group, *Down at the Lake: A Historical Portrait of Linden Hills and the Lake Harriet District* (Minneapolis: Linden Hills History Study Group, 2001), 24, 71, 73–75.

8. *Minneapolis Tribune*, 14 August 1902, 5; and 1 August 1915, A3.

9. *Minneapolis Tribune*, 4 April 1920.

10. Isaac Atwater, ed., *History of the City of Minneapolis, Minnesota* (New York: Munsell and Co., 1893), 1:379–86.

11. Smith, *City of Parks*, 14–15; Lakewood Cemetery Association, *Haven in the Heart of the City: The History of Lakewood Cemetery* (Minneapolis: Lakewood Cemetery, 1992), 24–25, 29.

12. Lanegran and Sandeen, *Lake District of Minneapolis*, 14–16, 38–39.

13. *Minneapolis Tribune*, 24 February 1900, 1.

14. Atwater, *History of Minneapolis*, 2:667–68; Lanegran and Sandeen, *Lake District of Minneapolis*, 99–100.

15. *Western Architect*, December 1903, 18.

16. Alan K. Lathrop, *Minnesota Architects: A Biographical Dictionary* (Minneapolis: University of Minnesota Press, 2010), 167.

17. *Minneapolis Tribune*, 11 July 1905, 6.

18. Imboden and Phillips, *Uptown Minneapolis*, 35; *Minneapolis Star*, 30 September 1939; and 28 September 1955.

19. Bob Glancy, "Gates: The Man and the Mansion," *Hill and Lake Press*, 2 March 1991, 8–9.

20. Bob Glancy, "Florence Flirts with Fame and Fortune: Minneapolis's Richest Widow," *Hennepin History*, Winter 2007, 18–35.

21. Penny A. Petersen, "Great Mansions of Minneapolis, The Gates Mansion," *Lake Area News*, April 1991, 24–26, 35.

22. Peter B. Wright, "Residence of Mrs. H. L. Judd, Minneapolis," *Architectural Record* 41, 4 (April 1917): 291–304.

23. "The Gates Mansion: A History and Description," pamphlet, Junior League of Minneapolis, 1933.

24. *Minneapolis Journal*, 21 August 1923.

25. *Minneapolis Journal*, 29 December 1932, 1.

26. *Minneapolis Tribune*, 25 January 1933; and 15 July 1956.

27. Glancy, "Florence Flirts with Fame," 34.

12. Nicollet Island, Northeast, and University

1. Penny A. Petersen, *Hiding in Plain Sight: Minneapolis' First Neighborhood* (Marcy-Holmes Neighborhood Association, n.d.), 8–22, 58.

2. Michelle M. Terrell, Two Pines Research Group, "Literature Search for Archeological Potential, De La Salle High School Athletic Field," 2005, 23–28.

3. Christopher and Rushika Hage, *Nicollet Island: History and Architecture* (Minneapolis: Nodin Press, 2010), 55–81, 98–101.

4. Larry Millett, *AIA Guide to the Twin Cities* (St. Paul: Minnesota Historical Society Press, 2007), 135–40.

5. Doug Hoverson, *Land of Amber Waters: The History of Brewing in Minnesota* (Minneapolis: University of Minnesota Press, 2007), 249–51.

6. Hage and Hage, *Nicollet Island*, 55–57; David C. Smith, *City of Parks: The Story of Minneapolis Parks* (Minneapolis: The Foundation for Minneapolis Parks, 2008), 6–7.

7. *St. Paul Pioneer Press*, 17 June 1881, 6.

8. *Daily Globe* (Minneapolis edition), 1 May 1889, 8.

9. Hage and Hage, *Nicollet Island*, 65–70.

10. Terrell, "Literature Search," 35–37.

11. Brian Leehan, *Pale Horse at Plum Run: The First Minnesota at Gettysburg* (St. Paul: Minnesota Historical Society Press, 2002), 56–81.

12. Horace B. Hudson, ed., *A Half Century of Minneapolis* (Minneapolis: Hudson Publishing Co., 1908), 152; Marion D. Shutter, ed., *History of Minneapolis, Gateway to the Northwest*, 3 vols. (Chicago and Minneapolis: S. J. Clarke Publishing Co., 1923), 3:823–24.

13. Richard Moe, *The Last Full Measure: The Life and Death of the First Minnesota Volunteers* (New York: Henry Holt and Company, 1993), 268.

14. *Minneapolis Star*, 3 June 1947.

15. Petersen, *Hiding in Plain Sight*, 80–83; Shutter, *History of Minneapolis*, 2:6–11.

16. Isaac Atwater, ed., *History of the City of Minneapolis, Minnesota* (New York: Munsell and Co., 1893), 2:591–99.

17. "Notable Buildings of Minneapolis," Bulletin No. 57, Minneapolis Board of Education, 1942, 8–9.

18. *Minneapolis Journal*, 19 October 1901.

19. Hildegard Binder Johnson. "The Germans," in *They Chose Minnesota: A Survey of the State's Ethnic Groups*, ed. June Drenning Holmquist (St. Paul: Minnesota Historical Society Press, 1981), 169.

20. Hoverson, *Land of Amber Waters*, 167, 249–51.

21. Hudson, *Half Century in Minneapolis*, 403–4; Roland C. Amundson, "Listen to the Bottle Say 'Gluek, Gluek, Gluek,'" *Hennepin History* 48, 1 (Winter 1988–89): 4–9.

22. *Minneapolis Tribune*, 24 July 1966.

13. *Suburban Minneapolis*

1. Beverly O. Ewing, ed., *Hopkins, Minnesota through the Years* (Hopkins, Minn.: Hopkins Historical Society, 2000), 17–20, 73–75.

2. Paul Clifford Larson, *A Place at the Lake* (Afton, Minn.: Afton Historical Society Press, 1998), 27–69.

3. Leo C. Meloche, *Lake Minnetonka, 1850–2000: A Pictorial History of Things and Places on Lake Minnetonka* (Shorewood, Minn.: In-Depth Publishing, 2003), 75–76; Ellen Wilson Meyer, ed., *Picturesque Deephaven* (Excelsior, Minn.: Excelsior–Lake Minnetonka Historical Society, 1989), 22–23.

4. Thelma Jones, *Once upon a Lake* (Minneapolis: Ross and Haines, 1957; rev. ed., 1969), 5–6, 309, 332–33.

5. Marion D. Shutter, ed., *History of Minneapolis, Gateway to the Northwest*, 3 vols. (Chicago and Minneapolis: S. J. Clarke Publishing Co., 1923), 3:778–85.

6. John W. Diers and Aaron Isaacs, *Twin Cities by Trolley: The Streetcar Era in Minneapolis and St. Paul* (Minneapolis: University of Minnesota Press, 2007), 219–21.

7. Helen W. Blodgett, *Robbinsdale Then and Now* (Robbinsdale, Minn.: Printing Arts, 1983), 13–16, 20–28.

8. Tim Brady, *The Great Dan Patch and the Remarkable Mr. Savage* (Minneapolis: Nodin Press, 2006), 69–81.

9. Charles Leerhsen, *Crazy Good: The True Story of Dan Patch, the Most Famous Race Horse in America* (New York: Simon & Schuster Paperbacks, 2008), 240.

10. Brady, *Great Dan Patch*, 61–68, 161–72.

11. *American Architect*, October 1910.

12. Brady, *Great Dan Patch*, 191–224.

13. Shutter, *History of Minneapolis*, 2:771–72.

14. *Minneapolis Tribune*, 26 January 1911, 6.

15. George E. Hopkins, "100 Bloomington Historic Sites," 1968, at www.bloomingtonhistoricalsociety.org.

16. Scott Donaldson, "The Making of a Suburb: An Intellectual History of Bloomington, Minnesota," 1964, 39–40, at Hennepin History Museum; Charles E. Wales, "Notes in Reference to the Wales Properties on the Minnesota River," ca. 1920s, at Hennepin History Museum.

17. Waconia Heritage Association, *Waconia, Paradise of the Northwest: The Lake and Its Island* (Waconia, Minn.: Waconia Heritage Association, 1986), 85–102.

18. Larry Millett, "Past Lies in Ruins of Coney Island," *St. Paul Pioneer Press*, 2 September 1990, 1B.

19. Horace B. Hudson, ed., *A Half Century of Minneapolis* (Minneapolis: Hudson Publishing Co., 1908), 233–34.

20. Jones, *Once upon a Lake*, 332–33; Meloche, *Lake Minnetonka*, 59–60.

21. Larson, *Place at the Lake*, 58–60.

22. Hudson, *Half Century in Minneapolis*, 376–78.

23. Larson, *Place at the Lake*, 60–62; Meloche, *Lake Minnetonka*, 130–33.

24. F. H. Nutter, "Highcroft, Lake Minnetonka, Minn.," *Western Architect*, February 1903, 16–17.

25. *Minneapolis Journal*, 30 December 1901, 1.

26. Ellen Wilson Meyer, *Tales from Tonka: Stories of People around Lake Minnetonka* (Excelsior, Minn.: Excelsior–Lake Minnetonka Historical Society, 1993), 103–5.

27. O. N. Nelson, ed., *History of the Scandinavians and Successful Scandinavians in the United States*, 2 vols. (Minneapolis: O. N. Nelson & Company, 1900, second rev. ed.), 1:485–86.

28. Larson, *Place at the Lake*, 58, 60, 62; Meloche, *Lake Minnetonka*, 157–58.

29. *Minneapolis Tribune*, 15 June 1897, 3.

30. *Picturesque Minnetonka: Its Natural Beauties and Attractions* (Minneapolis: S. E. Ellis, 1906; reprint, Excelsior, Minn.: Excelsior–Lake Minnetonka Historical Society, 1975), 38–39.

31. Jones, *Once upon a Lake*, 367–70.

32. H. Allen Brooks, *The Prairie School: Frank Lloyd Wright and His Midwest Contemporaries* (Toronto: University of Toronto Press, 1972; New York: W. W. Norton & Company, 1976), 131–34.

33. William Purcell, "Parabiographies," 1913, William Gray Purcell Papers, Northwest Architectural Archives, at www.organica.org.

34. Brooks, *Prairie School*, 206–12; *Western Architect*, January 1913 and July 1915, plates 6–13, in *Prairie School Architecture, Studies from "The Western Architect,"* ed. H. Allen Brooks (Toronto: University of Toronto Press, 1975), 74, 119–26; Mark Hammons, "Purcell and Elmslie, Architects," in *Art and Life on the Upper Mississippi, 1890–1915*, ed. Michael Conforti (Newark: University of Delaware Press; London and Toronto: Associated University Presses in association with The Minneapolis Institute of Arts, 1994), 250–51.

35. David Gebhard and Patricia Gebhard, ed., *Purcell & Elmslie: Prairie Progressive Architects* (Layton, Utah: Gibbs Smith, 2006), 85, 88, 90–92, 107–9.

36. William Millikan, *A Union against Unions: The Minneapolis Citizens Alliance and Its Fight against Organized Labor, 1903–1947* (St. Paul: Minnesota Historical Society Press, 2001), 241.

37. Irene Stemmer, "History of Bushaway Road and Its Neighborhood, 1858–2009," prepared for Wayzata Heritage Preservation Board, 2009, 32–34; Larson, *Place at the Lake*, 69.

38. Meryle Secrest, *Frank Lloyd Wright* (New York: Alfred A . Knopf, 1992), 202–15.

39. William Allin Storrer, *The Frank Lloyd Wright Companion* (Chicago: University of Chicago Press, 1993), 66–67, 174–75.

40. "Francis Little House," in "Unified Vision: The Architecture and Design of the Prairie School" at www.artsmia.org/unified-vision.

41. Frank Lloyd Wright, *An Autobiography* (New York: Longmans, Green, 1932; Duell, Sloan and Pearce, 1943; Horizon Press, 1977), 304.

42. "Francis Little House."

43. Jane King Hession, Rip Rapson, and Bruce N. Wright, *Ralph Rapson: Sixty Years of Modern Design* (Afton, Minn.: Afton Historical Society Press, 1999), 146–67.

44. Linda Mack, "Pillsbury House's Time Running Out," *Star Tribune*, 11 November 1996, 1B.

ILLUSTRATION CREDITS

The University of Minnesota Press gratefully acknowledges the following institutions and individuals who provided permission to reproduce the illustrations in this book.

Carver County Historical Society: page 321

Hennepin County Historical Society: pages 264 (bottom), 276

Hennepin County Library, James K. Hosmer Special Collections Library: pages 13, 190 (bottom), 329 (bottom)

Hennepin County Library, Minneapolis Collection: pages 2 (bottom), 15, 105, 172, 181, 182, 201, 210, 214, 217, 224 (top), 228, 237, 240, 244, 275, 284, 288, 290, 305, 329 (top), 338

Hopkins Historical Society: page 302

James Ford Bell Library, University of Minnesota: pages 136, 207

Paul Clifford Larson: pages 137–39, 141–43, 146, 149–52, 157, 169, 204, 206, 208, 223, 224 (bottom), 247, 256, 262, 282 (bottom), 284, 312–15, 322–23, 325–27, 331, 333–36, 339

Metropolitan Museum of Art: page 337 (copyright The Metropolitan Museum of Art/Art Resource, NY)

Minnesota Historical Society: pages 2 (top), 4 (photograph by William H. Jacoby), 5, 7 (photograph by Walter N. Trenerry), 8 (photograph by A. F. Raymond), 10–12, 17 (photograph by Lee Brothers), 24, 26–28, 30–32, 34–35, 38, 39 (photograph by William Henry Illingworth), 40–42 (all photographs by Northwestern Photo Company), 43, 44 (photograph by Paul L. Schuler), 45, 48 (photograph by *St. Paul Pioneer Press*), 49, 50 (photograph by A. F. Raymond), 51, 52–53 (photograph by Arthur C. Warner), 55, 56 (photograph by James Taylor Dunn), 59 (photograph by Charles P. Gibson), 60 (photograph by A. F. Raymond), 62–66, 67 (photograph by A. F. Raymond), 69 (photograph by Charles P. Gibson), 70 (photograph by *St. Paul Pioneer Press*), 71, 74–77, 78–79 (photograph by Charles P. Gibson), 81–85, 86 (photograph by *St. Paul Pioneer Press*), 88–89, 90 (photograph by A. F. Raymond), 91, 94 (bottom), 97, 98 (photograph by Haynes), 100–101 (both photographs by William J. Hoseth), 104, 106–7, 108 (photograph by Rodolph W. Ransom), 109, 111–13, 115, 116 (photograph by Camera Shop), 118–20, 122, 123 (photograph by Edward Augustus Bromley), 128 (photograph by Alonzo H. Beal), 130, 131 (photograph by Joel Emmons Whitney), 132, 134, 135 (photograph by Harry Darius Ayer), 140 (photograph by *Minneapolis Star Tribune*), 147, 152, 153 (photograph by Lord & Burnham Company), 155–56, 159–60, 166 (photograph by *Minneapolis Star Journal*), 167–68, 170, 173–75, 177 (photograph by William H. Jacoby), 179 (photograph by Hibbard & Potter), 184, 188 (photograph by Charles J. Hibbard), 189, 190 (top), 192 (photograph by Alonzo H. Beal), 194–95, 197–98, 200, 202, 203 (photograph by Hibbard Studio), 205, 209, 212 (photograph by Lee Brothers), 215 (photograph by Sweet), 216, 220–21, 226 (photograph by Haas), 227 (bottom) (photograph by A. F. Raymond), 230, 232 (photograph by Sweet), 233 (photograph by Hibbard & Potter), 236 (photograph by William H. Jacoby), 238–39, 242–43, 246 (photograph by Sweet), 248–50, 252–55 (all photographs by Charles J. Hibbard), 257, 258 (photograph by Edmund A. Brush), 260–61, 264 (top) (photograph by Charles J. Hibbard), 265, 267

268 (photograph by *Minneapolis Journal*), 270 (photograph by William H. Jacoby), 271, 278–79 (both photographs by Charles J. Hibbard), 281–82 (all photographs by Charles J. Hibbard), 286–87, 291 (photograph by A. F. Raymond), 292, 293 (photograph by William H. Jacoby), 294 (photograph by A. F. Raymond), 295, 297, 299, 303–4, 308, 310–11 (photograph by Charles P. Gibson), 316–17 (both photographs by Hibbard Studio), 318, 320, 324

Northwest Architectural Archives, University of Minnesota: pages 183, 193, 332

Toby Rapson: pages 340–42

Robbinsdale Historical Society: pages 306–7

INDEX

Larry Millett is an architectural historian and the author of *Lost Twin Cities, Twin Cities Then and Now,* and *AIA Guide to the Twin Cities*. He has also written six mystery novels featuring Sherlock Holmes, all but one of them set in Minnesota. He lives in St. Paul.